BACKDOOR REVOLUTION

BACKDOOR REVOLUTION

The Definitive Guide to ADU Development

Kol Peterson

Building anADU.com

Accessory Dwelling Strategies, LLC, Portland, Oregon

Unless otherwise noted, all images in this book are courtesy of the author and Jeff Freeman (jeffreyfreeman.com).

Cover photo by Thad Peterson.

Editing and design by Indigo: Editing, Design, and More

ISBN: 978-0-692-05351-5

Contents

Introduction

In 2010, I relocated to Portland, Oregon, after a seven-year hiatus living in Boston and Washington, DC. In recognition that housing was likely the single largest expense I would have in my life, I sought a financially sustainable housing situation. I explored tiny houses on wheels and house-sitting, as well as converting a school bus, but ultimately I landed on the idea of buying a house and building and living in an accessory dwelling unit (ADU).

After visiting over fifty residential properties in inner Northeast Portland, I found one that I really liked and was the first to bid on it. The house was built in 1906 and had four bedrooms in very good condition. The backyard of the 5,000 sq. ft. lot had a fair-sized lawn that was edged with shrubs and a couple of trees. The backyard abutted five neighboring properties but still felt secluded, due to the orientation of the windows and entries of the houses and to the visual privacy created by sheds on several of the adjacent properties. A large cherry tree on the south side of the backyard enshrouded the lawn with its massive canopy. This would become the site of my future home and the beginning of what would become a rich source of personal, academic, and professional fodder for me.

That year, 2010, was the lowest point of the Great Recession in Portland. With a shortage of construction work, designers and builders were readily available to work. While living in the primary house with my then-girlfriend, who is now my wife, I worked with a designer that

I found on Craigslist. He had never designed an ADU before but longed to do so. That's also where I found a general contractor—again, one who had never built an ADU before but was intrigued by the idea of building a house from scratch, as he'd only previously worked on remodels.

My designer and I careened our way through the ADU design process for three months. I assumed all the while that I would ultimately be able to build my ADU for $40,000. It ended up costing closer to $120,000. This dramatic cost adjustment was just one of hundreds of things I began to learn about ADUs as I plodded my way from being a web manager with little development experience into becoming an amateur housing developer on my own property.

I catalogued the whole development experience thoroughly on a blog, transparently open-sourcing my experience for the benefit of whoever might care to learn more about it. After completing the ADU and realizing that I had become quite knowledgeable on the subject, I began to teach a daylong class on my property about the ADU development process for other homeowners around Portland. Then, with a couple of fellow ADU advocates in Portland, I helped launch a website called AccessoryDwellings.org, which became the go-to online resource for current ADU information. I then started to teach an ADU class for real estate agents. In 2014, I started a citywide ADU tour, an event that regularly draws nearly 1,000 attendees. In addition, I started an ADU consulting company through which I do on-site ADU consultations as well as a variety of educational and speaking events.

To this day, my wife and I live in that 800 sq. ft. detached ADU—our dream house. I had met Deb when she was living in a wonderful garage-conversion ADU that she had built and lived in for several years prior to our meeting. We make a joke that I first fell in love with her ADU before I fell in love with her.

But I actually began writing this book while sitting in a 120 sq. ft. tiny house on wheels. This tiny house on wheels is one of six located at Caravan- The Tiny House Hotel. I started this experimental boutique hotel with my wife in the summer of 2013. The hotel was the first of

Image 0.1. The ADU in which the author and his wife live.

its kind in the world, a retail manifestation of the huge demand to experience tiny houses on wheels firsthand. Many of our guests stay at Caravan to test out what it is like to live in a 100 sq. ft. house before making the leap to radically downsizing. For me and Deb, Caravan provides a retail platform for education, policy, and advocacy around small urban infill housing, in addition to showcasing the craftsmanship of a variety of designers and builders. I can think of no more appropriate location to write the inaugural words of this introduction.

Living smaller has intrinsic values that tiny houses on wheels and ADUs share. Both ADUs and tiny houses on wheels can be independent dwellings with their own six walls. They represent smaller forms of dwellings than are typical in the United States, hence they are much more energy efficient than the average house. As with regulations for tiny houses on wheels, regulations for ADUs vary by municipality. For example, ADUs are not allowed in many places, and where they are legal, they remain a relatively rare form of housing. They lend themselves both to being used for urban infill housing and as enticing financial alternatives to purchasing conventional, larger houses located on expensive full-sized lots.

Image 0.2. Caravan- The Tiny House Hotel.

Beyond these similarities, tiny houses on wheels and ADUs are extremely different from one another. Most significantly, permitted ADUs are legal, permittable dwellings that can be legally insured, rented, appraised, assessed, and financed. As of the writing of this book, tiny houses on wheels are typically classified as vehicles, not buildings. They're rarely legal to live in; cannot be appraised, assessed, or added to the property tax roll; and cannot be easily financed by a mortgage. By placing a dwelling on wheels, it becomes untethered from conventional planning, zoning, and building regulations, a freedom that many craftsmen actually enjoy. However, placing the dwelling on wheels also brings the dwelling out of the oversight of building-code development regulations and out of the conventional regulatory framework and mainstream institutional systems with which most dwellings on residential properties must comply.

An ADU, on the other hand, is a legal, self-contained dwelling unit either internal to, or detached from, the primary dwelling on the lot. As such, it can be legally hooked up to the municipal infrastructure: water, sewer, electric, and gas utilities. The regulated planning and construction process provides a safety net for the developer, the owner, and the occupant of the permitted dwelling; a permitted ADU can be legally rented and insured. The status of ADUs as a legal form of housing allows them to potentially become widely adopted and built, as they can fit within the accepted institutional framework of conventional housing systems and development processes.

I first moved to Portland after college in 2001 but left in 2003 to attend graduate school at the Harvard Graduate School of Design in Cambridge. My master's degree was focused on environmental planning, watershed planning, transportation planning, and geographic information systems. Following graduate school, I landed a dream job in the Office of Water at the US Environmental Protection Agency in Washington, DC. In addition to working on water issues, I learned from urban development policy experts throughout the EPA who focused on ways to build better cities—cities that are walkable, bikeable, and foster a sense of community.

While living in DC, I bought a row house in Capitol Hill; it was considered a fixer. I purchased it when I was twenty-five, my first foray into home ownership. Owning my first home changed my perspective on many things. I fixed up the house, which meant managing large improvement projects that included finishing out the basement into what functionally served as a separate apartment. I sublet two rooms in my house, which taught me the value of generating passive income. I was amazed to be living in a really nice house essentially for free. Previous to living in that house, I had been paying $600 a month to share a room with a friend in Dupont Circle, an expensive DC neighborhood. In the new house, my mortgage was fully covered by my roommates, and all of my employment income was going straight into retirement savings and other investments. Older federal colleagues marveled at me. I marveled back—why would anyone choose to pay for their housing in any other way?

Seven years after first leaving Portland, I worked my way back to a town I sorely missed. I had only left because I initially lacked the credentials to land a good job there; the city had a scarcity of good jobs at the time. In 2010, I leaped at a job opportunity with a federal government office.

Since then, Portland has undergone dramatic changes. Portland was growing into a metropolitan city seemingly overnight. It is simultaneously sad and heartening to witness, and I am a part of those changes. I have been on the front edge of ADU education, advocacy, and consulting in Portland for the past six years. I now find myself in a unique position to speak to those changes and to contextualize the roles that ADUs play in the development of infill housing in a growing city.

Based on economic, social, and geographic trends, I believe ADUs are on the precipice of massive revitalization and that they will become much more prominent in many US cities over the next few decades. This book is an attempt to help homeowners build an ADU for themselves in their community and to guide policy officials in other cities. It is not an attempt to convince cynics of the merits of ADUs nor to turn cities and towns that ban ADUs outright into paragons of ADU development. Rather, my hope is that this book may assist homeowners who feel overwhelmed by the ADU development process and also assist citizens and jurisdictions that are considering how to embrace the revitalization of this intriguing housing option.

PART I:

THE HOMEOWNER'S GUIDE TO ADU DEVELOPMENT

Chapter 1

What Is an ADU?

ADUs ARE RELATIVELY RARE, SO THIS FIRST CHAPTER PROVIDES SOME context about what they are, what they're called, what they look like, what their function is, and why anyone would care about them. This chapter also lays out a broad policy vision for ADU development in American cities and towns. It closes with definitions of terminology that will be used here as well as the contextual framework and limitations of this book.

Defining an ADU

An accessory dwelling unit, or ADU, is a secondary housing unit on a single-family residential lot.

ADUs have notable characteristics (which we'll cover in detail in future chapters) that help further define, differentiate, and distinguish them from other housing types.

- ADUs are accessory and adjacent to a primary housing unit.
- ADUs are significantly smaller than the average US house.
- ADUs tend to be one of two units owned by one owner on a single-family residential lot.
- ADUs are most often built by homeowner developers after the primary house has already been built—the two units are developed asynchronously.

- Zoning regulations vary considerably in how they treat ADUs, yielding a wide range of types, styles, and uses.
- Vast numbers of informal ADUs exist compared to permitted ADUs.
- ADUs are a grassroots housing development form.

Other Terms Used for ADUs

The term *accessory dwelling unit* is an institutional-sounding name, but it's the most commonly used term across the country to describe this type of housing. While the full name is a mouthful, the shorthand *ADU* is better. However, there are at least sixty-five synonyms for these dwellings (see appendix 3).

By default, this book refers to permitted, secondary housing units on single-family lots as ADUs. Sometimes, I use the names of the secondary units as they are referred to in a particular jurisdiction; the terms *secondary units*, *accessory structures*, and *accessory units* help convey the legal or regulatory status of the units. These terms can offer a subtler but better picture of how the units are being used. I'll refer to the main house on the lot as the *primary house*.

The names used for ADUs vary depending on the city in which they are built, whether they are permitted units or not, who owns them, their physical and structural form, and the period in which they were built.

The term *ADU* is fairly new. The earliest reference I found to it was in the late 1980s, although ADU-type housing forms were common in the United States since at least the mid-1800s; American examples such as Thomas Jefferson's small house at Monticello and servant quarters stretch back further. The most common name since the 1980s—a name that persists in many jurisdictions to this day—is *accessory apartments*. However, as the name evokes, this apartment form is limited to internal ADUs. Indeed, new, stand-alone, detached ADUs were not allowed to be built in almost all US jurisdictions as late as the 1980s.

The lack of a common name for ADUs makes it difficult to aggregate cross-jurisdictional knowledge, strategy, and research about ADUs. It makes both web research and book research challenging. Couple this lack of cohesion and dearth of current legal ADU development with the fact that ADUs are innately a cottage industry and it becomes clear why this form of housing does not have a strong, nationally aligned stakeholder group, lobbying body, or association as a champion of its interests. There are a handful of fledgling nongovernmental organization initiatives that have made some strides toward galvanizing local efforts around building ADUs, but these initiatives and efforts have not coordinated nationally.

The lack of a common name creates some challenges, but there may be some justification for maintaining localized names that help contextualize the use and form of the ADU program to a particular locale. A "carriage house" makes sense in Charleston, South Carolina, where relic ADUs may have been converted from old horse stables. "Laneway houses" make sense in Vancouver, British Columbia, where the majority of the residential grid consists of avenues and lanes and where detached ADUs are only allowed to be built off of the lanes. "Accessory apartments" make sense in cities such as Newton, Massachusetts, where detached new-construction ADUs are not allowed but internal ADUs are.

What's in a Housing Unit?

To help differentiate ADUs from other alternative habitable dwelling spaces found on residential properties, let's consider what actually defines a housing unit from a regulatory perspective.

In the broadest sense, planning and building codes state that a housing unit must have habitable living space that allows for living, sleeping, cooking, eating, and sanitation. *Living space* is a term that refers to interior conditioned spaces that are built to code with permits and are intended for habitation.

There are two core and distinct building-code elements that permitted housing units all share: a kitchen sink and a stove connection.

These are not typically permissible in other separate living spaces, such as art studios, guest rooms, or finished basements. An art studio may have a separate entrance and its own bathroom, but it is still not classified as an ADU. What differentiates that art studio from an ADU is the kitchen sink and the stove connection. Even if an independent living space has sleeping quarters and a bathroom, it is not an ADU unless it has a kitchen sink and a stove connection.

STRUCTURAL FORMS OF ADUs

There are several types of structural forms for ADUs:

Detached new-construction ADUs (see image 1.1)
Garage-conversion ADUs (see image 1.2)
ADUs above a garage or workshop, or attached to it (see image 1.3)
Addition-to-ADUs or "bump-out ADUs" (see image 1.4)
Basement-conversion ADUs (see images 1.5 and 1.6)
Internal "carve-out" ADUs, where part of the primary house is converted to an ADU (see image 1.7)

Even when a range of ADU types are allowable by zoning, homeowners usually lean toward a form that would work best for their particular circumstances. Beyond zoning regulations and spatial constraints on a property that may limit the structural type of ADU (see chapter 8), differences in construction costs may help steer a homeowner toward a basement conversion or garage conversion rather than a detached new-construction ADU (see chapter 4).

THE MULTITUDE OF BENEFITS OF ADUs

Backdoor Revolution is targeted to the homeowner who wants to build an ADU. It was also written for planners and advocates to understand why so few permitted ADUs are being built in all but a small handful of

Image 1.1.

Image 1.2.

Image 1.3.

Image 1.4.

Image 1.5.

Image 1.6.

Image 1.7.

cities. I want to help those readers learn how to foster more permitted ADUs in their jurisdiction.

Backdoor Revolution was not written to convince readers about the merits of ADUs or to persuade towns to adopt zoning codes and regulations that allow their development.

My assumption is that readers of this book are peripherally aware of the many personal and policy benefits of ADUs. Professionals reading this book may have already reached the conclusion that ADUs may be a useful policy implementation tool for their jurisdiction, even if relatively few permitted ADUs exist there currently.

Nonetheless, for readers who are new to the subject, here's a list of benefits that ADUs provide.

Economic

- ADUs provide flexible dwelling options in neighborhoods by utilizing existing governmental infrastructure (e.g., roads, sewers, schools), and they reduce the demand for expanding infrastructure in far-lying reaches of a developed metropolitan area.

- They create housing near employment, retail centers, and transit corridors, where there is need for additional affordable housing options.
- They generate jobs for construction. Approximately half of the cost of new construction goes toward labor, and half goes toward materials. ADU construction labor is inherently a local job, so when an ADU is constructed, money is kept circulating in the community.
- New dwelling units generate more tax revenue and more taxable income for a city, increasing its property tax base.
- They are a wealth-building opportunity for homeowners who use one of the units for rental income. They can also stabilize housing costs for homeowners.

Environmental

- ADUs create housing with a relatively small environmental footprint. New detached ADUs provide rental housing that is smaller per capita than standard, new single-family rental units. And new ADUs overall provide housing that is smaller per capita than standard, new single-family units. In a building life cycle, smaller residential spaces use less energy in construction, deconstruction, and habitation.
- They reduce energy use for heating and cooling, which account for the majority of the energy used in the life cycle of a building. Smaller buildings require substantially less energy. Residential buildings are responsible for approximately 22% of the energy used in the United States.
- ADUs tend to be built where there is an active market demand for rental housing in residential zones. These neighborhoods tend to be where residents can choose to walk, bike, or ride public transit to work, oftentimes in central city neighborhoods. Transportation is responsible for 33% of the energy used in the United States. As

a by-product of their location efficiency, ADU occupants tend to use less transportation energy than is used as a by-product of most new single-family housing developments.

Social

- ADUs provide one- or two-bedroom housing units in residential zones, which are generally in short supply relative to demand. US housing stock does not match housing demographic trends. More and more individuals and households are seeking smaller, central-city residences.
- They provide more affordable housing options in a residential neighborhood without dramatically changing a neighborhood's character.
- They provide a unique configuration of housing for multigenerational households. This can provide a comfortable, affordable, accessible, and practical housing option for families who may be dealing with child care, special needs, or elderly members.
- They create spaces for groups and individuals to live in close proximity and share with one another but maintain their own distinct, private living quarters.
- They enable active seniors nearing retirement to find viable options to downsize, control costs, and remain in a familiar neighborhood.

Policy Goals

The innate characteristics of ADUs lend themselves to being an economically, environmentally, and socially corrective housing tool. The potential benefits of ADUs are enumerated in many publications, including professional urban planning articles, academic publications, news articles, zoning documents, and municipal housing policy documents. However, these serve largely as academic platitudes, since relatively few permitted ADUs exist today.

It is a grander policy challenge for governments to steer individuals toward personal choices that result in the best societal outcome and to purposely induce the virtuous choice by making it a passive choice. A passive choice is the expected behavioral choice that a self-interested or apathetic person might reasonably make. Optimally, those individual passive choices collectively result in the best societal outcome.

It is in society's best interest to design systems where individual passive choices are the most regenerative for society's greater policy goals. Collectively, people in government and advocates can design regulations and programs that facilitate the market adoption of individual behaviors that virtuously benefit everyone, whether or not the individual is actively choosing to be virtuous. As a tactic that can lead to beneficial economic, environmental, and social outcomes, I believe that ADUs could reasonably be considered a policy goal.

Terms You'll Find in This Book

The focus of *Backdoor Revolution* is on ADU development in centrally located, walkable, and bikeable neighborhoods in cities and towns. This is where most ADUs will tend to be built, and how many of the economic and environmental benefits mentioned above will come to pass. While the development of ADUs in rural areas is not a focus of this book, much of the information found here is transferrable to them.

Backdoor Revolution covers both detached and internal ADUs, but the two types have a range of substantive differences that will become clear in future chapters. While it was important to capture both types in a single work, there is enough differentiation between their development, costs, regulations, design best practices, and legalities that separate books could be written about each option. This book focuses more on detached units than internal units in certain sections, as detached ADUs can illustrate some of the principles in a more clear-cut manner. They also represent a more politically challenging goal as far as ADU zoning and financing barriers are concerned. But rest assured—both internal and detached ADU development are covered in great detail.

For the purposes of this book, I'm limiting the ADU history and concept to North America. Cities here are generally subjugated to single-family residential zoning land-use divisions, so it is fair to characterize these secondary housing units on single-family residential lots as ADUs, regardless of their structural form and the local building-code definitions of a housing unit. Other nations may not have similar zoning regulations that would lend themselves to the concept of an ADU; Australia is a notable exception, with its ample ADU development in certain provinces.

There is a limited set of North American cities with active permitted ADU development, since ADUs were effectively banned in most cities after World War II. The limited pockets of permitted ADU development are used in this book as references from which to draw lessons and best practices regarding permitted ADUs. However, many cities have a bounty of informal ADUs, and economic and social trends can be extrapolated from this form of development as well.

Given my personal, professional, and substantial firsthand experience with ADUs and ADU owners in Portland, a recognized leader of ADU development in the United States, this book draws primarily on the depth of information that I have learned here.

This book uses the term *homeowner developers* frequently. The term refers to the individual who owns and lives on the property, aspires to build the ADU, funds the project, oversees the project, and manages the development process to build the ADU.

I'll use a capital *C* in *City* when referring to a city's governing body and a lowercase *c* for *city* when referring to the place.

One final note: I've met many great people in my work, and many of them have shared their stories on my website, AccessoryDwellings.org. I've used some of their testimonials and tribulations throughout *Backdoor Revolution*. Unless otherwise noted in the citations at the end of the book, these stories come from those fine folks, and I thank them all for sharing with me—and with you.

Chapter 2

Timeline to Design and Build

There are two things that homeowners underestimate in planning to build their ADU: how much time it takes and how much money it costs. Costs will be covered in the next chapter, but first, I'll review the steps and timeline for developing an ADU.

The time frame for ADU development can range from as little as two months to as long as two years, with an average of one to one and a half years. The development process can be broken down into three major phases: design, permitting, and construction.

The following sections outline the basic steps to design and build a new detached ADU construction project. The average time-frame estimates in these examples are for a moderately aggressive pace of development. Overall, designing a new detached ADU commonly takes two to three months, including the schematic site-design phase and development of permit-ready drawings. However, the design phase can be completed in as little time as a week, or it can take a year. This is one part of the process over which the homeowner has some control, depending on the agreement with a designer. Homeowner developers should be extremely thoughtful during the design phase, as they are going to get exactly what is designed. The best advice for homeowners is not to rush the design phase.

Permitting time varies greatly by jurisdiction. Some jurisdictions offer over-the-counter, same-day permits, while in others it can take a year or more of permit processing time that requires a conditional review process.

A new detached ADU takes longer than structural conversions to design, permit, and build, and will be on the longer end of the time-frame estimates. There are average-length delays during design, permitting, and construction to figure into these timelines. If there is already an existing, structurally sound building envelope—for example, a garage or basement conversion—the total time for conversion to an ADU may be shorter.

Design and Permitting Process

(Two weeks to one year; average three to six months)

- Ensure that you have ready access to sufficient funds.
- With your rough budget in mind, brainstorm the project scope.
- Talk to a City planner to determine feasibility. Ascertain municipal standards for the regulatory issues.
- Uncover any major property-specific design or cost red-flag issues, such as
    - a buried oil tank or cesspool. These systems may have to be removed if they are close to where a foundation will be placed.
    - a poor sewer line. If the existing sewer line is in a state of deferred maintenance, the ADU could trigger the need to update it. Sewer work in the public right-of-way is notoriously expensive.
    - special restrictions that go beyond those listed in the standard municipal zoning ADU code. These may include, but are not limited to, deed restrictions; homeowners associations with covenants, conditions, and restrictions; historic design overlays; and conservation or wetland overlay districts.
- Create rough sketches for site plans.
- Talk to neighbors for early feedback and identify objections or potential conflicts.

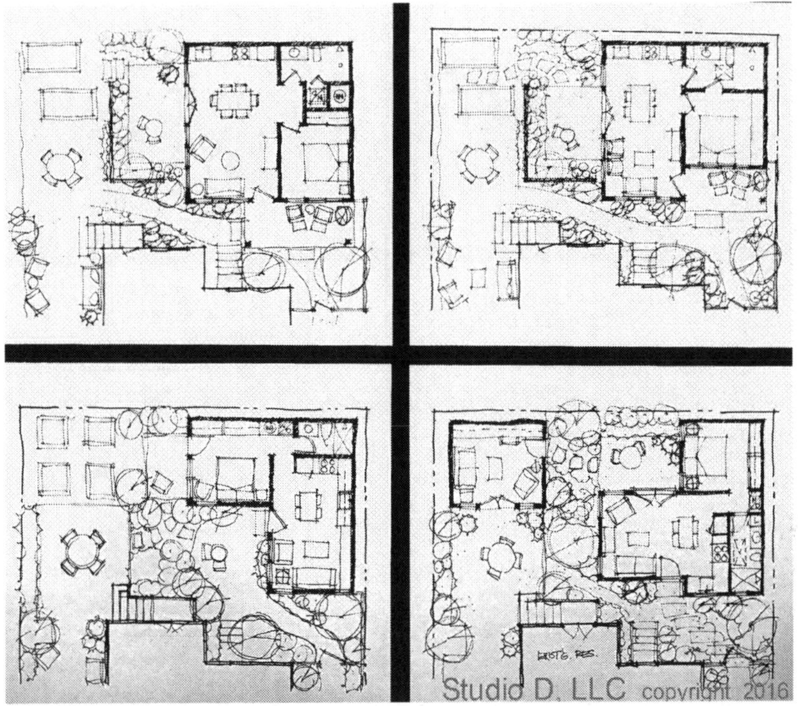

Figure 2.1. An example of schematics showing options for possible ADU site plans. (Image courtesy of Studio D Design LLC, www.studiod.ws.)

- Interview architects or designers. Optimally, select professionals who have a passion for or knowledge about small-space residential design or have experience with ADU design.
- Find reputable builders or general contractors and subcontractors. If you, the owner, are acting as the general contractor, identify a licensed plumber as well as mechanical and electrical subcontractors. You may base your assessment of them on costs, references, and communication skills.
- Access financing as needed for the design and permitting phase.
- Get schematic drawings (or rough 3D models) from the designer based on your project goals and preliminary sketches.
- Review and revise the plans using an integrated design process. Meet with the designer, builder, and subcontractors to

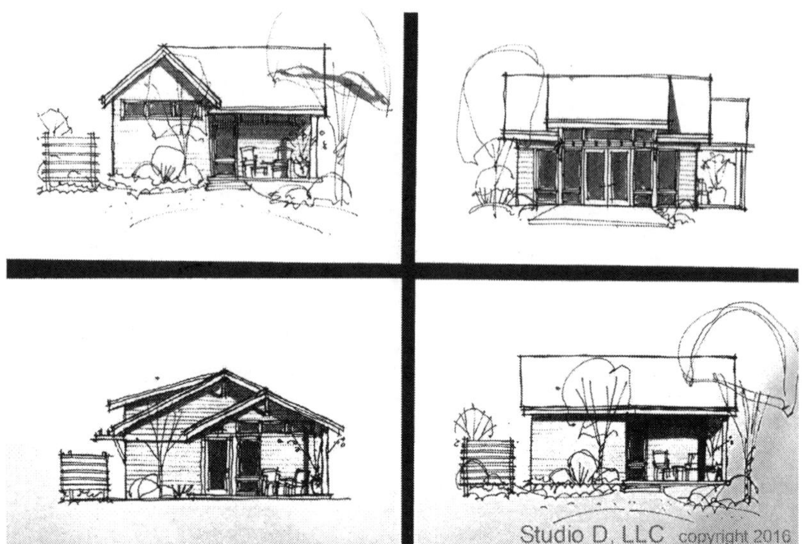

Figure 2.2. Schematic options for ADU elevations. (Image courtesy of Studio D Design LLC, www.studiod.ws.)

talk through objectives and schematics. Get input and feedback about the schematic design. Review heating and cooling and utility connection needs with the subcontractors, the designer, and the builder.

- Work with the designer to refine schematics. The designer may also build a 3D model of the design and finalize it based on feedback from you and the builder.
- In accordance with code requirements, develop drawings and structural engineering calculations and other documentation to support your permit application.
- Submit drawings to the City or County for permit.
- Hire a land surveyor to determine property line locations and install survey pins. Install construction staking if the City requires it before allowing the foundation to be poured.
- Obtain permits.

Construction Process

(Three months to two years; average three to eight months)

Depending on the existing site conditions, construction methods, weather conditions, and crew management, the construction steps and timeline for ADU projects will vary.

The following checklist was developed during construction of my ADU, which was built in Portland, Oregon, in 2011. It was a fairly standard ADU construction technique for the area: a detached new-construction, two-story ADU with a slab-on-grade foundation.

Weathertight Shell: The Structural and Infrastructural Elements of a Building

- Break ground
- Excavation
- Foundation
    - Set concrete forms
    - Pour foundation wall
    - Pour concrete slab
        - Gravel
        - Water/vapor barrier
        - Rigid foam
        - Rebar
        - Pour slab
- Rough-in utilities
    - Sewer, electrical, water, gas
- Framing
    - Framing the structure
    - Sheathing
    - Roof
    - Stairs
    - Windows
- Roofing

- Weather-resistant barrier
    - Rain screen on walls
- Siding

Interior Work

- Rough plumbing
- Mechanical systems
    - HVAC, ventilation, water heater
- Install wiring
    - Light fixtures
    - Electrical outlets and switches
- Air sealing
- Insulation
    - Rigid foam, spray foam, blown-in insulation, or batt insulation
- Drywall
    - Sheetrock, mudding, sanding, primer
- Flooring
- Tiling
- Painting
- Cabinets, shelving
- Install plumbing fixtures
- Install electrical and lighting fixtures
- Certificate of occupancy issued by the jurisdiction
- Modifications
- Furnish
- Move in!

Chapter 3

Financing

ADUs OFFER A PREDICTABLE PATHWAY TO WEALTH CREATION WITH ancillary benefits. They can offer a safe, secure, productive, long-term investment. Depending on housing costs, the rental market, the cost of construction in a market, and the intended use of the units, the return on investment can range from good to incredible for ADUs. They provide a route to minimize, reduce, or eliminate personal housing costs, which tend to represent the single largest monthly expense for most Americans.

In talking to more than two hundred ADU owners, I've never met anyone who had financial regrets about building their ADU. In fact, it is common for owners to express that it was the most financially life-enhancing move that they ever made.

For the annual ADU tour that I manage, I ask the hosts to answer a number of questions for the benefit of the attendees, including, "What was the most surprising thing you learned during the ADU design-build process?" Here's how host Bryan Scott responded:

> How much it would change our lives and lifestyle completely. Our ADU home has become the roof over our heads, our livelihood, and our retirement plan.... We designed and built our first ADU as our personal home as part of downsizing and simplifying our lifestyle. We realized the freedom (financial and otherwise) that could come by living in our

> ADU and renting out the primary house to cover the mortgage. Designing, building, and living in our ADU completely changed our lives.

How ADUs Build Wealth for Their Owners

There are several common ways to own, manage, and build wealth with a residential property. Owning and living in a property with an ADU is substantially the same as owning and living in a duplex, triplex, or fourplex in a residential zone.

Historically, owning an ADU provides a similar wealth-creation model to duplex ownership.

> The period between about 1870 and 1940 was the heyday of medium-scaled housing in American cities. In Chicago at the turn of the 20th century, two-flats (two-story houses with an apartment on each floor) multiplied; for that city's Eastern European immigrants, buying a two-flat and renting out half of it was a rung on the ladder of social mobility.[1]

ADUs fit into a form of housing that Opticos Design principal Dan Parolek has termed "missing-middle housing." Missing-middle housing promotes housing that is at the scale of a single-family house but has multiple units inside. ADUs, duplexes, triplexes, and courtyard apartments are all examples of this. Modern zoning ordinances severely limit where duplexes, triplexes, and fourplexes are allowed. Relic examples of these housing types are now commonly classified as nonconforming uses and could not be built today on the same property.

Fortunately, ADUs are allowed in more areas than some of these other housing types. ADUs also offer a compelling suite of economic and social benefits that entice homeowners to develop a small housing unit, even if they would not otherwise consider become housing developers.

ADUs as an Investment

Because ADUs do not necessarily add immediate resale value that is commensurate with the cost of their construction, the tendency is for owners to develop the ADU and hold on to the property. The economics of ADU development lends itself to those who want to hold their property long term. ADUs are not an effective way to turn a quick profit.

There is no standard method for looking at the financial viability of an ADU, but here are some ways to think about it:

- reduced mortgage payments
- years to break even
- return on investment

Later, I'll discuss some of the common ways ADUs are used for income generation and the financial pros and cons of those approaches.

The first models presented below illustrate how readers may think about the financial returns of ADUs as an investment. These initial methods account solely for the cost of construction and the rental income potential. They assume that the ADU was built with cash and that the extra unit will rent out at a market rate. These calculations do not account for factors that vary by jurisdiction, such as property tax changes or increases in utility costs, nor do they account for loan repayments or income tax impacts. Professional real estate investors may incorporate all of these variables when determining whether an investment makes sense for them.[2]

Reducing Mortgage Payments

Some homeowners primarily consider how the ADU affects their overall monthly housing expenses.

For example, say a homeowner named Greg develops a $160,000 ADU and it rents out for $1,500/month. Greg's existing primary house mortgage is $1,800/month. If he plans to continue to live in the house and to rent out the ADU, the rental income effectively reduces his personal mortgage payment from $1,800/month to $300/month. When doing the math, Greg may also consider potential rental vacancies, increased property taxes, insurance, and maintenance as a more seasoned real estate investor would.

Alternatively, some homeowners opt to live in their ADUs and rent out their primary house—potentially a more profitable approach. After the ADU is built, the rental income from the primary house is available. Let's assume that Greg could rent out his house for $2,000/month. In this scenario, he has not only just entirely covered his property's mortgage payments, but he's also making an additional $200/month. Greg has permanently eliminated his housing mortgage payments as long as he chooses to live there, plus he has created an additional income stream of $2,400 each year.

Here's one example of this perspective from owner Amanda Punton:

> To recoup the cost of the ADU investment through long-term rental, we're looking at a couple of years, but it's hard to say because meanwhile we're increasing the value of the house. We won't know how much value we've added to the house until we sell it. Right now the ADU covers the mortgage, not the taxes and insurance, but it's pretty nice for the cash flow.

Here's another example of this perspective from homeowner Blake Clark:

> The investment has been phenomenal. It's probably our best-performing asset. We more than cover all the expenses with the rent. We've built up a sizable reserve for issues that come up. We're not retiring on the income, but it's been a good investment.

Breaking Even

Some homeowners consider how long it will take for the ADU to generate sufficient rental income to entirely pay for itself based on the initial cost of its development. Looked at this way, any profit from the additional rental income after the break-even date represents pure profit. It is no longer paying for the cost of construction; it is simply income. Here are two examples:

- In the case of living in the house and renting out the ADU for \$1,500/month, \$18,000/year of net rental income means that a \$160,000 ADU construction cost would break even in 8.9 years (\$18,000/year × 8.9 years).
- In the case of living in the ADU and renting out the house for \$2,000/month, \$24,000/year of net rental income means that a \$160,000 ADU construction cost would break even in 6.7 years (\$24,000/year × 6.7 years).

According to host Bryan Scott:

> In our minds, this project was an investment in our freedom and our future. Had we decided to simply move back into the house... we would have spent the same funds on our mortgage over the next 2.5 years. As it currently stands, our tenants are paying our mortgage, and if we live in our garage-conversion ADU at least that long, the project will have been free. Every day after that or each time we rent the garage during our travels is simply a gift.

Homeowner Tatiana Xenelis-Mendoza's basement ADU, which ended up costing \$55,000, will take a little longer to break even than planned:

> It took us six months longer than anticipated because we ran out of money. We thought we could do it for \$35,000, but

> the electrical cost was quite sizable. That was nearly as much as excavation and pouring the new slab. However, it's still a good return on investment. We anticipate it will be a 3.8-year payback period.

When I was developing my own ADU, I initially thought about the ADU break-even terms even more conservatively. My wife and I live in the ADU and rent out the primary house. I only counted any rental income from the primary unit that was above and beyond the property's mortgage as supplemental passive income. Because the house rents out for significantly more than its thirty-year mortgage monthly payments, the supplemental passive income alone paid for the cost of the ADU in 4.5 years.

In my mind, after the 4.5-year mark had passed, I had financially caught up in my savings and retirement accounts to where I'd been prior to building the ADU. From that point forward, we were living for free in our dream ADU. The rental income from the primary house now represents significant, ongoing, positive cash flow. Indeed, the ADU is why I now have the freedom to write this book instead of working at a regular nine-to-five day job.

So far, these examples have not accounted for any additional contributory value that the ADU adds to the real market value of the property. If the property were to be sold, the new sale price would reflect the market value that was added by the ADU. The major property improvement can significantly add to the potential resale value of the property.

I asked Vince Kingston, a mortgage lender who specializes in renovation loans for ADUs, about this. He explained that not including the principal value of the ADU "would be like investing in a stock and then pretending like you're never going to get your initial investment back. You'd only be judging your return by the incremental pennies instead of also including the principal investment. That's what people do in real estate. They totally dismiss the value that is sitting there."

Provided there is no requirement for owner occupancy, the addition of an ADU should add significant contributory value to the property. At present, though, there is not yet an established method or rule of thumb to determine the contributory value. Owner-occupancy requirements may undermine the contributory value of an ADU. (Read more about this in chapter 8. For information about the valuation of properties with ADUs, see appendix 1.)

For example, let's assume that the ADU Greg built for $160,000 added $120,000 of resale value to the property. When accounting for the contributory value of the ADU, Greg would have to recover only $40,000 from rental income before he reached a break-even point. Notably though, that $120,000 of resale value is tied up in the ADU, so it's not the same as having the money to invest elsewhere.

- In the case of living in the house and renting out the ADU, $18,000/year of rental income means that a $160,000 ADU construction cost would break even in 2.2 years ($18,000/year × 2.2 years).
- In the case of living in the ADU and renting out the house, the break-even point would be 1.7 years ($24,000/year × 1.7 years).

Return on Investment

For these simple ADU models, I have narrowly considered the economics of the ADU in terms of construction costs vs. the potential rental income. When considering the return on the investment (*Return on Investment*, also known as *ROI*, is determined by dividing annual income by capital cost), professional developers consider not just these variables but also a range of other costs that factor into ROI calculations for the annual income.

These factors collectively are called *net operating expenses* and include additional property taxes, utility costs, property management fees, maintenance and repairs, property insurance, and projected vacancy gaps. These additional expenses should be considered, and they certainly temper the ROI. However, they probably do not temper it enough to alter the fundamental viability of ADUs as a wealth-building investment.

Consider some very conservative operating costs for an example ADU. For the next two scenarios, assume the ADU was built with cash instead of using a loan. First, imagine if the owners lived in the primary house but still paid all the utilities and used a property manager for the ADU.

Expense	**Amount**
Additional property taxes	$1,000/year
Utility costs	$500/year
Maintenance and repairs	$1,000/year
Property insurance	$300/year
Property management fees	At 8% = $120/month, $1,440/year
Rental vacancy rates	1 month/year, or $1,500/year
Net operating expenses total	**$5,740/year**

Rental income	$18,000
Net operating costs total	-$5,740/year
Net operating income	**$12,260/year**

ROI calculation	$12,260 ÷ $160,000 = 0.077
ROI	**7.7%**

When renting out the ADU and accounting for net operating income, the ROI is 7.7%.

Consider if the owners use a property manager to rent out the primary house and live in the ADU. The first costs are still added costs from the ADU development, but the property management fee and vacancy rates are now derived from the primary house:

Expense	Amount
Additional property taxes	$1,000/year
Utility costs	$500/year
Maintenance and repairs	$1,000/year
Property insurance	$300/year
Property management fees	At 8% = $160/month, $1,920/year
Rental vacancy rates	1 month/year, or $2,000/year
Net operating costs total	**$6,720/year**
Rental income	$24,000
Net operating costs total	-$6,720/year
Net operating income	**$17,280/year**
ROI calculation	$17,280 ÷ $160,000 = 0.108
ROI	**10.8%**

If the owners rent out the primary house, the ROI is 10.8%.

What if a loan was used to develop the ADU, such as financing through a home equity line of credit (HELOC)? In this example, the owners—let's call them the Chows—use a $100,000 HELOC, pay $60,000 in cash, use a property manager because they dislike property management, and pay for all the property's utilities, and the ADU is vacant a month each year.

If they opt to pay off the principal HELOC loan balance along with the 4% interest, the monthly payments for the $100,000 ten-year loan is about $1,000/month.

That debt service reduces their income by $12,000 per year, leaving the Chows with an annual cash flow of $260 ($18,000 - $5,740 - $12,000) in that first year. Each year, if the rent increases, so will cash flow. In ten years, the Chows will own their ADU free and clear. The Chows generate a little income each year until the loan is paid off and end up with a debt-free ADU in ten years. If they hold on to the property for that full ten-year period and make those monthly payments, that's a pretty good deal. And after that point, they can make $12,300/year ($18,000 - $5,700) or $17,300/year if they live in the ADU ($24,000 - $6,700) for as long as they keep the property.

Alternatively, they could also have opted to pay the HELOC as an interest-only loan for only $400/month. For that ten-year period, they would make $7,500 in income each year ($18,000 - $5,700 - $4,800). But, at the end of that ten-year HELOC period, they would still owe the $100,000 principal loan balance.

To better understand how a professional developer might look at an ADU as an investment and make sure my understanding of the ROI of ADUs wasn't fatally flawed, I spoke with a professional developer. Chris Botero of Stumptown Equity Solutions has built a few basement ADUs as his own investment properties. I asked Chris to explain what he'd think about the return on investment for an ADU development if he was building a $160,000 ADU that would get $1,500/month in rental income.

In roughly five seconds and without blinking, Chris said that a 6% interest-only rate on a $160,000 HELOC would be an $800/month payment, which would be roughly equivalent to a thirty-year fixed amortized payment. He went on,

> You're bringing in $1,500 a month, and you're paying out $800 a month, plus taxes, plus insurance, plus a few other things. So let's round it to $1,000 or even $1,200 a month. Now you've borrowed 100% of the money, you've paid nothing out of pocket, you've built this thing, and this thing now pays you net $300 a month or whatever it might be. And maybe it's paying itself off.
>
> I would do a billion of those. Take money that's not yours, invest it in something that creates income, you pay a chunk for that debt service, and you keep the rest.[3]

Even when fully accounting for the net operating expenses, if you compare ADUs against other long-term, common investment options, ADUs seem to fare extremely well.

Another less calculable but very real factor that must be considered is the substantial energy, effort, and stress that comes with the development of an ADU. This may be one of the largest side projects most people will ever undertake.

PAYING OFF THE ADU

Homeowners will have varying circumstances and comfort levels regarding how quickly they want to pay off any debt service they accrue to build an ADU. I asked Chris about what factors a homeowner should consider regarding how quickly they should pay off the debt service.

> It's kind of this descending thing. If you go from an interest-only loan to a forty-year amortized loan, your payment goes up a little bit, but you're making headway on the principal balance. With a thirty-year amortized loan, your payment goes up a little bit more, but you're making more headway. With a ten-year HELOC, you're talking about a ten-year payoff. Your monthly payment is going to go way up, but you're paid off in ten years. So, you make nothing or you're actually out of pocket a little bit for ten years, but then you have no debt on it.
>
> It's small bits of money now, versus larger bits of money later. For instance, if you're amortizing the loan over thirty years, you're making more each month, but your payoff is drawn out longer. So, you might make $400–$500 a month for thirty years, and then you'd make $1,500 a month once the thirty years is up because you have no debt service.
>
> Compare that to a ten-year payoff. Let's say you just break even for ten years, but then, at the ten-year mark, you have no debt service, and you make the full $1,500 a month.

So it really comes down to whether you're looking for cash flow or a quicker payoff and equity. The faster you amortize it, the quicker it's paid off, and some people like to pay things off. It all just depends.

FINANCING AN ADU

Imagine if a regular middle-income homeowner was told that they had to suddenly come up with cash to pay for a Lamborghini. Or imagine they had to pay quadruplets' private college tuition for a year. Most would laugh and say, "No way. That's impossible. Well, I suppose maybe I could afford to pay for that if I could finance it."

The prospect of buying a Lamborghini or paying out of pocket for private college for quadruplets is roughly how much a homeowner must anticipate having to pay to build an ADU in the course of one year. Unlike the option of dealership financing for a new car or obtaining financial aid and student loans for college, it can be difficult or sometimes impossible to obtain conventional financing through a bank for ADU development. Even if an individual's economic or social motivations to build an ADU are pure, clear, and strong, financing the capital cost of building an ADU still proves to be challenging for most people.

In ADU classes that I have taught in Portland over the last seven years for thousands of homeowners, capital cost is consistently cited as the most common barrier to construction of an ADU. In the ADU websites I manage, pages about the costs and financing of ADUs are consistently among the most visited. Even homeowners who were able to successfully build ADUs listed cost as the biggest obstacle they faced. (For more on this challenge, see "The Challenge of Financing ADUs" in chapter 7).

Because traditional bank financing options are not widely available for ADUs, homeowners must become creative with how they fund ADU development. The process of building and finishing construction for these projects can commonly force a homeowner to tap into and extend their financial resources, such as personal loans, cash-out refinances, and HELOCs, as shown in figure 3.1.

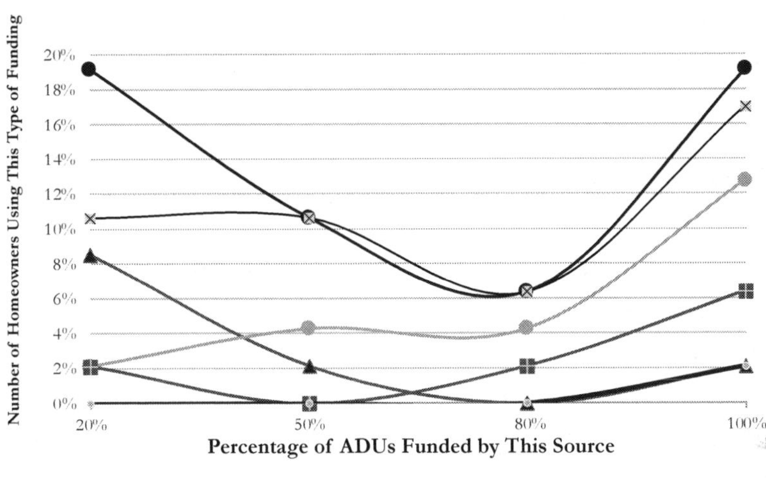

Figure 3.1.

Typically, homeowners use a patchwork of two to four creative financing sources to overcome this formidable barrier to entry—the capital cost of ADU construction.

In the Portland area, for those who build in order to rent out either the ADU or the primary house at market rates, the ROI ends up penciling out very well. However, a solid understanding of the potential return on investment does not necessarily help people figure out how to pay for it. Next, I'll cover some of the common and creative methods that homeowners typically use to finance the cost of ADU development.

Cash Savings or Other Liquid Assets

Using cash savings is the most obvious option. Indeed, most people use some personal cash savings to partially pay for an ADU. Owners may also have stocks and equities that they can easily liquidate.

Some 401(k) plans offer ways for individuals to take out money from their retirement savings as a low-interest loan to be repaid to themselves without any penalty as long as the money is used to build a primary residence. That's a loan against your future self, a potentially liquid asset.

I used this method to help pay for my ADU and aggressively paid off all the 401(k) loan debt in four years. I'm sure that many conventional financial advisers would adamantly warn against ever using retirement funds for anything other than guarding it for retirement. But I'm confident that they could not find me a reliable investment with at least a 45% ROI.

Home Equity Lines of Credit

As land values escalate over time in a real estate market, home equity lines of credit (HELOCs) play a more and more significant role in ADU development. HELOCs are a flexible and common tool used to finance projects like these.

HELOCS essentially work like this. If someone owns more than 10% equity in their primary residence, a bank can likely offer them a loan for an amount up to that 10% threshold. Let's say Elaine owns a property, and she wishes to build an ADU in her backyard. Elaine had put $15,000 (i.e., 5%) down initially when she bought the house for $300,000. Now, after she has lived in the house for a number of years, the house is worth $400,000, and Elaine's equity position has gone from $15,000 to $115,000, or from a 5% equity position to 28.75% ($115,000 ÷ $400,000 = 0.2875). This means that Elaine is potentially eligible to borrow up to 18.75% (28.75% - 10%) of the total value of the house, or $72,188 [($400,000 - $15,000) × 18.75% = $72,188]

Home Equity Line of Credit	**Amount**
Initial investment or initial equity position	$15,000 (or a 5% down payment) on a $300,000 property
Current real appraised value	$400,000

Home Equity Line of Credit	Amount
New equity position	$115,000, or 28.75% (up from her initial 5%)
Eligible to borrow	$72,188, or 18.75% of the total property value

After the HELOC is approved, the lender would provide Elaine a checking account with a $72,188 starting balance. To initiate a HELOC, the current value of a property is established by an accredited appraiser through the bank or credit union providing the HELOC. Elaine pays no initiation fees for the loan. When Elaine starts to actually spend the money from her HELOC, she begins to pay off the loan interest only over a period of ten years before she must start paying principal and interest (loan terms will vary). At a 4% interest rate, the monthly interest-only loan payments for a $100,000 HELOC would be approximately $400/month.

The equity-line checking account sits there at no cost until Elaine chooses to tap into it. This flexibility means that she can strategically use those funds only when needed, which keeps her loan interest payments as low as possible.

The loan amount depends on how much money was put down on the property initially and how much value the property has accrued since it was purchased. Given their flexibility, HELOCs can play a very significant role in financing ADUs. They commonly represent the most substantial portion of a homeowner's ADU-fund portfolio. One downside is that most HELOCs are variable-rate mortgages.

First Mortgage Cash-Out Refinance

This is a potentially good option for those who want to refinance their house and lock into a better mortgage loan interest rate or change the terms of their loan. To take advantage of a cash-out refi, as it's known, the homeowner must own at least 15% equity in the property to obtain any liquid cash benefit from a refinance.

In the scenario described above, Elaine could refinance her property and obtain the difference between her equity position and 15% of the value of the property as a cash payout from the refinance (terms may vary).

Since Elaine owns $115,000 in equity ($15,000 down plus $100,000 in accrued equity), she could potentially take out $55,000 as a cash withdrawal. Here's how the math works out: $340,000 (85% of the current $400,000 value) - $285,000 (current remaining mortgage) = $55,000.

The benefit of a cash-out refinance over a HELOC is that Elaine can pay a fixed, amortized interest rate on all of it.

HELOCs are typically ten-year adjustable-rate interest-only mortgages; then they are fixed into longer-term fixed mortgages. Some homeowners opt to use a HELOC for ADU development then do a cash-out refinance after construction, using their newly updated property to show an improved equity position. At that time, they can bundle their other construction debts (e.g., HELOCs, personal loans, credit card debt) into a single, fixed, amortized loan.

With a cash-out refinance, Elaine begins to pay interest on the full loan amount immediately, regardless of how quickly she can use the cash-out withdrawal for her ADU development. If her ADU takes a couple of years to complete, her new cash-out refi debt service would have higher carrying costs than the HELOC may have had. With a HELOC, if the homeowner does not use the money or does not know when they will need it, there is no carrying cost associated with allowing the account funds to sit idle. There is more flexibility built into a HELOC than with a cash-out refinance. There is also an initiation fee of $3,000–$5,000 for refinancing a first position loan, whereas HELOCs typically do not have initiation fees.

Family-and-Friends Loans

While banks may be reticent to provide nonsecured loans for ADUs, family members may not have as much hesitation about helping out with a low-interest loan (0%–8% annual interest). In fact, an older individual with retirement savings may have the bulk of their financial portfolio in low-interest-bearing money market accounts or bonds (1%–3%), investment vehicles that may actually be earning less than the rate of inflation. Homeowner developers can offer that family member agreeable loan terms that are higher than what the family member could receive from a traditional bank or conservative bond investment yet far lower than what the homeowner developer can get from a credit card, conventional lender, or hard-money lender, generally in the range of 8%–18%.

Because the borrower and lender would trust one another in a family arrangement, this loan can be as informal or as formal as the two parties require to feel comfortable. It can be finalized with a handshake or completed with assistance from lawyers, who would most likely advise that a contract be drawn up for such a loan. This type of family-and-friends loan can end up being a great way for a parent, relative, or friend to make a real lifelong difference for someone they care about. It can work very well between family members or between trusted friends.

Again, conventional financial advisers may warn against peer-to-peer loans because of the risk of the loan repayment going awry. This option can work well for ADU development when other options do not. Large personal loans such as this may not be considered initially because the borrower might be embarrassed to ask to borrow large sums of money from family. However, if the homeowner (borrower) considers that they may actually be assisting another family member (lender) financially, this in-family lending strategy may ultimately help convert shame into a sense of mutually regenerative grace. It's a financing situation that cuts corporate lenders out of the mix.

Most homeowners who build ADUs finance them by using a mixture of these four methods. Beyond these common options, there are also some less common financing options.

Nonsecured Loans and Credit Cards

I am personally cautious with money and hesitate to broadcast the idea of using a credit card, due to their high interest rates. But the fact is that some people do use credit cards to pay for a portion of ADU construction. Credit cards may play a crucial role for homeowners to pay for the materials in the finishing stages of development. If a homeowner is smart about using a credit card toward the end of the project, they can quickly do a cash-out refinance once the improvements are completed using their new after-completed value. This consolidates their debt, which allows the homeowner to quickly pay off a high-interest credit card debt or another higher-interest bridge loan.

As of the writing of this book, Home Depot has a Project Loan credit card that might offer another option for ADU development. The customer can get a credit line based on their income level to purchase up to $55,000 in goods and services from Home Depot (according to 2017 promotional materials). The customer pays interest only (7.99%) for those first six months. After the six-month period, customers must begin paying off the principal and interest on their debt. Lowe's offers its own financing options for large purchases.

Other regional options may exist for nonsecured loans from banks and credit unions. Some banks provide personal loans solely based on an individual's debt-to-income ratio, credit score, and liquid assets. For example, in Oregon, Umpqua Bank has a line of credit called Executiveline that provides loans of up to $100,000.

Renovation Loans

Renovation loans, sometimes called rehab loans or construction loans, are a type of conventional financing method that bases a loan on the future value of a property after an improvement is made. Using Elaine's scenario described earlier, the bank's appraiser said Elaine's ADU would value the $400,000 property at $500,000 after it is completed.

Renovation Loan	Amount
Current property value	$400,000
After-construction appraised value	$500,000
Total loan value	$190,000 (95% of future value - current mortgage debt, or $475,000 - $285,000)
Total loan value with conforming loan limit	$168,100 ($453,100 conforming loan limit - $285,000 remaining mortgage debt)

Even with the conforming loan limit, $168,100 may provide sufficient funds for Elaine to build an ADU.

Renovation loans seem great, but in all likelihood, this type of loan option would be difficult to get except in areas where ADUs have become a more established building type. For this type of loan to work, a bank must understand and trust in the value of the building product against which they are offering a loan. Unfortunately, ADUs are not a well-known building type nationally. Banks are conservative and do not look favorably on what they deem to be an unknown risk. Depending on a homeowner's historic business relationship with a local bank or local credit union, it may be possible to work out a renovation loan with them.

Renovation loans have other drawbacks. The homeowner must have permitted drawings to show to the bank before they can feasibly qualify for the loan. The project must be completed using a licensed general contractor from start to finish, which means that homeowners cannot use their own sweat equity to help defray construction costs. The general contractor takes deposits from the bank after each phase of the work is completed instead of being paid up front, which contractors generally prefer. And lastly, the work is supposed to be completed within a six-month time frame.

Because of these factors, renovation loans may make this form of financing less desirable. In certain markets, though, this is a great option for owners with no significant home equity or other financial assets to apply toward an ADU.

Construction Loans

Construction loans are more commonly used by professional developers in building a new house and an ADU from scratch. These loans have higher interest rates and would make sense only if the property is going to be sold or refinanced upon completion. In this way, the initial construction loan can be quickly repaid to the lender and becomes a form of bridge financing. Very few homeowners use this type of financing.

Chapter 4

Costs and Management of Development

PROBABLY EVERYONE WOULD LIKE TO BUILD THEIR ADU FOR AS LITTLE money as possible. This chapter attempts to break the huge range of development costs into practical, tangible chunks of information. By reading this chapter, you will be able to understand what an ADU is likely to cost.

Without a lot more information about the specifics of a construction job, most builders and authors would not want to give cost estimates as this book does. Rather than provide generalized information with no pragmatic value, *Backdoor Revolution* offers specific cost estimates, with the reader's understanding that these numbers can vary tremendously based on a multitude of variables. I have found that providing actual, real numbers is far more useful than not providing numbers at all. Through no fault of their own, many people have a distorted understanding of how much it costs to develop housing or make a major home renovation.

Based on having taught this material to thousands of people in classes, I am certain that the benefit of providing more precise estimates and cost ranges outweighs the drawbacks of doing so. By sharing this, my hope is that homeowners can use my rough estimates and use a rough coefficient against them to gain a better sense of what different things may cost in their location. A coefficient for construction costs should work over both time and space and provide the reader with approximate ADU development cost estimates.

What ADUs Cost to Build

Imagine that someone was going on vacation and asked you to estimate how much an average vacation costs so they could budget for it accordingly. You might reasonably guess anywhere from $100 to $10,000, which is a wide range. There are too many factors, variables, and assumptions to take into account before anyone can really answer that question.

The average cost to build an ADU also varies significantly. An ADU could easily range from $20,000 to $400,000, a twenty-factor difference in cost. This chapter provides some examples of average costs for ADU construction in Portland, Oregon, in 2016. We'll examine some of the variables in ADU development to help understand the wide range of costs.

With those caveats in mind, here are some average figures for all construction expenses from start to finish, but not including the design and permitting.

Size (sq. ft.)	Type	Total	Cost per square foot
800	Detached new construction	$160,000	$200
400	Detached new construction	$120,000	$300
400	Garage conversion	$80,000	$200
800	Basement conversion	$80,000	$100

The Costs of Development for Your Locale

A large factor in development cost relates to the economics in a given location. For example, it is far more expensive to build in Vancouver, British Columbia, than to build in Portland. And it is more expensive to build in Portland than to build in Phoenix, Arizona.

In Vancouver, detached ADUs, called "laneway homes," commonly cost C$350,000 to build. This may sound extremely expensive to most of us, but for middle- to upper-income homeowners in Vancouver, it is affordable housing. The average single-family residential property in Vancouver sold for roughly C$1.5 million in 2016. Developing a small house for C$350,000 on that C$1.5 million property would seem relatively inexpensive by comparison. Similar costs exist in the San Francisco Bay Area market.

ADU construction costs are largely tied to local construction economics. When discussing the cost of ADU construction, it's best to use local construction costs as a baseline for construction of an ADU in a given locale. As a rule of thumb, readers can benchmark costs against the cost examples in this book.

The best way to compare the cost estimates provided in this book is to determine the cost for the design and development of a two-story, 800 sq. ft., standard stick-framed house with moderate finishes in your area. In Portland in 2016, this would have cost approximately $160,000 to construct.

The permit costs and utility connection (or "hookup") costs for an ADU need to be determined separately by the homeowner, as ADU fees are generally treated differently than single-family homes. As a reference point, the permitting and utility connection fees amounted to an additional $10,000–$15,000 in Portland. Often, neither designers nor builders have a reliable sense of what these fees might be. These permit and utility connection fees should be far less than the comparable fees for a new single-family house on an empty lot, but they may not be. Fees could range anywhere from $10,000 to $60,000. See the section called "Keeping Administrative Fees at Bay" in chapter 11 for questions you should ask the City.

The best people to ask for construction cost estimates are small, residential design-build companies. If they are reluctant to provide off-the-cuff estimates, explain that you will not hold them to it, that this is just a way to gauge the financial feasibility of a future project, and that you're just seeking a ballpark range. When obtaining the construction cost estimates, include design work and all construction costs, plumbing, electrical, finish work, and appliances. Do not include landscaping the property, furnishing the unit, or the carrying costs of a loan in the design and construction estimate.

If, after several conversations with design-builders, you learn that an 800 sq. ft. house would cost $250,000 to construct, assume that construction costs are more expensive than in Portland in 2016 by a coefficient of 1.56 ($160,000 × 1.56 = $250,000). You may also learn that permits and utility connection fees would cost $30,000, rather than $10,000, bringing the estimated total development costs to $280,000. Conversely, if you learn that an 800 sq. ft. house would cost $100,000 to construct, use a coefficient of 0.63 ($160,000 × 0.63 = $100,000). That cost coefficient can help you start to develop an idea of what your proposed ADU may cost to design and build in your area.

Average ADU development costs can fluctuate quickly along with local economic conditions. In 2011, the average cost for the same 800 sq. ft. ADU in Portland was closer to $120,000. The average costs for construction of the same structure in 2017 have increased to $180,000—a full $60,000, or 33%, more than in 2011. The years 2010 and 2011 were the lowest point for Portland's real estate following the Great Recession, and professional labor and building materials were both more readily available and affordable then. By 2017, Portland was experiencing rapid population growth and a subsequent construction boom; professional labor and materials were more scarce and expensive. These rapid local economic changes show that these numbers can change regularly and dramatically, so there is no way to provide generic estimates nationally. By determining a coefficient to benchmark against the $160,000 figure, you can start to develop a realistic budget for the project.

FIXED COSTS: SMALL IS EXPENSIVE

Kitchens and bathrooms are the most expensive parts of a home to build or renovate. Each ADU, by definition, must contain a kitchen.

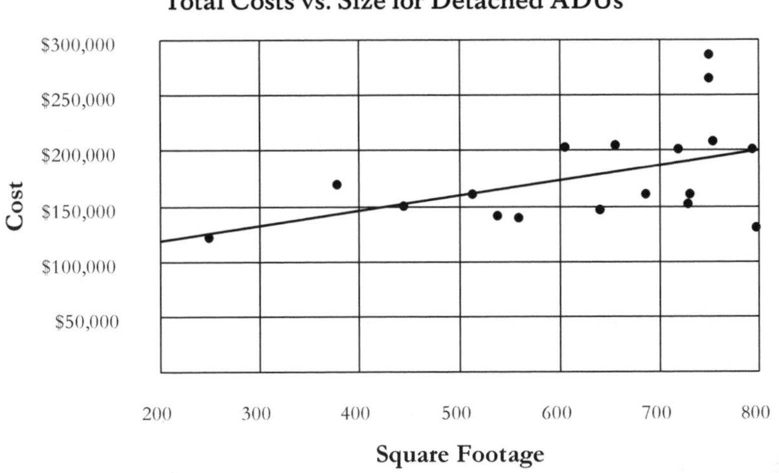

Figure 4.1. The cost of detached ADUs, from the 2016 and 2017 ADU tour in Portland, Oregon.

No matter how large or small a house, it generally has a single kitchen. A full kitchen with moderate finishes and appliances is going to cost in the range of $10,000–$20,000. Whether a kitchen is in a 400 sq. ft. house or a 2,500 sq. ft. house, the kitchen is still likely going to cost $10,000–$20,000. It is helpful to think of the kitchen as a fixed cost. New detached ADUs in Portland typically require new or upgraded electric service to the property. Upgraded electric service work costs $2,000 in Portland. When building even a very small house such as an ADU, you must account for fixed costs like these that would be associated with the development of any house.

Anytime a crew is sent out to a job site, there is a fixed cost, as the subcontractors must order and pick up materials for the project, transport their crew to the site, and do the setup and breakdown of their trade work for the job. These are all fixed costs to them, and the fact that an ADU is small does not reduce these job costs.

The same fixed-cost principle applies to design work for an ADU. In fact, from an architectural perspective, designing an ADU is often more challenging and labor intensive than designing a standard four-bedroom detached house on a standard 50-by-100-foot lot.

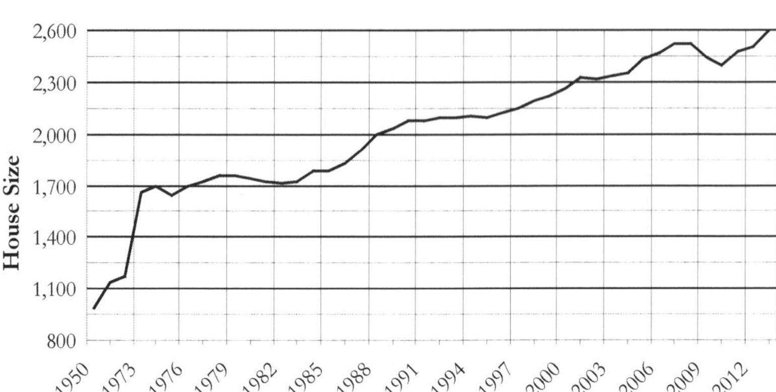

Figure 4.2. Average US house sizes grew 2.6 times between 1950 and 2013. (Data from "Median and Average Square Feet of Floor Area in New Single-Family Houses Completed by Location," United States Census Bureau, https://www.census.gov/const/C25Ann/sftotalmedavgsqft.pdf.)

While it may be convenient to think of construction costs as being proportional to the size of the project, it's more accurate to think of it in this way: there is a baseline cost for any new detached unit. In addition to that fixed cost, there is a marginal increase in total cost as you build upward in size.

In Portland, that baseline cost for a new detached 400 sq. ft. ADU was approximately $120,000 in 2016. While the overall costs for smaller units are less expensive, larger detached units are only marginally more expensive (an extra $40,000 for an additional 400 sq. ft.). All housing unit development has a baseline cost. Adding size adds marginal costs, but the fixed costs make ADU development expensive on a cost-per-square-foot basis. (See figure 4.1.)

I caution homeowners to be realistic and understand that they will not be able to accomplish building an ADU for far less money than everyone else. I state this explicitly because there is rampant and very misleading misinformation available that leads people to think that they can build a house for anything from $10,000 to $40,000. In reality, the materials alone to build an ADU will cost more than $40,000, even for an extremely modest ADU. If you can find someone

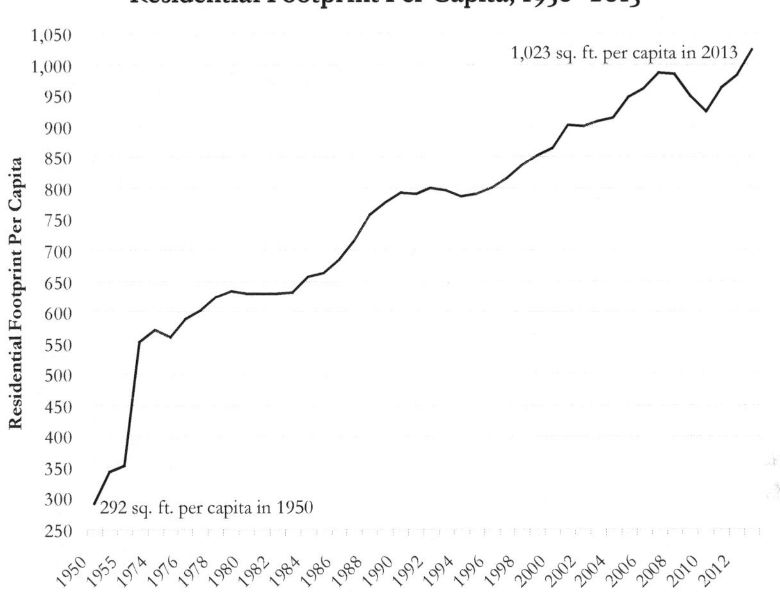

Figure 4.3. Meanwhile, average household sizes between 1950 and 2013 have decreased. As a result of increased home sizes and shrinking household sizes in that time frame, residential footprints per capita have increased from 292 to 1,023 square feet per capita.

who claims that they can actually build you an ADU for that price, hire them—but be sure to use a fixed-price contract! Personally, I would view that type of bid as a major red flag.

What Type of ADU to Build

With all the ADU structural forms available to a homeowner, there are theoretically many ways to build one on a property. In Portland, the three most common ADU forms to develop are as follows (see figure 4.4):

- detached new construction (representing about 50% of ADUs in Portland)
- garage conversion or ADU above/next to a garage (25% of ADUs)
- basement conversion (25% of ADUs)

From a developer's perspective, additional square footage is the cheapest thing to add to a house. Homebuyers pay significantly more for larger homes in a manner that is proportional to the size or number of bedrooms in the home, which sets up an unfortunate economic dynamic. This scenario compels residential developers to build larger homes to recoup their investment costs and earn a decent wage or perhaps even a significant profit.

In general, if a City wants to dramatically rein in oversized homes or spur more small housing development, it could consider dramatic size-based permit fee structures to level the playing field. Or a City would have to create regulations that explicitly restrict home size. Otherwise, developers will likely continue to build larger homes than what the market actually commands because unfortunately this is where opportunity for a decent profit margin lies. This is one reason why house sizes have swelled so dramatically since the 1950s. From 1950 to 2013, the average single-family house in the United States increased by 264% (from 983 sq. ft. to 2,598 sq. ft.). (See figures 4.2 and 4.3.)

Other less commonly built structural forms in Portland for ADUs are as follows:

- internal ADUs (converting a portion of the current living space to an ADU)
- addition-to-ADUs

Here, we'll discuss some of the cost considerations for each type.

Detached New Construction

The cost of detached new construction should theoretically be the least complicated to estimate among the three most common types of ADUs, but even those costs tend to vary wildly.

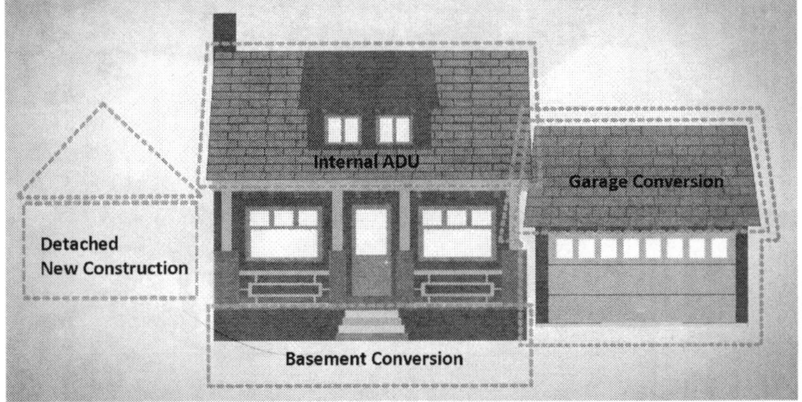

Figure 4.4. Different ADU structural types. (Data from "Accessory Dwelling Units — Take the First Step," video by Paper Crane LLC, https://www.youtube.com/watch?v=-rqtpem82-Q.)

The National Association of Home Builders (NAHB) estimates that the national average for detached new construction was $95 per square foot in 2015. This cost was for houses whose average size was 2,607 sq. ft. Due to fixed costs described earlier in this chapter, ADUs will always cost much more on a square-foot basis than the local average construction costs for current average-sized (2,400 sq. ft.) new homes.

A typical 800 sq. ft. ADU in Portland in 2016 had a baseline construction cost of $200 per square foot, and the total construction cost ranged between $120,000 and $250,000.

NAHB breaks down the general construction costs for detached residential construction in 2015 as follows (percentage of the total cost, from most to least):

Interior finishes	(29.3%)
Framing	(19.1%)
Exterior finishes	(14.4%)
Major system rough-ins	(13.4%)
Foundations	(9.5%)

Site work	(6.8%)
Final steps	(6.6%)
Other costs	(0.9%)

These percentage breakdowns by phase and trade shown in figure 4.5 and summarized above provide a sense of how ADU construction costs may stack up. (See figure 4.5.)

Conversion of Preexisting Structures

Converting an underused existing space seems like a winning idea for creating an ADU. Repurposing an existing space may result in adding substantial value to an area that is not being used to its highest and best use. This also has some significant waste-reduction benefits over building detached new construction. Unfortunately, it's rarely straightforward to execute the repurposing of underutilized space into a permitted ADU.

Homeowner developers often hold unrealistic expectations about the cost savings associated with converting such spaces to a permitted ADU. To their surprise, the cost savings to convert a preexisting, nonhabitable structure such as a garage to a habitable, finished, permitted ADU are often not much cheaper than building a detached ADU from scratch. This section describes some of the common surprise costs that occur with conversions of existing structures into permitted ADUs.

Garage Conversions

It's very common for homeowners to want to convert a garage to a permitted ADU. Converting a garage to an income-producing ADU seems like a good idea to many homeowners who are not using their garage for its intended purpose. Due to building-code requirements for habitable spaces, garage conversions like this often end up being nearly as expensive as new construction, commonly costing $100,000 or more to convert a 400 sq. ft. existing garage to an ADU. This up-front realization deflates the initial appeal of the project by eliminating the financial savings homeowners assumed they'd realize by converting a preexisting

Table 1. Single Family Price and Cost Breakdowns 2013 Results		
Average Lot Size:		14,359 sq ft
Average Finished Area:		2,607 sq ft
I. Sale Price Breakdown	**Average**	**Share of Price**
A. Finished Lot Cost (including financing cost)	$74,509	18.60%
B. Total Construction Cost	$246,453	61.70%
C. Financing Cost	$5,479	1.40%
D. Overhead and General Expenses	$17,340	4.30%
E. Marketing Cost	$4,260	1.10%
F. Sales Commission	$14,235	3.60%
G. Profit	$37,255	9.30%
Total Sales Price	**$399,532**	**100%**
II. Construction Cost Breakdown	**Average**	**Share of Construction Cost**
I. Site Work (sum of A to E)	**$16,824**	**6.80%**
A. Building Permit Fees	$3,647	1.50%
B. Impact Fee	$3,312	1.30%
C. Water & Sewer Fees Inspections	$4,346	1.80%
D. Architecture, Engineering	$3,721	1.50%
E. Other	$1,799	0.70%
II. Foundations (sum of F to G)	**$23,401**	**9.50%**
F. Excavation, Foundation, Concrete, Retaining walls, and Backfill	$23,028	9.30%
G. Other	$373	0.20%
III. Framing (sum of H to L)	**$47,035**	**19.10%**
H. Framing (including roof)	$36,438	14.80%
I. Trusses (if not included above)	$5,461	2.20%
J. Sheathing (if not included above)	$2,332	0.90%
K. General Metal, Steel	$1,604	0.70%
L. Other	$1,201	0.50%
IV. Exterior Finishes (sum of M to P)	**$35,474**	**14.40%**
M. Exterior Wall Finish	$16,867	6.80%
N. Roofing	$7,932	3.20%
O. Windows and Doors (including garage door)	$10,117	4.10%
P. Other	$557	0.20%
V. Major Systems Rough-ins (sum of Q to T)	**$32,959**	**13.40%**
Q. Plumbing (except fixtures)	$11,823	4.80%
R. Electrical (except fixtures)	$9,967	4.00%
S. HVAC	$10,980	4.50%
T. Other	$189	0.10%
VI. Interior Finishes (sum of U to AE)	**$72,241**	**29.30%**
U. Insulation	$4,786	1.90%
V. Drywall	$9,376	3.80%
W. Interior Trims, Doors, and Mirrors	$10,536	4.30%
X. Painting	$8,355	3.40%
Y. Lighting	$3,008	1.20%
Z. Cabinets, Countertops	$12,785	5.20%
AA. Appliances	$4,189	1.70%
AB. Flooring	$12,378	5.00%
AC. Plumbing Fixtures	$4,265	1.70%
AD. Fireplace	$2,057	0.80%
AE. Other	$506	0.20%
VII. Final Steps (sum of AF to AJ)	**$16,254**	**6.60%**
AF. Landscaping	$5,744	2.30%
AG. Outdoor Structures (deck, patio, porches)	$2,891	1.20%
AH. Driveway	$3,741	1.50%
AI. Clean Up	$2,261	0.90%
AJ. Other	$1,617	0.70%
VIII. Other	**$2,265**	**0.90%**
Total	**$246,453**	**100%**

Figure 4.5. Average costs of home construction in the US. The absolute costs may not be relevant, but the percentage breakdown is useful. (Data from Heather Taylor, "Cost of Constructing a Home," National Association of Home Builders, January 2, 2014, http://nahbclassic.org/generic.aspx?genericContentID=221388.)

structure. Half of my ADU consultations are spent on reviewing options for garage conversions and informing clients about shortcomings of a garage conversion. This often pops the dreams of a conversion.

Here are the factors involved. The foundation walls of old garages are usually not up to current building code, which you can easily see when the garage settles in one corner. The stud walls or roof joists may be rotting or moldy or not sufficiently safe to bear any additional forces that will take place once the structure is repurposed.

Retrofitting the foundation or the structural framing and fastening elements to comply with current building-code standards can end up costing as much as starting an ADU building shell from scratch. If new interior lofts are added, vertically loaded structural systems need to be upgraded. If new exterior doors or window fenestrations are added, then additional plywood sheathing for wind-shear strength may be required. Other times, there is a musty smell in garages, indicating that there may be some damage from long-term water intrusion. This means that in addition to re-siding the structure and/or replacing the roof, interior framing members may also need to be replaced.

To further dampen the dream, many experienced builders and architects are less inclined to work on conversions of nonhabitable space to living space because of the unpredictability of the development and construction involved in garage conversions. There is simply no way for anyone, including a builder, to know what issues may crop up as the renovation unfolds. In addition to this unpredictability, the homeowner ends up with an ADU that was not initially sized or laid out for human habitation. Raising the roof or changing the roofline, adding a second story, or building an addition are all common ideas that effectively nullify any potential financial savings of a garage conversion.

In these instances, converting a garage will cost $5,000 more than new construction. That's because the owner is going to have to pay $5,000 to demolish and remove the old garage in order to build a new detached ADU.

When converting any permitted, preexisting structure (such as an art studio, office, or workshop) to an ADU, this same set of cost

Image 4.1. A 180 sq. ft. garage-conversion ADU in Portland, as viewed from the backyard.

principles holds true. If the structure was not permitted, or it is already failing structurally in any of the ways just described, the costs are likely to be closer to the cost of new construction.

That's the unfortunate outcome for most of those who initially consider converting their garage. However, if the building envelope does not need to be retrofitted and can be converted without having to repair or upgrade the structural envelope—that is, the foundation, framing, siding, or roof—it may be possible to safely convert to simple living space at a substantial cost savings over new construction. Newer garages or other accessory structures that were constructed with permits in the last few decades likely fall into this category.

If the garage is ultimately preserved and converted instead of torn down and replaced, a garage conversion tends to be significantly less expensive than new construction. For a typical garage-to-ADU conversion (180–576 sq. ft.), the range in Portland in 2016 was $70,000–$120,000. The least expensive permitted garage conversion I've seen in Portland was $40,000 in 2017, and I've seen several others that

Image 4.2. Interior of a 400 sq. ft. studio-style garage-conversion ADU.

kept their costs at around $50,000. However, the average cost runs closer to $100,000.

The key to keeping costs down is to do a true garage conversion; that is, not to change the exterior structural form of the garage at all. If the roofs are not altered and no additions or lofts are added, it is more likely that the garage can be converted at a more reasonable cost. Another trick is to use existing structural openings, such as the existing garage door opening, as the locations for the future windows and doors of the ADU.

Basement Conversions

From a purely financial perspective, basements tend to be the least expensive way to develop ADUs. Statistically, basement conversions cost less than half of detached new construction, but these amounts may also vary wildly. I've seen basement conversions that cost as little as $20,000 or as much as $260,000. Here are the major variables that factor into the huge range for converting a basement.

As with garages, basements already have a floor, walls, and a ceiling. If the home's foundation walls are not already structurally sound, the primary house may have bigger issues to face than the owner's aspirations to convert the basement to an ADU. Retrofitting failing foundation walls could cost up to $50,000 and would easily bring the total cost of an ADU project well past the $100,000 mark. More commonly, though, the foundation walls are structurally sound. The integrity of a questionable foundation should be evaluated by a foundation specialist.

Moisture intrusion is another ailment found in some basements in temperate or wet regions. Whereas having episodic water intrusion is common in unfinished basements, it is not tolerable to have water intrusion in finished basement spaces. The musty smell of an unfinished basement is a simple indicator of ongoing moisture vapor intrusion. If this issue is not addressed before the basement is converted to living space, the inside of the finished walls will eventually start to develop mold, creating indoor air-quality issues. This can lead to respiratory problems or other health issues for the future resident of the ADU. Water and moisture intrusion issues must be resolved before proceeding and could cost $5,000–$20,000 to fix.

The next big-ticket item is headroom. In Portland, rooms are required by code to have a minimum of 6 feet, 8 inches of headroom to be counted as permitted living space. This means the basement must start off with a floor-to-ceiling rafter-bottom height of at least 6 feet, 10 inches. This building-code height requirement varies by state or jurisdiction. In Portland, some basements' heights do not meet this standard, and the basement must be excavated and a new concrete slab poured. This costs roughly an additional $20,000.

When creating a habitable unit, there must be a code-compliant entry and stairway to the unit. Many existing basement entries are not up to current code, and creating a code-compliant stairway that leads to the basement is the next-largest expense. For the excavation and concrete work, building an exterior stairway may cost $10,000–$15,000. Notably, when just finishing out the basement to create additional living space such as a bedroom or an entertainment room—but not a basement ADU—the owner may not be required to retrofit the stairs to meet current stairway code or entry requirements. A stairwell that is not code compliant may be grandfathered in this case, but not for an ADU.

In Portland, the ADU code requires that for the basement unit, which is a separate dwelling unit, heating systems and other utilities are accessible by the ADU tenant, and that the tenants should not have to enter the primary housing unit upstairs to gain access to these utilities. The occupant of Unit A should never have to enter Unit B to turn their utilities off or on. Similarly, the occupant of Unit B should never have to enter Unit A to turn their utilities off or on. Therefore, the water heater, electrical panel, and central-air mechanical system for the primary house cannot be located within the basement ADU.

In homes with basements, the primary housing unit typically has its heating system, ductwork, water heater, and electrical panel in the basement. Updating all of these infrastructural elements for the primary unit so that they are not located within the basement ADU can be expensive. Repositioning, relocating, updating, and replacing the primary unit's infrastructural elements to meet the separation standards required by ADU building code can commonly cost $5,000–$20,000.

The occupant of the ADU must be able to control their own heat independently from the primary unit, so any ducted vents from the central-air system for the primary unit running through the ceiling joists in the basement must be capped off so they do not ventilate into the ADU. More significantly, the central heating system for the primary unit typically must be totally repositioned or replaced with another system altogether, such as a ductless mini split system.

There are two common ways to accomplish the separation of the infrastructure access for the two distinct units. Either the infrastructure can be located within what is classified as a common space, or the infrastructure can be located within each of the respective units. Common space is a partitioned, firewall-rated portion of the primary house that the ADU occupant can also access. Though less common, it's also possible to place the electric panel for both the primary house and the ADU outdoors, where it would be accessible to both sets of

Image 4.3. Basement bedrooms require egress windows, which run $3,000–5,000 due to the concrete cutting and the work involved in building concrete walls for the window wells.

occupants. More information about the utility separation is located in appendix 1.

Window wells from the basement bedrooms, required by building code for egress in the case of a house fire, are fairly expensive as well. Each egress window cut into concrete may cost $2,000–$5,000 to cut, excavate, and build out.

If none of these expensive retrofitting variables is required, converting the basement to an ADU might cost as little as $20,000 or as much as $50,000. This range would depend on how finished the basement was already and the scope of the basement ADU conversion. If the space was already finished and in excellent shape, and all that was required was a kitchen, firewall separation, a heat source, and electric utilities, a basement ADU may only cost $20,000. However, it's far more common that homeowners who wish to do basement conversions will deal with one or more of the issues described above and also have to entirely finish out the unfinished basement, and this will cost $70,000–$120,000.

The technical building elements that distinguish permitted ADUs from informal in-law units are discussed in the "Technical Issues in Basement ADUs" section in chapter 5. Given the steep costs of jumping through the ADU building-code requirements (namely, separation of the infrastructural and utility systems required to develop a permitted basement ADU), developing basement ADUs may not always be a homeowner's most rational choice. Rather, it may make more sense to build and rent out a bedroom in the basement. This bedroom may have a separate and dedicated entrance, a separate bathroom, and additional living space, but since it does not have a kitchen, it is not classified as a separate housing unit from a regulatory perspective. It's just classified as finished living space that is legally part of the primary house.

> If [the ADU is in] an existing home, there's always the potential for something to present itself to you. There may be structure missing or rotten sill plates. Often, there are old junction boxes buried in walls. If it's a basement we have to figure out how to fit everything in the space to avoid soffits. It can be challenging to figure out a way to run a pipe around a joist or beam because it's load-bearing.
>
> —JOSH SALINGER OF BIRDSMOUTH CONSTRUCTION

Incidentally, this type of basement living space commonly evolves into an informal in-law apartment. That is, a finished basement space that functions like an ADU but was never permitted as such and does not meet all of the actual ADU building-code requirements. If a finished basement with egress windows already exists, then to build an informal in-law unit is just a matter of building or improving separate entry access and adding in functional kitchen elements, such as a bar

Image 4.4. A basement ADU. (Image courtesy of Tatiana Xenelis-Mendoza.)

sink or an illicit secondary kitchen sink. This type of informal ADU development is covered in more detail in chapter 12. Depending on the current condition of the basement, a minor update like this may only cost $2,000. This low cost is why there are thousands or even tens of thousands of basement ADU–like units in every major city in the US where homes have basements. These types of improvements may have been done with permits; however, if a kitchen sink and stove are present, those may not have been originally permitted. These two elements commonly require the space to be officially built to the ADU standards described earlier, with official permits.

Internal ADU Conversions

Other internal ADUs, such as carving out portions of the main floor or building an attic-conversion ADU, would be similar in scope to a basement-conversion ADU. This work would also cost in the range of

Image 4.5. A challenging exterior stairway design that leads to a finished attic in-law unit in Port Townsend, Washington.

$20,000–$140,000, depending on the scope and the level of finish in the space being converted. Adding a code-compliant separate access to the new unit is a notable challenge and expense for an internal ADU, especially in an attic-conversion ADU.

Addition-to-ADUs

An addition-to-ADU is likely to be a little more expensive than the cost of detached new construction. When building an addition to the primary house, the shared structural wall and roof must be opened up, reengineered, and retrofitted. Legacy building-code issues on the primary house, such as asbestos or lead paint, may need to be appropriately remediated or mitigated. The rest of the ADU construction cost would be equivalent to new construction. Therefore, an addition-to-ADU is likely to cost $15,000–$30,000 more than construction for a comparable detached new ADU.

Large Variables That Drive Costs of Construction

Unfortunately, there aren't many secret tricks to reducing most ADU construction costs. Modular construction is not cheaper, nor are shipping-container conversions or off-the-shelf ADU designs that typically require modifications for the site. While true structural conversions are less expensive than new construction, complex structural conversions and new additions commonly cost as much as new construction. A few of the big-ticket variables that factor largely into such a construction budget include who is hired, how the project is managed, and what types of materials are used.

> I saw many people investing $150,000 or more in ADUs and planning for a 10-year return on investment. We wanted to do it more affordably so focused on a basement ADU, which requires much less cash upfront....
>
> When we decided to build an ADU, we focused on properties having a basement with an exterior entrance and adequate head height. It took a while but we did ultimately find one.
>
> —John Hayden, basement ADU owner

Designer and Builder

There is no magic or universal formula to find an ideal, affordable design team and construction crew. Here are some common-sense vetting tips that a homeowner can use to help find the right team to design and build their ADU.

In general, less accomplished designers and builders are likely to cost less than more established designers and builders. The larger and more well-known the company, the more overhead expenses they are likely to have.

Homeowners will find that bids for construction vary significantly. The cheapest bids may seem to be the most attractive. However, chasing the lowest bid may not always be the smartest choice. In addition to looking at the cost and thoroughness of a bid, a homeowner should check references to see whether recent clients were satisfied with the builder's capacity to finish the work on budget and on time, and the homeowner should also observe the communication skills of the builder during initial conversations. Good communication and speedy responses can be critical to a positive working relationship with your designer and builder.

The builder does not need to have any ADU-construction building experience. There are no major differences between ADU construction and standard residential construction, except for the utility connections. ADU utilities are connected differently, but they are not especially challenging. Homeowners should not feel that they must restrict their builder search to ADU builders.

Although not requisite, having a passionate small-space designer or an experienced ADU designer can be very helpful. ADU design is both different and more challenging than standard residential home design; read chapter 5 for more insights.

A homeowner may be able to find a gem: a novice but competent design-and-build team that is able to do the job for a good price. Homeowners should understand there is also more risk involved with using less-experienced companies.

Developer, General Contractor, Builder

Homeowners can directly manage the ADU construction project themselves to varying degrees as the general contractor (GC) if their City code allows this. General contracting project management is a full-time job that involves finding the subcontractors, coordinating between trades, setting up schedules, making payments, negotiating subcontracts, ordering materials and supplies, setting up building inspections, and managing quality control.

There are three approaches that a homeowner developer may use in project management. All three approaches have their merits.

1. Become the general contractor yourself for the entire project.
2. Use a general contractor for the weathertight shell, and become the general contractor for the finish work.
3. Use a general contractor from start to finish.

Become the General Contractor

Providing project management for the construction of an ADU is a daunting task for homeowners. Beyond the satisfaction of managing the development of an ADU, managing one's own project can save a homeowner roughly 15%–25% of the total project cost—the amount a general contractor typically charges to manage a project.

It may work for a homeowner to act as their own general contractor if they are ambitious, very knowledgeable about building, have a lot of building skill, have tools, and have a solid break from a regular work schedule for 4–6 months. However, without a substantial break from other day-to-day employment, general contracting on the weekends, evenings, and during vacations ends up causing a typical ADU build period to last 1–2 years instead of the average build period of 3–8 months. Bearing this in mind, the 15%–25% savings gained by not hiring a general contractor is effectively lost due to lack of rental income during the additional year or more of construction. However, some owners admirably opt to be their own general contractors in order to intimately learn the skill sets of building a home and save that 15%–25% in out-of-pocket expenses.

I tend to caution most people away from acting as the general contractor for new construction, largely to counter the unrealistic expectations that exist among homeowners about the ease of self–general contracting the development of an ADU. The reality is that the excavation, concrete formwork, foundation, and framing involved for a permitted, weathertight shell are quite technical. Any mistakes can become extremely costly or be very labor-intensive to fix. Self–general contracting a weathertight shell is not advisable for most novice homeowner developers.

Conversely, if the ADU is being created from within a solid, structurally intact, and permitted space—a garage or a basement—general contracting the conversion job is much more attainable for homeowner developers. That conversion project management scope would be akin to the work associated with a major gut rehab. Some homeowners may have managed such projects when remodeling a basement or another part of their house.

> Allow a year from initial planning to completion of building—and more if you're a do-it-yourselfer.
>
> —JOE ROBERTSON OF SHELTER SOLUTIONS LLC, AN ADU DESIGN-AND-BUILD COMPANY

The terms *builder* and *general contractor* are used synonymously, but being the general contractor does not necessarily mean swinging a hammer or doing any physical work at all. Construction labor should be understood as distinct and different from general contracting, which is actually project management. However, typically a general contractor does some or even the bulk of the construction labor. A homeowner may not play the role of general contractor but may choose to do a lot of construction labor. Or a homeowner may act as a general contractor but contribute no manual labor whatsoever. Both approaches are totally valid.

Use a General Contractor for the Weathertight Shell; and Become the General Contractor for the Finish Work

A weathertight shell refers to all major residential structural building elements. This work includes excavation, foundation, framing, sheathing, weather barrier, siding, ground-work plumbing, mechanical systems, and windows and doors, and could also include plumbing rough-in, electrical rough-in, insulation, and hanging drywall. A homeowner may not feel comfortable taking on project management for the weathertight shell but may be able to do so for the finish work, such as the cabinetry, painting, staining, appliance installation, trim, and landscaping.

This split general-contractor approach is quite common for ADU construction; it's what I did on my project. During the construction, I referred to the weathertight shell as "Phase I" and the finish work as "Phase II." Although I wished that I had been able to general contract my whole project to learn all of the trades, after observing the amount of work involved in construction of a small house, I was really glad that I hired a professional builder to manage the construction of the weathertight shell.

Weathertight shell construction typically involves renting heavy equipment, such as excavators, concrete forms, and concrete delivery trucks, as well as efficiently managing two- to six-person crews to complete large tasks (the foundation, framing, and roofing). While each and every part of the construction is important, the foundation, framing, plumbing rough-in, and electrical rough-in in particular must be sequenced, tightly coordinated, and executed correctly.

If there are any mistakes during this first stage, they are likely to become very big mistakes. For example, a foundation wall must be totally level from one end of a house to the other. Pressure-treated lumber and framing for the stud walls are fastened directly to the foundation walls. The tolerance of level for the foundation wall affects the house framing, roof, drywall, and cabinetry, which must ultimately be square, level, and plumb. Minor differences in foundation wall heights from one end of the house to the other are not acceptable.

In many ways, the finish work (cabinetry, painting, flooring, and trim) that is done during the latter phase of construction is the fun part of construction for most homeowners. Unlike the weathertight shell, it is much easier to fix mistakes that occur with finish work. In addition to project managing the finish work, my wife and I also did a lot of finish labor on the ADU ourselves. My wife created a beautiful wraparound tile mosaic in the bathroom tub, and I managed contractors or personally worked on the flooring, trim, exterior staining, cabinets, closet shelving, kitchen counters, and appliance installations, as well as electrical and plumbing fixture installations.

With a month off between jobs, I spent ten to sixteen hours a day working on the ADU finishes. I hired friends, laborers, and even my general contractor, who did the weathertight shell, to help me on an hourly basis on bigger jobs as a subcontractor during the finish work. I estimate that my wife and I invested approximately $15,000 of sweat equity during the finishing phase of construction. While this approach "saved" $15,000 in out-of-pocket expenses, these sweat-equity savings were possible only because I had a month available between full-time day jobs.

Use a General Contractor for the Entire ADU

Hiring a general contractor to manage the entire job from start to finish is the last of the three approaches. Using this approach, the homeowner leaves the construction entirely in the hands of building professionals. This approach costs more money out of pocket; however, depending on the professionalism of the general contractor, the work is more likely to be done faster and correctly.

This approach results in less stress on the homeowner, who still may be involved intimately as the developer, but who is not required to be on-site to oversee or do any of the construction labor. With a detailed set of construction plans and a reputable general contractor, the homeowner could theoretically skip town for six months and come back to a move-in-ready ADU, although I've never seen this scenario actually happen. Homeowners are heavily invested both emotionally and financially in their ADU and generally want to be around to bear witness to the ADU birthing process.

Another advantage of this approach is that the contract can require the general contractor to warranty the work. If a general contractor is reputable, they should be willing to do this. However, if a homeowner does some of the work themselves, this type of warranty cannot be written into the contract.

A design-build company handles both the design and the construction of a project. Because project management is handled from start to finish and the company is more accountable for the entire process, this type of approach tends to cost more. There is comparatively little required of the homeowner using such a process. This is the best approach if the homeowner has sufficient funds and does not have the ability, time, or interest in being heavily involved in managing the project.

If the homeowner is going to hire the builder and the designer independently from each other, I recommend that the homeowner interject a design-build process. That is, the builder would be involved in the design phase, and the designer would help with construction oversight to some degree. This means you must identify a builder before there is even a project to bid on, which can seem a bit counterintuitive. An experienced builder should be able to give cost-range estimates before any plans have been drawn up. Selecting a builder who is involved in the design helps reduce lost-in-translation problems that commonly arise during the more conventional, linear designer-to-general-contractor approach.

Defraying Development Costs through Sweat Equity

The dream of building one's home elicits American, self-sufficient, do-it-yourself symbolism best characterized by Henry David Thoreau's romantic reflections on his experience building a cabin on Walden Pond in Concord, Massachusetts, in 1854. However tempting it may seem, building a permitted house from the ground up is an enormous job and not necessarily feasible for someone with little or no building experience. Most homeowners do not have anywhere near the experience, capacity, or skills required to build an ADU themselves.

That said, as a rule of thumb, half of the cost of construction is for materials and half is for labor. To the extent that a homeowner does some amount of the labor themselves (referred to as sweat equity), this can save significant out-of-pocket cash. A homeowner could theoretically cut their out-of-pocket development costs in half by doing all of the labor themselves. For each hour the owner is not working at another job, they are, however, losing that source of income. Depending on their income, interests, skills, time, and capacity, it may or may not make financial sense to do a portion of the construction labor themselves.

It is very common for homeowners to do some amount of the construction, typically in the finishing stages. From a survey of ADU owners in Oregon, we know that owners contributed an average of ten weeks of their time to construction of the ADU. This is a substantial amount of energy and reflects just how personal these projects are—or how desperate homeowners may be to reduce the tremendous out-of-pocket capital expenses.

When accounting for total ADU development costs after a project is complete, I include an estimated value for the sweat equity that homeowners contributed to the construction. For example, my wife and I put $15,000 of sweat equity into the finish work of our ADU, and I added that sweat-equity estimate to the total out-of-pocket expenses to come up with the total construction cost. Through sweat equity, homeowners are sometimes able to defray their out-of-pocket budget expenses proportional to the amount of work they do themselves.

Self-designing the ADU is another way that homeowners may save money. ADU design is quite technical, so it's best to use a designer who has had years of training and experience. When there is a preexisting structural envelope to be converted (such as a basement or garage) that does not require any reengineering, it is easier to draw and submit those designs without the aid of a professionally trained designer.

Level of Finish

When shopping for finish materials, there are several tiers of quality and price for every element of finish work. The homeowner is constantly faced with deciding between certain price points for finish products such as trim board, paint, countertops, tiles, flooring, light fixtures, and kitchen appliances. NAHB estimates that finish work accounts for 30% of the total project cost. Each decision in the selection of finish material collectively amounts to a significant portion of the total project cost.

The level of quality and cost of the selected finish materials is entirely up to the discretion of the homeowner developer. If the ADU may one day serve as a primary residence for the owner or a family member, the homeowner developer may choose to purchase higher-end materials to use throughout the entire project. Conversely, if the ADU is intended purely for renters, the homeowner developer may be inclined to opt for lower-end builder-grade materials throughout the entire project.

> We try to use salvage and reused building materials.... We've done well there with doors and tiles. It's more difficult doing this for all of our clients because it's so time-consuming. It's too expensive for them to pay us to look for materials for them. Sometimes we just buy something and store it, and if we can use it in a project later we do.
>
> —Paz Pozarycki of UDU Design LLC, an ADU design-build company

---

Salvaging Finish Materials

There can be significant savings through the selection of budget materials or salvaged materials. Unfortunately, most of the materials used for the construction of a weathertight shell during new construction (concrete, insulation, framing, roofing) cannot be easily or cheaply salvaged from another project and reused on a new project. However, many finish materials (flooring, cabinetry, doors, countertops, tiles, knobs) can be salvaged and reused. This can save money and reduce waste.

With salvaged materials, the items need to be selected before the drawings are done and submitted to the City for plan review, as they affect the architectural design of the ADU. There are several finish items in particular that can save a homeowner significant money:

1. New windows and doors for detached new-construction ADUs can range from $3,000 to $12,000. It is possible to find a similar set of good-quality, discounted windows for $1,000–$5,000.
2. New kitchen cabinets can run from $5,000 to $12,000. Used cabinets range from $1,000 to $4,000. The initial ADU kitchen layout must be designed around cabinets that are purchased.
3. Bathtubs may cost $1,000–$2,000. A used tub may run $100. Tub dimensions must be determined before the bathroom design is done. A used tub must be selected during the design phase.
4. Flooring, doors, sinks, toilet, and vanity can cost more than $1,000 each new. Salvaged flooring, doors, sinks and faucets, toilets, and vanities may each cost under $100. These items can all be purchased after the weathertight shell is complete. Most cities should have some kind of local, salvaged building supplies resource (e.g., Habitat for Humanity's ReStore or deconstruction resource center). If no such store exists in the area, scouring Craigslist is typically the best approach to seeking salvaged materials.

Chapter 5

Design Principles

CHAPTER 5 WILL COVER SOME BEST PRACTICES FOR DESIGN THAT CONsider the distinctive attributes of infill ADUs. Homeowners should consider how to apply these concepts in their projects. This is not intended to be an exhaustive depiction of all best residential design practices; rather, designers should consider incorporating these concepts into their ADU design.

There are many books and websites about small-space design, the most popular of which are a series of books authored by Sarah Susanka. You can find some of these ideas represented in coffee table books and discussed in great detail in other design-focused literature. This chapter complements the plentiful graphic, diagrammatic, technical print literature and websites by adding a customized set of ADU design principles and nomenclature. I've curated these ADU design principles by visiting hundreds of ADUs and well-designed small houses over the years, speaking with designers who focus on ADUs, and consuming a host of small-space design literature myself.

Small-Space Design Principles for ADUs

- When limited to a small space, it is critical to spatially join the kitchen, living room, and dining room into one great room to create a psychological sense of larger space, as well to leverage additional functionality by overlapping them. These spaces should be

Image 5.1. An ADU great room, with varied colors, textures, and ceiling heights throughout.

separated visually by varied wall colors, ceiling and floor heights, lighting, textures, and furniture. Otherwise, a great room feels plain or unimaginative. (See image 5.1.)

- Tall ceilings make small spaces feel much larger. Consider designing the structure with cathedral and vaulted ceilings instead of standard flat ceilings. While the minimum height required for ceilings may be 6 feet, 8 inches or so, strive to incorporate ceilings of at least 8 feet and up to 10 feet in portions of the great room. Varying the ceiling height adds visual interest. (See image 5.2.)
- Consider the view from various key locations within the ADU. Aim to create some long and expansive sight lines if possible, including out of windows. (See image 5.3.)
- In temperate or cold climates, which exist across the majority of the United States, it is generally best to place most of the glass windows and doors along the south-facing wall. This allows for improved passive solar heating and natural lighting.
- High windows allow the sun to cast light across small spaces and give a greater sense of volume to a small space. High windows are

Image 5.2. This single-story ADU has 10-foot ceilings, giving it a sense of spaciousness.

available in several forms, including skylights, clerestory windows, and floor-to-ceiling windows. Skylights with flared shafts are particularly effective at capturing larger volumes of natural light. (See images 5.4 and 5.5.)

- There are several kinds of lighting functions: ambient, accent, safety, and task. Consider the lighting function before defaulting to ambient lighting. Use dimmer switches to integrate even more lighting mood options. Do not skimp on adding ample lighting fixtures during the design and construction of the ADU; too many lighting options are better than too few. Utilize natural lighting in darker spaces such as bedroom closets or bathrooms by incorporating conventional skylights or tubular skylights. (See image 5.6.)
- Small homes should attempt to layer or stack the functionality of spaces. This design principle is commonly used within tiny-house-on-wheels design and boat design. Examples may be an office that easily doubles as a guest room, or the placement of large pieces of furniture in a great room on caster wheels to more easily reconfigure the space for different purposes. (See images 5.7 and 5.8.)

Image 5.3. A view from the bedroom loft to the end of the ADU, through the south-facing French doors, and into the backyard.

Image 5.4. Two skylights bring natural light and a sense of volume into a 290 sq. ft. ADU.

Image 5.5. A close-up of a flared skylight shaft.

Image 5.6. South-facing glazing, pendant lights over the kitchen bar, and standing lamps in the living room collectively add a range of light textures into the ADU great room.

- Within small homes, it is wasteful to have space solely dedicated to getting people from room to room. The various functions of rooms in an ADU should be stacked to effectively merge the functions of a home into common spaces. (See image 5.9.)
- Luxurious, large-sized bedrooms do not make sense to prioritize in space-constrained ADUs. In an ADU, the square footage for a bedroom space generally should take a back seat to additional square footage for the great room. The largest ADU bedrooms only need to be about 150 sq. ft. (See image 5.10.)
- Ample storage is vitally important for long-term residents. While it may seem frustrating to allocate precious square footage to storage, occupants use and value storage space. Don't let any unused space go to waste. Consider options such as drawers in stairs. For innovations on storage design, look to the tiny-house-on-wheels movement or boat design for inspiration. (See image 5.11.)

Image 5.7. This rolling island on casters creates a kitchen nook, but it also allows for the kitchen to open up space when needed.

Image 5.8. A Murphy bed with a fold-out table in a studio-style garage-conversion ADU.

Image 5.9. This ADU has no hallways. All circulation occurs within rooms.

Image 5.10. This bedroom is small but adequate for its purpose.

Image 5.11. Most of the kitchen wall space in this ADU has vertically stacked layers of shelving and storage. The fridge is recessed under the stairway, and the rest of the space under the stairwell is cleverly used for a cabinet.

Image 5.12. A small storage shed in the backyard can be a very useful addition if the garage-turned-ADU can no longer be used for storing lawn and garden equipment.

- Both the primary house and ADU occupants need long-term storage. If the primary house has a basement, it can play a vital role for both units. If the basement or garage is being converted to an ADU, or the property does not have dedicated long-term storage space, an exterior storage shed may be a useful addition to the property for storage needs for both housing units. (See image 5.12.)

Design Principles for Detached ADUs

Detached ADUs have several special architectural design considerations that standard residential design generally does not need to take into account. In particular, when determining where windows and doors should be placed, there are several dynamics to consider.

- A detached ADU is likely to be adjacent to a rear yard or garden. It is best to use full-light French doors or sliding glass doors to create an intimate connection to the rear yard from the ADU great

Image 5.13. South-facing French doors lead into the backyard, creating an intimate connection with the outdoors and making the interior space feel larger.

room. This makes the ADU great room feel larger and establishes a visual connection with greenery in the surrounding landscape. Avoiding steps up or down from the building interior to the exterior can help facilitate a more direct connection with the outdoors. (See image 5.13.)

- Depending on the desired social relationship between the occupants of the two dwellings, it can make sense for both to have access to a shared courtyard or for one house or the other to benefit more from having yard access primacy. In some multigenerational family settings, for example, both the primary house and ADU may have French doors that face each other across a shared yard, creating a sense of a family compound. However, it is more common in ADU development for the owner to prefer established privacy for each unit by not facing large windows or French doors directly toward each other.
- Vegetative screening, hedgerows, and lattice screening and fencing can be used to effectively create courtyards, privacy control,

and noise abatement. The use of these landscaping techniques can be considered initially, or they can be used retroactively to address privacy concerns that arise after the construction of the ADU. Landscape design can help augment the aesthetics of the property, helping to ensure that the yard is used and not wasted. (See image 5.14.)

- Most new homes have views from the inside to the outside that are worth enhancing and other views that are best to obscure. While desirable and undesirable views from the ADU can be dealt with retroactively using blinds, curtains, and window film, it is best if the windows are intentionally placed to take advantage of the best available views.
- If there is a pleasant canopy view or a great urban streetscape, for example, consider how to best orient the windows and glazing to take advantage of these features. Conversely, consider where to place windows to block poor views. A clerestory window may let in a lot of natural light, provide a view of a tree canopy and the sky, and yet may strategically obscure the view of an unsightly structure next door. (See image 5.15.)
- Because ADUs are inherently a form of infill housing, they are likely to be built in close proximity to neighbors, as well as to the primary house. Therefore, consideration should be given to how the placement of windows can impact the privacy of the ADU residents and their neighbors. For example, ensure that the ADU's bathroom windows do not face directly into the kitchen of a neighboring structure. While neighbors should not be allowed to exert control over the design of a neighboring property's ADU, it is the design responsibility of the ADU developer to ensure that the new building creates as little aesthetic harm to neighboring properties as possible. Respect for neighbors in design is sometimes even codified directly into the ADU development regulations, dictating where and how ADU entries and windows must be oriented to avoid any privacy encroachments.

Image 5.14. Cedar screening creates small, quasi-private courtyard spaces for the occupants of the ADU and the primary house.

Image 5.15. This tactfully placed large window provides an upward view of a tree canopy from the living room of this ADU. What you do not see is that there is a storage shed on an adjacent property less than 10 feet away from this window.

- When converting a garage or another accessory structure, it is typically easiest and cheapest if the kitchen and bathroom plumbing can be joined along an exterior wall that is proximate to the primary house. This reduces the amount of concrete trenching and repair work required inside the ADU. For example, it may cost $1,000–$3,000 more to plumb a bathroom on the opposite side from the kitchen in a garage conversion due to the additional concrete work and plumbing involved.
- Small homes with open floor plans amplify sound that bounces around freely throughout the dwelling. This is not a problem if the ADU is designed for only one full-time occupant. But if the ADU is

Image 5.16. The lofted bedroom of this ADU has a window that allows natural light from the skylight to come in.

built for two full-time occupants, it is important to consider sound privacy. Without any walls to obstruct its path, sound moves freely from room to room. Thus, the two occupants lose their sound privacy entirely, unless rooms with doors and insulated walls are built explicitly to address sound privacy issues. There is a design tension at play here because open, lofted designs look wonderful and make small spaces feel larger, but the lack of sound privacy resulting from an open floor plan can be cognitively and emotionally problematic for two-person households. For example, one person making breakfast in the morning may easily wake up the other person, as it will sound as though the person is cooking, eating, and washing dishes next to the bed. Phone conversations, music, and TV will be heard by the second person. This audio privacy issue may ultimately result in the need to wall off a bedroom instead of keeping it as an open, lofted bedroom space. Using physical barriers with insulation and mass can attenuate sound. (See images 5.16 and 5.17.)

Image 5.17. Whenever acoustic privacy is desired, the sliding wood panels in the bedroom are closed, as shown above.

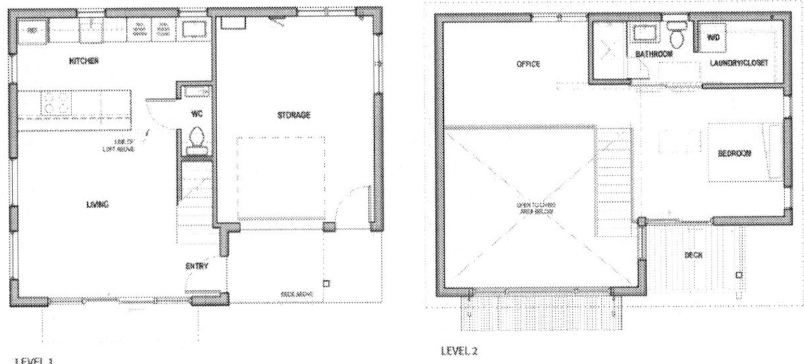

Figures 5.1 and 5.2. A lofted floor plan. (Images courtesy of Polyphon Architecture and Design.)

- In particular, one interior floor plan for detached, two-story, one-bedroom ADUs in particular seems to work well. The layout has an open first-floor plan with a lofted bedroom over half of the ground floor. Beneath the loft are exposed beams with decking used for the ceiling above. There are numerous iterations of this basic layout, but one example, a lofted floor plan, is shown in figures 5.1 and 5.2.

ADU Design Tips and Tricks

- By code, ADUs are size constrained and height constrained. ADUs built from converted garages are always constrained in these ways. To make a code-compliant bedroom on the second story may be impossible. Even if it's not entirely impossible, building a code-compliant stairway may ruin both the first-story and second-story floor plans. Thus, many ADU owners are effectively forced into building non-code-compliant sleeping lofts, which must be classified as "storage lofts" or "attics" in architectural drawings. These sleeping lofts are often accessed by alternating-tread stairs or ladders and are often wonderful and cozy spaces, but they are not yet generally permittable as legal bedrooms.[4] Code officials cannot condone these storage lofts as habitable living spaces, so

Image 5.18. A ladder that goes to a storage loft...which might be used for sleeping space too.

the homeowner would proceed with this design at their own risk and complete this work after the inspections are complete. (See image 5.18.)

- Alternating-tread stairs, also known as Jefferson stairs, and ladders are a steeper and more space-efficient alternative to stairways. There are many beautiful alternating-tread stair images to use as inspiration on the web. These alternatives are not code compliant, so they cannot be used to access habitable space, but they can be used to access storage lofts or attics. In some cases, a spiral staircase can help create a code-compliant stairway where a linear or winder stairway does not fit. (See images 5.19 and 5.20.)
- Exposed wood beams used with tongue-and-groove decking as the ceiling finish can serve as the flooring for a lofted second-story bedroom. These are a great way to add visual character to the first floor and to gain an additional six inches to a foot of visual headroom on the first floor. This design works well to make a height-constrained space feel larger. The drawback of this design is that there is not much sound isolation when the ceiling of the first story is also the floor of the second story. (See image 5.21.)

Image 5.19. Alternating tread stairs that lead to an attic storage space.

Image 5.20. A spiral staircase can be used to create a code-compliant stairway in a compact house.

Image 5.21. Exposed wood beams are structural, attractive, and add vertical headroom in the kitchen.

- Pocket doors are a wonderful feature to utilize in bathrooms of ADUs. In some designs, pocket and barn doors can be used for closets and bedrooms. They often add character to an ADU, since they are less common than hinged doors. Most importantly, they save door-swing space, making it easier to open and close the bathroom door. This option also allows space in the adjacent room or hallway where the door would normally swing open to be utilized for other purposes. (See images 5.22 and 5.23.)
- Placing a pocket door between the toilet/tub and the sink, or between the toilet and the tub/sink, allows the toilet to be used privately by one person while another person is brushing their teeth. This is a great trick to pack more utility into a bathroom without adding any additional space to it. A second door can be added to wall off the entire bathroom if the owner desires to preserve shower-toilet-sink privacy. (See image 5.24.)

- ADUs typically have to be positioned away, or set back, from adjacent property lines by 3, 5, or 10 feet—or more—depending on the local zoning regulations. However, although structures can't be placed within the setback, that doesn't mean the setback space is wasted. It can be elegantly hardscaped with pavers or used as a patio or pathway or to store large items such as ladders or a canoe. In some cases, the ADU entry can occur on the side within this setback. (See image 5.25.)
- While an ADU has official square-footage limitations, there are ways to add useful square footage without it being classified as "livable space," helping to circumvent the limit on total square feet. Storage lofts, short closets, recessed shelving, and spaces located under lower sections (less than about 5 feet) of an angled knee wall are all examples of spaces that do not officially count as livable space but can nonetheless add functional space to a house. These tricks are relevant if the ADU size limits are measured and limited by the interior livable space, but they're not relevant if the size limits are determined by the exterior wall dimensions. (See image 5.26.)

Image 5.22. A pocket door that does not take up any room space. Note the sink that would be blocked off if the door swung inward to the left.

Image 5.23. A pocket door hides the laundry closet.

Image 5.24. A pocket door to the bathroom, and a second pocket door within the bathroom on the left side that isolates the toilet from the sink and shower. This design allows the toilet to be used privately while others may still access the sink.

Image 5.25. An effective and attractive hardscaping makes efficient use of the 5-foot setback requirement. The door toward the back right is the entry to this ADU.

Image 5.26. Though the storage in the repurposed kitchen cabinets is highly functional, it's recessed under a 5-foot portion of the kneewall. Thus, none of that square footage is counted in the limit for a 800 sq. ft. interior.

Technical Issues in Basement ADUs

Basement ADUs have their own technical idiosyncrasies, many of which may be familiar to contractors who have done basement renovations to create habitable living space. Water intrusion is a common issue that must be dealt with when converting a damp basement space. Window wells are required for egress from any bedroom in the basement. Large basement windows add ample visual and psychological value to a basement ADU, even if they are not required in a given space. The following is a list of technical issues that commonly arise for basement ADU conversions.

- Recessed lights are critical to use in basement ADUs due to the inherently height-restricted space that basement ADUs are built in. Avoid flush-mounted ceiling light fixtures or hanging ambient light fixtures, except for kitchen pendant lights over a counter or bar. (See image 5.27.)

Image 5.27. Recessed lights in the ceiling in a basement ADU. (Image courtesy of John Hayden.)

- Typically, basement ADU codes require that the two units are separated by a one-hour firewall. This commonly means that there must be two layers of five-eighths-inch drywall separating the downstairs unit from the upstairs unit. All spaces between the two units must retain this fire-rating standard, including around recessed light fixtures. Recessed LED fixtures should be considered to reduce the difficulty of fireproofing a box around conventional recessed canned light fixtures.
- Insulation, mass, and resilient channels should be used to attenuate sound between the two stories. It is difficult to get rid of all bass sounds, such as someone jumping on the floor in the upstairs unit, but with sufficient insulation, much of the noise between the two units can be reduced.

- Basements tend to stay at a fairly even, cool temperature year-round. They are cooler than the rest of the house during hot summer days, so they generally do not require air-conditioning. Due to the already temperate conditions of a basement, many basement ADUs can get by using simple, inexpensive, electric resistance heating systems such as cadet heaters or radiant panels instead of using more elaborate and expensive centralized heating systems.
- *Common space* refers to a space that is firewall-separated from both the primary house and the ADU. The most typical common space is in a portion of the basement of the primary house, though it could also be a shared utility room on the property. Common space is accessible to occupants of both units on the property, and any utilities for both units can theoretically be housed within it. When building a basement ADU, it is typical to have a common space in which the electric service panels for both units are housed. Other large or noisy mechanical system elements, such as the central heating system furnace, the water heater, or a shared washer and dryer, can also be housed in common space.

In addition to these design tips, tricks, and ideas, there are some technical issues relating to utilities and infrastructure that need to be considered during the design phase. This information is located in appendix 1.

Chapter 6

Income Models

THERE ARE MANY WAYS TO POTENTIALLY USE AN ADU: PRIMARY DWELLing, rental housing, or office. Indeed, their flexibility of use is one of the primary drivers of their development. However, ADUs are an enormous investment, and homeowners generally build them with a goal of recouping their expenses.

According to the 2013 Oregon Department of Environmental Quality (DEQ) survey of ADUs,[5] the primary motivation for ADU development was rental income from the additional unit (46% of respondents) followed by the ability to provide a separate living space for a family member (26% of respondents).

The proximity of the landlord and tenant with an ADU and a primary house provides a built-in framework for a social and economic dynamic that is different from conventional landlord-tenant dynamics. This chapter describes some common trends in how ADUs are typically used after construction in order to generate passive income and provide housing flexibility.

Common Models for ADU Ownership

These are some of the most common ways that homeowners choose to use their ADUs:

1. Rent out the ADU long term at market rates.

2. Provide the ADU to family or friends at a rate that is either significantly lower than market rates or for free.
3. Rent out or provide the furnished ADU occasionally to family or friends at lower-than-market rates, and then use it for flexibility as desired, potentially as a guesthouse or as a short-term furnished rental at market rates.
4. Rent out the furnished ADU short term at market rates.

Owners can also live in the ADU and rent out the primary house. Because the primary house is larger than the ADU, it generally brings in more rental income. Here are some examples of this setup:

1. Live in the ADU, and rent out the primary house at market rates.
2. Rent out the primary house at market rates. Live in the furnished ADU part-time, and when living elsewhere, rent out the ADU part-time at market rates.
3. Live in the ADU and rent out the primary house to family or friends at below-market rates.

If there is no owner-occupancy requirement, then both the primary house and the ADU can be rented out as standard investment rental units.

Market-Rate Rentals

According to the 2013 Oregon DEQ survey, 80% of ADUs were used for long-term housing. In the San Francisco Bay Area, 86% of the informal ADUs were used primarily as long-term rental housing.[6] Renting out the ADU at market rates is the most common use for ADUs.

For those considering renting out an ADU, the best way to estimate rental income potential is to look at rental rates for comparably sized apartments in that area. Based on the Oregon DEQ survey, the difference in rental rates between apartments and ADUs appears to be statistically insignificant. A new 800 sq. ft. one-bedroom apartment in a given neighborhood would rent for approximately the same as a new 800 sq. ft. one-bedroom ADU. To get a sense of the local apartment rental market rates, query real estate agents or websites such as Zillow or Craigslist.

Where an owner lives on the property, it's possible for the second unit to capture higher-than-average rental market rates, depending on how the unit is advertised and managed. The mere proximity of the second unit makes it easier to manage, and it is possible to use this proximity to add value to the renter of the second unit. Many owners opt to pay the utilities for both units and build that "utilities-included" and yard-maintenance convenience factor into a slightly higher rental rate. For example, most primary houses and ADUs share wifi and trash services, and some share laundry facilities.

It is easy to fully furnish an ADU with relatively little furniture. Most ADUs are small enough that only certain pieces of furniture in particular configurations will work. This one-time furnishing cost ($1,000–$10,000) can also help fetch more rent in a niche furnished rental market than comparable unfurnished rental units.

I'm not going to delve into the duties involved in being a landlord. Being a landlord isn't for everyone. Relative to other forms of work from which one can derive comparable income, being a small-scale landlord is relatively simple. There's a reason why rental income is called "passive income." However, if being a landlord is not something that the owner wants to do, they can use a property manager instead. Property managers typically charge a percentage of the monthly rent as their fee.

Short-Term Rentals

Short-term rentals (STRs) are an emerging hot topic for ADUs, due to the growing prominence of Airbnb and an increasing demand for vacation housing in residential neighborhoods. Short-term rentals in general—and short-term rentals in ADUs in particular—have become targeted by City Councils and neighborhood citizen groups concerned with affordable housing. Their position is that ADUs are intended to provide long-term housing. Using them as short-term rentals has forsaken their intended use and takes away valuable long-term housing stock.

The political arguments against the use of ADUs for STRs unveil assumptions as follows:

- the assumed purposes of ADUs
- the very limited political constructs of ADUs' role as affordable housing
- the overall economic impact of STRs on market rental rates, which have not yet been scientifically established

Exploring the politics and economics of this emerging market and its intersection with ADUs is challenging, as social and political standards around STRs are still emerging. This is an evolving and dynamic issue without established answers, though I can offer a few insights.

Because the short-term rental market is emergent and the regulations are quickly shifting to deal with it, and because short-term rental host management may not be a desirable homeowner duty in the long run, it would be wise for homeowners generally not to model ADU income around any assumptions regarding short-term rental income potential. For homeowners, I recommend using a conservative, long-term rental income assumption when considering whether an ADU makes financial sense or not. I caution all homeowners not to bank on a short-term rental income stream, even if it is a strong motivation for ADU development.

For policy makers, the benefits and drawbacks of short-term rentals exist with or without the presence of a permitted ADU. Perhaps ADUs should not be treated differently than other residential housing forms in terms of how they can be used. The same long-term and short-term rental regulations that apply to single-family homes and duplexes should be applied to properties with ADUs.

If there is a lot of resistance to ADUs largely based on the fear of STR use, a horse trade could be made to disallow STRs in ADUs so that ADU regulations can be made otherwise more flexible. The elimination of short-term rental use is unlikely to greatly quell homeowner demand to build permitted ADUs. Beware that political compromises that specifically treat ADUs like the ugly stepchild compared to all other housing forms will collectively stall permitted ADU development overall.

Before a City leaps to judgments about ADUs and STRs based on assumptions and anecdotes, it would be wise to gather data and create better policy. It may be best to holistically address the short-term rental issue on its own standing rather than entangling STR policy with ADU policy. Perhaps putting all short-term rental tax revenue into an earmarked fund dedicated to affordable housing would more succinctly address the policy challenges at hand rather than banning short-term rentals in certain districts or certain housing types.

Or Do Not Rent It

The fluidity and ease with which ADUs can change use over time is one of their unique characteristics. Due to the proximity of the owner to the accessory unit, as well as the flexibility, privacy, and modest size of the unit, it is relatively easy to utilize and manage the ADU for a variety of uses. It is not uncommon for there to be three or four uses for an ADU over the course of a single year (longer-term rental housing, guesthouse for family, short-term rental, office). This compelling flexibility attribute should be heralded.

Evidence suggests that most ADUs will likely be used for long-term housing for the majority of their life span. The DEQ survey found that 80% of permitted ADUs are used as long-term housing. The vast majority of ADU development is motivated by either the flexibility that the ADU affords for an additional family member or by the rental-income potential of the extra unit. Long-term housing will likely be the most significant use over the life span of the ADU.

However, not all ADUs are used for housing at a given point in time. In the 2013 DEQ survey, roughly 15% of ADUs were not used as housing at all at the time of the survey. The study found that 11% were used as offices, while 4% were used as "other" guest housing, free temporary housing, and short-term rentals. ADUs may serve as long-term housing most of the time, but the living arrangement may easily change over the course of a year—and will likely change over the course of a few years or a decade. Whether informal or formal, ADUs can turn into housing or other uses depending on the changing needs of the property owners.

Informal ADUs, which dwarf the numbers of permitted ADUs nationwide, also appear to be commonly used primarily for long-term housing. These may also be used for a range of flexible purposes, including offices, guest rooms, and family housing. The Bay Area survey on informal ADUs found that 86% were used as housing and 14% had an alternate use, a similar statistical finding to the Oregon DEQ survey of permitted ADUs.

The Social Relationship of the Residents

There are some unique characteristics of ADUs that impact how they're used. For example, the Oregon DEQ survey found that 26% of those who rent ADUs are family or friends of the property owners and that in these situations, ADUs often rent for free or at far less than market rates.

But the majority of ADUs are more standard rentals. The occupants of the two units have a fairly modest level of involvement and interaction with one another. In fact, it is common to have dynamics where the occupants of each unit rarely bump into one another; the secondary unit functions more like a house next door.

ADUs are independent from the primary unit, and the occupants of the two units do not necessarily visit one another's living space.

The privacy, independence, and social dynamic of the occupants of both units can be set according to the property owner's wishes and are informed partially by the site design. The desired dynamic can be incorporated into the design and development of the architectural relationship between the ADU and the primary unit. This is done through the placement of a shared courtyard and shared common space, as well as window and door placement, alignment, and glazing.

Some owners opt to physically separate the two units so that it is not even evident that they're on the same property. This type of detached-ADU site plan is very easy to design on corner lots or on properties with alleys, where the unit entries may actually face different streets or rights of way. This type of site design does not necessarily take advantage of the social relational characteristics that ADUs can have with the primary house, but it does result in the ADU feeling entirely distinct from the primary house.

ADUs provide the potential to create a more intimate form of relationship with the occupants of the primary unit. ADUs can provide a compound-like atmosphere if the homeowner wishes to use the property that way. Generally, ADUs are not designed to function like an intimate extension of the primary house, though ADUs often share some common property elements as well as some architectural features. The dynamic is explicitly up to the owner's preferences. The owner determines and designs the physical relationship between the buildings, and it is also at the owner's discretion to establish appropriate social boundaries between the occupants of the two units.

Due to the proximity of the residences, the owners who live on-site may end up going into the rental unit to manage it more often than a typical rental. For example, I live in an ADU but go into the primary house two or three times a week to check in on things—take out the trash, change light bulbs, say hello to the tenants, and so on. I make this dynamic known to those who wish to live in the primary house before they choose to live there. The dynamic is like an owner living in a group house, except that I have as much privacy as I want in my ADU.

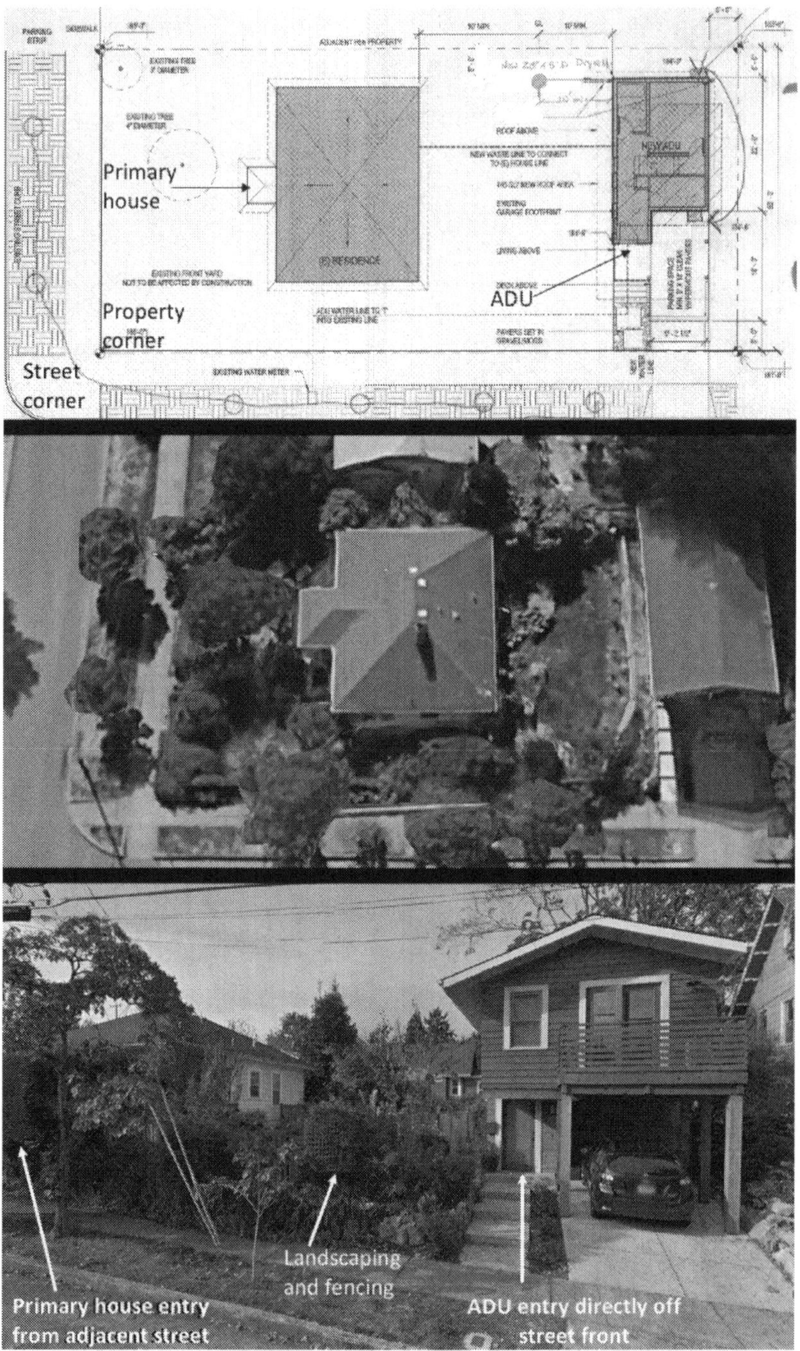

Figure 6.1. Site layout and landscaping can make an ADU feel as an entirely distinct unit from the primary house if that aesthetic is desired by the owner.

Image 6.1. The primary house and ADU have matching roof pitches, siding, and coloring, allowing the two units to visually complement each other.

When a tenant texts me about a broken light bulb, I'm often able to replace that light bulb within minutes. When I run household errands for my ADU maintenance needs, I also run household errands for the primary house maintenance needs. This is a far higher level of service than I'm capable of providing to a conventional rental property. Meanwhile, my wife and I borrow and return household items from the primary house as needed, such when we're having company in the ADU and need extra chairs.

Being so close to the rental unit, whether it's the primary house or the ADU, makes it easier to manage it in an intimate way. This means that it is possible to change the use of the second unit with relative ease during housing transitions.

While living under the same roof as one's parent may not be appealing for many American adults, living in close proximity to a parent can be very appealing for a range of pragmatic reasons. For example, it is a fairly common arrangement for grandparents to help finance an ADU on their kid's property and then relocate to it to help raise their grandchildren—the quintessential granny flat. Simultaneously, the kids are able to look after their aging parent.

ADUs can be used in unusual, socially niche ways that other home configurations cannot as easily facilitate. In addition to the more common example of grandparents living in the ADU, ADUs provide good options for grown children who have developmental disabilities to live in the ADU next to their parents or siblings. Here's one example from Vancouver, Washington.

> His 288-square-foot accessory dwelling unit is attached to his parents' house in east Vancouver. Even though he's lived in the unit for a little over a year, Yung Ting still calls his place "new house" and his parents' "big house."
>
> When people initially heard that Yung Ting was getting his own place, many were taken aback. The 23-year-old has autism and Down syndrome.[7]

Numerous creative relationships can exist on properties with ADUs. I know of middle-aged people who own a property with an ADU but have their twentysomething-year-old children live on and manage the property, providing training-wheeled guidance to property ownership. I also know of a separated couple who live in adjacent units on the same property; perhaps this arrangement has occasional appeal to many happily married couples as well. There's also the bartering possibilities of using the ADU for an au pair, a live-in nurse, or a property caretaker.

Typically, ADU owners live on the property and manage the rental unit themselves. But one set of vagabond ADU owners I know uses a property manager to manage the rental unit (the primary house, in this case) simply because they do not want to deal with the work involved in being landlords when they're traveling. They also do not want to set up a social-hierarchical dynamic with the primary-unit

Image 6.2. A cottage-style ADU with its owner. The primary house is shown to the right. The ADU was built primarily for their son, who has a disability.

renters; those renters don't even know that the occupants of the ADU are the property owners.

I know of another arrangement in a relatively urban residential neighborhood where two single moms each lived with their children of similar ages in the primary house and the garage-conversion ADU, respectively. The women, both renters in this instance, built a magical play space and garden in the rear yard, complete with ducks, a hot tub, and a swing set. They took turns looking after each other's kids, who played together. This type of social cohousing arrangement could not exist, physically or economically, as fluidly in any other housing form in this neighborhood.

The reality of ADU ownership is that the property owner can set up the social dynamic between the two units however they wish. The customized microeconomics that can happen on a property with an ADU are useful for the occupants, but this housing relationship can also fill niche roles in community building for a city at large. ADUs can help facilitate all these niche, critical, social functions at no subsidized cost.

Bonnie Roseman, a real estate agent in Portland, tells the story of how she became an ADU owner. She came around to developing an addition-to-ADU with and for her mother. The pass-through doorway between the primary house and the ADU allows the familial occupants to walk from the house into the ADU without going outside. Because of this setup, Bonnie's mom actually uses a primary-house bedroom as her library and study—in effect, an extension of her 800 sq. ft. ADU. Bonnie's daughter also lives in the primary house, so it has become a three-generation household. This narrative is representative of many of the organic social and economic relationships that happen with ADUs.

> I came up with this idea that if we could buy a duplex, we could both afford something better than we could afford on our own and help each other. We searched and searched and could not find a duplex. So in the end, we were like, okay, let's buy a home and build an ADU. We lived in this house while we built the ADU as an addition to the house. Then, after the addition was completed, we went through the formal steps to turn it into an official ADU.
>
> My mom will be eighty this year. It was five years ago that we were planning it. She was turning seventy-five, in great shape, dancing all the time, going to lectures, very active, doing all kinds of things. But night driving was hard. My mom was very nervous about being around people because she had lived so long on her own. But, as it turned out, she's really happy that we did this. It's really fantastic that we did this not out of a necessity. In the last couple of years, my mom has had various health things come up—nothing life-threatening, but some incidents where she hasn't been well. And it's been amazing.[8]

Image 6.3. The great room in the Rosemans' attached ADU.

Fledgling Development Models

Other fledgling ADU development models are occurring in various cities. These are currently rare models, but condoization in particular is worth describing in more detail below.

Other efforts have looked at building ADUs as bona fide affordable housing. In Austin, Texas, community development corporations have built several ADUs as affordable housing units on properties they own through a program called the Alley Flat Initiative. In Santa Cruz, California, Habitat for Humanity is attempting to establish a model in which the ADU is developed and used as a form of affordable housing.

ADUs as Condos

This is an emerging topic for ADU development. The development of ADUs as condominiums is a legal mechanism by which the ownership of an ADU and the primary unit can be separated. The ADU can then

Image 6.4. An ADU as a condo in Portland, Oregon, that sold for $325,000 in January, 2017. (Image from Living Room Realty, http://www.livingroomre.com/homes-for-sale-sold-details/2835-SE-71ST-AVE-B-PORTLAND-OR-97206/16338428/54/.)

be sold separately from the primary house. This approach could result in the sale of a stand-alone ADU as a small and more affordable form of housing in otherwise expensive real estate markets.

This model may appear to be a way to make ADU development profitable for speculative developers. If this were true, then ADUs would be developed not only by those who wanted to hold on to the property for passive rental income; they would also be developed by those who saw profit margin potential in speculative ADU development.

While this approach is too embryonic to provide a critical analysis, there are a couple of variables that should be discussed. The positive aspect of this approach is that it could theoretically result in the production of more ADUs being built overall, as well as the production of relatively affordable housing stock for sale in residential zones.

Habitat for Humanity: ADU Development Assistance for Low-Income Families

Habitat for Humanity's My House My Home program is a partnership between the City of Santa Cruz, California; Senior Network Services; and Habitat for Humanity. This partnership program is designed to assist low-income senior homeowners age in place. The City and Habitat provide low-interest and no-interest financing, and Habitat's skilled volunteer construction crews handle the construction needs of the program.

The program targets seniors who are at risk of losing their homes because they can no longer meet the mortgage payments or can no longer use their homes because of changing handicap accessibility needs. The program aims to build seniors an accessible ADU into which they can downsize, then rehabs the primary house into an affordable rental to be managed by a property management company.

The primary house rental units serve households with incomes at or below 60% of median income, with rent set by the City. Over time, as the loans are paid back, or upon sale or transfer of the ownership, those loan funds go back into a revolving fund to help pay for future My House My Home projects.

This program allows senior homeowners to stabilize their housing costs so that they can age in place by providing an accessible, energy-efficient unit, and it adds new stock to the affordable rental market for low-income families.

The drawback of this approach is that it eliminates the organic, flexible, and changing functions that ADUs play over time for the long-term property owner. The ADU would more likely be owned and inhabited as long-term housing itself, but it likely would not be used as free housing for a family member.

Jake Wegmann, professor of housing, real estate development, and planning at University of Texas at Austin, shared an optimistic perspective about ADUs as condos.

> The way a lot of American cities continue to keep housing pretty cheap, as certain neighborhoods got denser with more development pressure, was to just keep re-subdividing the lots. I guess as far as I'm concerned, condoizing the lots is maybe the closest modern approximation to that. It seems like it might have some of the same benefits. I mean, it's just splitting one lot into two. It seems like a good idea to me.[9]

The reason that the ADUs-as-condos model is not necessarily as lucrative as it may seem at first blush is that the primary house, when sold as a condo, would be discounted from the market value it would have as a stand-alone fee-simple property. If the ADU is located in the backyard and partitioned as a condo, the primary-house owners would effectively lose the unencumbered use of a rear yard. Some buyers may prefer the simplicity of buying a fee-simple property over buying a condo to avoid additional administrative costs or the hassle involved with being part of a homeowners' association (HOA).

PART II:

THE PROFESSIONAL'S GUIDE TO ADU DEVELOPMENT

Chapter 7

What Is Distinctive about Developing and Inducing ADUs

ADUs ARE A RARE FORM OF HOUSING, AND THEY'RE UNLIKELY TO flourish under the common regulatory framework that most cities have instituted for housing development. This chapter offers considerations and insights into the following characteristics about ADUs:

- how ADU developers are distinct from those of other housing types
- why permitted ADUs are rarely found in today's housing stock
- what institutional elements are unique to their development
- what conditions will help them flourish

Amateur Homeowner Developers

ADUs tend to be extremely good long-term investments, but they are not particularly good short-term speculative investments. Therefore, those who opt to develop ADUs tend to hold on to the property and have a vested, long-term interest in the property.

Indeed, the average ADU developer—that is, the individual who initiates and finances the project—is typically the homeowner and resident of the primary house. From the Oregon DEQ survey, it was estimated that 70%–90% of ADU developers in the Portland market were homeowner developers.[10]

No other housing form is typically developed by amateur homeowner developers. Other housing types are generally developed by professionals who understand the process; it's what they do every day for a living. Homeowner developers are inherently amateur developers.

Homeowners are building an ADU on the property where they will likely live and which they will hold for a long period of time. They will derive income from the ADU, whether or not it will be their personal home, and beyond the finances, they will likely invest love, care, and attention to detail into the development of their ADU. As previously mentioned, the DEQ survey revealed that the average homeowner contributes ten weeks of sweat equity into the construction process.

The fact that amateur homeowner developers are excitedly executing these projects means that ADUs will have a more customized character than most speculative residential projects. This unique and custom quality is even more pronounced when the owner is going to use the ADU as a primary residence for themselves or a family member.

ASYNCHRONOUS DEVELOPMENT

ADUs tend to be built asynchronously from the primary house because they tend to be developed by the homeowner who has already purchased a finished primary house on the property.

The physical design of ADUs is typically responsive to existing site conditions and structures. As a result, ADUs tend to have interesting site constraints and specific landscape conditions inherent to the nature of backyard urban infill. Examples of the responsive nature of detached ADU design are described in the section "Design Principles for Detached ADUs" in chapter 5. In the case of basement-conversion ADUs, the most rational floor plans are largely determined by the existing location of an entry, the egress window opportunities, and the utility locations. The combination of preexisting site conditions and the amateur homeowner developer's

Image 7.1. Tiled winder stairs with undermounted LED light strips, white trim, and a salvaged steel guardrail and handrail.

design sensibility coalesces to form a small housing unit that is customized to the homeowner's property.

The nature of an ADU design means each space-efficient and customized urban infill ADU is one of a kind. I've visited well over two hundred ADUs, and I have never seen two that look alike.

> I've always enjoyed small dwellings carved out of forgotten urban spaces. Designing an ADU presents unique spatial challenges, which often result in a richer design solution.
>
> —JACK BARNES, PORTLAND ADU ARCHITECT

Customized ADUs on a property may tend to help a primary house persevere where otherwise equivalent homes in a neighborhood may be demolished.

FAITH IN GOVERNMENT

Building an ADU is likely the single largest cash investment a homeowner will ever make and possibly one of the most complex projects they will ever undertake.

An ADU could easily cost $160,000. By contrast, purchasing a $500,000 property with a conventional mortgage will only require about $25,000 as an up-front investment for a 5% down payment. In other words, developing a $160,000 ADU could easily require six times more cash on hand than is necessary to finance a $500,000 property with a conventional mortgage. This huge cash expenditure may feel intimidating and overwhelming for middle-income households.

As novice developers, homeowners are undertaking a complex and multifaceted housing development project, the likes of which they've never tried before. They understandably want a high level of predictability and certainty regarding the steps in the development process, the costs, and the eventual financial outcomes on what feels like a very risky undertaking.

Ideally, there will be some level of hand-holding for homeowners to assist them through what may be perceived as an ordeal. Specifically, homeowner developers need to have an accurate sense of how much these projects cost. In addition to grappling with the daunting construction costs, the homeowners also need to know permitting costs and development fees, and they need to have a clear sense of the property tax and income tax implications for the property. Homeowners need a sense of certainty from the planning and building department in order to help them work their way through the intimidating, overwhelming, and complicated permitting process. This is why discretionary reviews are problematic—they scare homeowners off (see chapter 8).

Having an accountable, transparent development process is key to providing the necessary faith in government that a homeowner must have to take this financial leap. Even today, I find many people consider skirting the development rules to build a unpermitted ADU simply because they do not want the City to regulate their property decisions, charge surprise administrative fees, or trigger property tax increases.

Some level of mistrust in government is a culturally intrinsic and healthy American condition. For some, the interaction with their City's planning and building department in the ADU development process is the most intimate interaction of their lives with a government. Others eschew the formal process because they do not understand why they must seek the City's blessing for their ADU project in the first place.

At best, a white-glove approach toward the homeowner developer could help, though this has not proven to be necessary in Portland or Vancouver, British Columbia. Predictable, reasonable, responsive, and transparent development processes that build faith in the intimidating and risky development process have proven to be invaluable in both jurisdictions.

The Challenge of Financing ADUs

Even if market and regulatory conditions are conducive for ADU development and the ADU zoning regulations are not too restrictive—even then—relatively few ADUs will be built. That is because ADUs are very expensive to build.

There is evidence from the DEQ survey that ADUs are developed by those who have an economic motivation or family need for the ADU. Yet ADUs can only be developed by people who have access to sufficient capital for this major investment and who can handle the complexity that comes along with managing such a multifaceted project.

Despite easy access to capital, it is less likely that extremely wealthy homeowners would develop an ADU on their property because they may lack the economic motivation that middle-class homeowners may have. For them, an ADU used as an investment might prove to be more labor intensive than other investment opportunities.

Conversely, it is rarely possible for those with little economic means to develop a permitted ADU. Building a permitted ADU to code is far more expensive than building an informal ADU without permits. It is likely that many who opt to build informal ADUs may be doing so partially for financial reasons. (See figure 7.1.)

Apart from regulatory barriers, financing ADUs through the capital cost of construction hinders their development. Even if the zoning code were very permissive, until loan financing options make some significant breakthroughs, permitted ADU development may remain relatively sparse. Homeowners cannot apply for a simple off-the-shelf ADU loan. A vast number of homeowners who want to build an ADU cannot obtain the necessary funds to do so.

My consulting practice deals largely with those who have not yet built an ADU but want to do so. I've now personally taught well over a thousand people about the ADU development process in full-day workshops. The workshop feedback forms ask, "What was your biggest barrier (perceived or real) to building an ADU?"

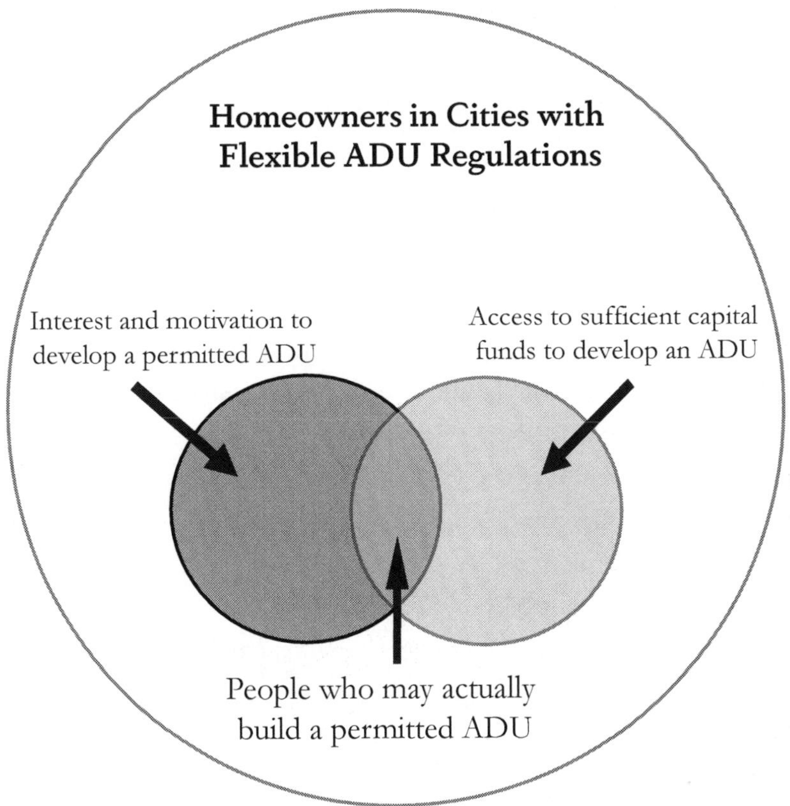

Figure 7.1. The overlapping category of those who may be both motivated to build a permitted ADU and financially capable of developing one is fairly limited.

It is clear from the answers that cost remains one of the largest barriers to development.

Portland's System Development Charge waiver temporarily reduced the capital development fees by $8,000–$12,000 starting in 2010, amounting to 5%–15% of an ADU project cost. This played a large role in spurring ADU development in Portland and serves as an economic indicator for how instrumental the reduction was to incentivizing more ADU development. (See figure 7.2.)

Even among those who were successful in building, 56% of respondents in the Oregon DEQ survey reported that financing was the largest hurdle to ADU development. They cobbled together financing, usually from a patchwork of personal savings, family loans, and home equity lines of credit.

- 24% of the DEQ survey respondents paid partially with family loans and credit cards.
- 40% paid with HELOC and cash-out refinancing.

Streamlined financing options for ADU development have not fully matured. National banks seem mostly incapable of providing financing products for these projects. It seems that for now, only local banks and credit unions sometimes may have conventional construction, rehabilitation, and renovation loan products that work for ADU development.

Until such options become available, only a limited pool of homeowner developers will be able to use their patchwork of funding sources, along with substantial sweat equity, to overcome the formidable cost of building an ADU.

Small Business Infrastructure

Because it is amateur developers who are doing a significant development for the first time, there is likely to be value in specialized, local ADU cottage-industry businesses that grow to support the development. ADU development ultimately lends itself best to boutique, small business operations. The need for specialized ADU expertise can be easily understood in planning and zoning, architecture, and building. There is also a clear need for ADU-educated real estate agents, appraisers, and financing.

This type of small business infrastructure is developing in Portland, but it is still nascent. I can think of tens of small design and building businesses that now primarily do ADU design and development work in Portland and Vancouver. This specialized industry could blossom

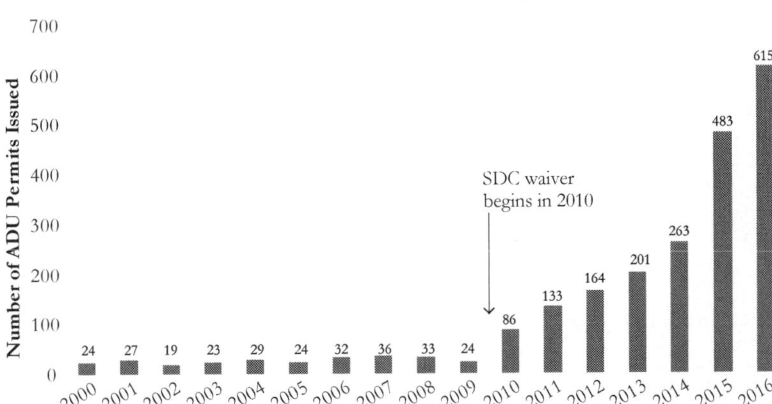

Figure 7.2. Portland's System Development Charge waiver was instrumental to kick-starting ADU development in Portland, Oregon, in 2010.

significantly as the movement grows. Eventually, there may be experienced ADU drafters, 3D modelers, interior designers, mortgage specialists, property managers, landscape designers, HVAC specialists, structural engineers, permit specialists, and educators, as well as other specialized consultants.

The lack of such specialists does not entirely prohibit ADU development, but it currently serves as an institutional barrier for already overwhelmed amateur developers. Most homeowners do not have the requisite time, energy, or expertise to be the first people in their area to break the ice with banks, architects, builders, building inspectors, and appraisers by having to explain basic information about the ADU development process.

Flexible Use

Flexible living arrangements are among the most appealing features of ADUs. This should be viewed as an asset not only by the individual but by a municipality as well. The ADU can become a form of unsubsidized affordable housing for relatives, or the primary house could become a new unit of market-rate rental housing if the homeowner decides to live in the ADU. When ADUs are not being used as full-time residences, they can also play a useful role as shorter-term housing for those in housing transition. Unlike other housing forms, ADUs can fluidly change their use to meet the highest and best use over time.

Homeowners commonly have a spare bedroom in their primary house that they may think of as "flex space" to use as temporary housing as needed. Housing a friend, family member, or renter in an ADU is less intrusive as it affords more privacy from the primary house than the habitation of the spare bedroom. Because it also has the capacity to be a stand-alone rental unit, an ADU is more likely to be utilized and valued than a spare bedroom. An ADU has intrinsically higher value as rental space on a property than an empty bedroom while simultaneously being more independent.

By living on-site, it is easier for a homeowner to change the use and management of a secondary house than if it were located on a different property. This also means that a homeowner can create value for the occupants of the secondary structure through their more immediate access, availability, services, and social relationship. Bartering for rent reduction or adding value for specialized accommodation services can serve niche, organic, social, and civic functions (see chapter 6).

This flexible-use aspect of ADUs is best left unhindered by overreaching specifications about what the use of the ADU must be (e.g., the ADU must be used as long-term rental housing). Not only do use restrictions limit the inherent capacity of the ADU to serve critical niche functions in the market, but use restrictions severely limit the motivation and ability of a homeowner to build an ADU in the first place (see chapter 8).

ADUs must be fostered in a manner that is different from other residential infill housing types. Indeed, they may need to be initially nurtured. Eventually, a variety of institutional and market actors can fill in the niche industry gaps. It is evident that in the cities where ADUs have actually flourished, whether by accident or design, these distinctive attributes were explicitly addressed by various institutions to coax ADUs into existence.

Chapter 8

Zoning Barriers

Mindless rules, not accountable officials, are the enemy of freedom.

—Philip K. Howard, *The Rule of Nobody: Saving America from Dead Laws and Senseless Bureaucracy*

Municipal regulations govern the planning and zoning codes that dictate the viability of ADU development in cities. While it may be theoretically possible to build an ADU in most cities, the regulations can be so onerous and restrictive that very few permitted ADUs, if any, are built under existing codes.

Even in a place where a model zoning code exists, the balance of economic and market factors that allow for an ADU movement to happen is delicate, and ADUs still may not be developed. For more information about the balance of preconditions necessary for development, see chapter 11.

Many communities ban ADUs outright. A 1990 study estimated that only 40% of municipalities allowed ADUs. Among those, it was estimated that roughly one permitted ADU was built for every 1,000 homes.[11] A 2005 study of 187 communities in eastern Massachusetts revealed that 107 (57%) allowed "accessory apartments," and of those municipalities that allowed (internal only) ADUs, many municipalities reported only one ADU being permitted every few years.[12] As of 2017, it is unknown what percentage of municipalities allow ADUs, though the number of cities has increased substantially in recent years.

More importantly, the vast majority of communities that claim to allow ADUs over-regulate them to such a degree that they may as well be banned. The extremely low annual development rate of permitted ADUs found in most jurisdictions (one to ten ADU permits per year) is largely attributable to restrictive ordinances and bylaws and long, involved, complex permitting processes. No wonder so few homeowners would dare to run the ADU development gauntlet; such formidable roadblocks stand in their way.

POISON-PILL REGULATIONS

The most damning of these ordinances are "poison-pill regulations," as they each effectively kill ADUs in their own right. If any of the poison-pill regulations exist, ADUs have little chance of flourishing. There are three extremely common poison-pill zoning regulations, ordinances, or bylaws that tend to stand in the way of a substantial number of permitted ADUs from being built. The bulk of this chapter will deconstruct these regulations:

- owner-occupancy requirements
- off-street parking requirements
- conditional or discretionary reviews

That these regulations kill ADUs is the most significant message for planning officials and advocates. My hypothesis is that if any of these bylaws exist, no viable movement can take place within a jurisdiction. The existence of these regulations prevents a jurisdiction from seeing positive ADU growth on a year-to-year basis.

These provisions seem innocuous, so it is hard to fathom how much they stymie permitted ADU development throughout this country. But the proof is in the pudding. Rather, the lack of pudding is the proof. It is by deeply studying the growth dynamics of permitted ADUs in several selected cities and then surveying the many counterfactual examples that exist everywhere else in the nation that it is possible to draw these conclusions.

Where ADU development is needed to help meet rental demand in single-family-zoning-dominated jurisdictions, these poison-pill regulations have the active effect of fostering informal ADU-like development. If a municipality wishes to foster more permitted and safe ADU development, these are codes that must be addressed.

These poison-pill regulations tend to be accidental regulations copied from adjacent towns without critical analysis of their impacts or deliberate regulatory approaches to dampen ADU development. This book is not intended to influence Cities who have consciously opted to stymie ADU development. It is intended to help the former—those who adopted and maintain such onerous regulations not by explicit intent but rather by accident.

It seems many cities have copied and pasted ordinances, bylaws, and ADU zoning regulations from neighboring jurisdictions. Once every other neighboring city and town had similar bylaws in place, the bylaws became the norm—accidental mindless regulations. Perhaps planners just copied model codes without truly analyzing them, not realizing that these cities had never spawned much ADU development themselves. Or perhaps with the growing domination of Euclidian zoning, starting in the mid-twentieth century, these were active measures used to suppress ADUs while not outright banning them.

Today, their origin and intent forgotten, such accidental regulations are perhaps assumed to be normal and well reasoned. I will do my best to show their inherent conflicts with regard to ADU development. When challenged, these poison-pill regulations can become lightning rod political issues that elicit very heated citizen opposition. So adamant and vocal are select groups of citizens in protecting these regulations that most local politicians lack the will to forge a more lenient development pathway. Instead, politicians cave to the vocal opposition, the regulations stagnate, and inevitably, few if any permitted ADUs are built. This is the karmic cycle in which many Cities find themselves mired and that this chapter may help break.

Following the three poison pills, I'll review a number of other development standards that also commonly hinder ADU development if the standards are prohibitively restrictive:

- setbacks
- size limits
- minimum lot sizes
- structural forms
- sewer and water connections, development fee costs

Owner-Occupancy Requirement

Owner-occupancy ADU bylaws state that an owner must live on the property if there is an ADU on it. This precondition is the default rule of the land for ADUs today in the United States. With this restriction in place, ADUs generally will not be built. City planners are able to recite this owner-occupancy bylaw, but they are not be able to justify why only properties with ADUs should be subjected to it.

Here's what a standard owner-occupancy requirement looks like:

> Owner occupancy required.
>
> The owner of the lot on which the second unit is located shall maintain either the primary single-family dwelling unit or the second unit as his/her/their principal domicile as long as the second unit exists on the lot.[13]

A 1981 study revealed a few underlying sentiments that spawned the first owner-occupancy requirements for ADUs. The "purpose of these provisions is to prevent speculation and to ensure that the appearance of the structure will be maintained."[14] Ten years later, the same author was describing this ordinance as the de facto standard for

ADUs, which indeed it had become.[15] A 2006 article from the *Boston Globe* quoted a City Commissioner from Franklin, Massachusetts, saying, "A new bylaw is needed to specify exactly who could live in the apartments to make sure people do not build them to generate rent money or to house relatives who just want a cheap place to live."[16] One city's 2002 Master Plan document stated, "The key to accessory apartments is that they should be in structures that are owner occupied so that they do not then become like apartment buildings."[17] Owner-occupancy regulations for ADUs appear to have been formed in the latter half of the 1900s, based on biases about renting and renters, and were seen as a way to eliminate the possibility of speculative ADU development.

The vast majority of American cities and towns now have an owner-occupancy bylaw for properties with ADUs. In the Pacific Northwest, a 2013 survey of town and city bylaws revealed that thirty of forty-six towns have owner-occupancy bylaws.[18] Even surrounding suburbs of Portland, such as Hillsboro and Lake Oswego, have owner-occupancy bylaws. And larger cities such as Eugene, Oregon, and Seattle, Washington, have owner-occupancy bylaws.

In a survey of 157 towns in eastern Massachusetts conducted in 2004–2005, 60% (107 towns) allowed some form of ADUs. Of those towns that ostensibly allowed ADUs, every community in the survey included owner-occupancy provisions. Limiting ADU utility even further, 46 of those 107 towns had bylaws that specified that residents of the ADU must be "related by family" (e.g., kinship, marriage, adoption). And some of the bylaws were even more restrictive than that. Regulations in Andover, Massachusetts, limited the use of the ADU to "relatives where there is a need by reason of illness, disability, or age requiring extended care or supervision of the relative. This use shall be subject to reasonable conditions and the requirement for renewable time periods not exceeding five years."[19]

In Baltimore, the ADU regulations state, "The accessory apartment shall only be utilized by immediate family members...and may not be used by any person other than an immediate family member for any other reason. If the accessory apartment is no longer occupied by any person named in the use permit or if the property is sold, the use permit shall terminate, and any proposed changes in occupancy to the accessory apartment by the property."[20] Other cities restrict ADU resident occupancy to particular age groups, or low-income groups, or specify that the unit cannot be rented out. Rules like these are so restrictive that it would be remarkable if any resident tried to develop a permitted ADU.

There does not appear to be any clear logic for why owner occupancy should be required on a property with an ADU when it's not required for any other type of housing unit, such as a single-family, duplex, triplex, fourplex, or larger multifamily house. ADUs appear to be singled out by regulations in a manner that infers targeted arbitrary treatment compared to any other type of housing unit. Owner-occupancy bylaws for ADUs were likely born partially from a fear of change and the perception that owner occupancy implied stability in neighborhoods, whereas rental housing implied transitional housing.

Owner-occupancy bylaws unfortunately strike directly at the heart of one of the greatest benefits of property ownership: the flexibility of choosing how to use the property. An owner can no longer opt to move away from the property without selling it. The owner cannot consider the option of the property serving a future use as an investment property. Eliminating these options from the possible uses of the property diminishes the flexibility of a property with an ADU.

Here's one property owner's take on his attempt to build an ADU in Madison, Wisconsin:

> There's one significant provision that completely spoils granny flats for me: on any lot that receives approval for a granny flat, the primary house must remain owner-occupied. In other words, if I build a granny flat, I am forced to either stay here in my house permanently or sell upon moving elsewhere.... If I go in for the significant investment of building a granny flat, I will have severely

> restricted my options down the road. This is not an insignificant calculation; one of my best friends just moved across the country after an unexpected job change. Rather than quickly sell his house at a loss, he decided to rent it out, and his mortgage is easily covered by the rental income. If I build the granny flat and find myself in a similar situation, I will likely not recover the costs of my significant investment, particularly given that many buyers in a neighborhood like mine are likely to view the granny flat as a liability, not an asset. If I stay put long enough, the financial math pencils out, but it's not a risk that I'm willing to take.[21]

For those who fear absentee landlords, there does not seem to be much logic in targeting ADUs. Though there is no owner-occupancy requirement, 64% of Portland owners currently live on the property. Even with no owner-occupancy requirement, limited evidence suggests that it is likely the owner will nonetheless choose to live on the property.

Perhaps the origin is based partially on anticipation of speculative ADU development. A recent article about regulations in Marin, California, elicited this concern: "Part of the logic is that without an owner-occupancy requirement, the property essentially becomes a duplex that could lure investment firms interested in turning it into upscale development to max out its value.... Requiring owner occupancy ensures that someone living on the property is keenly invested in the neighborhood."[22]

Assumptions about speculative ADU development likely are not based on real-life information about permitted ADUs because there are not sufficient numbers to speak of in any of these jurisdictions. Speculative ADU development appears to be relatively uncommon regardless of the owner-occupancy requirement. In Portland, where there is data about a substantial number of permitted ADUs, 70%–90% of ADUs were developed by the homeowners who lived there.

This is partly because ADU development tends to cost more than the contributory value that it adds to the resale value of property. In Portland, speculative developers have not yet figured out how to make

ADUs profitable. Purchaser financing for properties with ADUs has not matured to incorporate the future rental income of a new ADU, limiting the pool of buyers available for such a purchase. Even if and when ADUs are built by professional developers as speculative projects, the ADUs can still serve a role as a relatively affordable form of market-rate rental housing due to their small size.

One may have a bias toward grassroots ADU homeowner developers over professional speculative developers, as homeowner-developer ADUs will likely be built more often for altruistic reasons rather than solely to generate income. But from a City's housing policy perspective, it should not matter who develops the ADU as long as ADUs are built. Regardless of who builds ADUs, they still increase the supply of small, more affordable housing units available in the market. It is easy to view developers as the boogeyman, but someone needs to develop housing. This is how homes are built, after all.

If a City wants to restrict residential development solely to homeowners, then that rule should be applied uniformly across other types of housing and not arbitrarily target ADUs. Yet no City that I know of has a bylaw restricting single-family home development nor tenure solely to homeowners.

Would it even be constitutional to make a law that a house could not be rented out? And, is it constitutional to state that a homeowner must live in a house that they own?

The targeted and arbitrary nature of this ADU bylaw reeks of an antiquated classist attitude about renters and retains vestigial wafts of institutional racism. Nonetheless, this bylaw is found in the majority of US cities. City planners and elected officials should seriously consider the following two questions:

- Is there a justifiable rationale for a targeted owner-occupancy ADU bylaw—one that is not based on discrimination against renters?
- If so, why is that same bylaw not being applied to other forms of housing?

Owner-occupancy rules may also be based on a legacy attitude or perception toward property with informal ADUs that neighbors have observed. Perhaps they viewed these non-code-compliant informal ADUs as relic tenement housing. Laudable municipal planning efforts to create better ADU regulations commonly elicit neighbor comments like this one from a 2016 discussion about ADU regulations in Ann Arbor, Michigan: "My fear is that this will turn much of the west side into a mirror of the student slums south of campus with dilapidated rentals crowded onto lots with no parking available and everybody parking their cars on their lawns."[23]

Since permitted ADUs are so rarely found in America, most homeowners have little or no reference for them. Informal ADUs may be the only current reference point that residents in a community have. The transference of such perceptions to permitted ADUs is understandable, but it awkwardly puts planners, advocates, and officials in the impossible position of defending a housing type that does not actually yet exist in their jurisdiction. It is hard to defend a novel planning idea, such as making ADUs easier to build, when vocal people who are afraid of such changes baselessly compare it to developing a slum in their neighborhood. To the extent that there is any visual impact from this hidden form of housing, ADUs usually enhance the architectural fabric of a neighborhood.

Informal ADUs are not comparable to permitted ADUs because the former is not required to be built to the same level of quality or finish as the latter. They are not necessarily built to planning or building-code standards, and informal projects may cut many corners to save costs. This is not meant to disparage informal units but rather to suggest that the unexamined transference of such prejudices is not a just way to inform regulatory ordinances. Various types of informal ADU development are covered in the final chapter of this book, "Civil Disobedience and Accessory Dwellings."

Perhaps to the surprise of those who have never seen a permitted ADU, they are typically well built, and many are artistic and lovely.

The owners of ADUs have a heavily vested interest in a well-designed ADU. Furthermore, the relatively marginal costs of artistically detailing a smaller housing unit tends to result in charming-looking dwellings. Lastly, permitted ADUs are new construction built to current building-code standards, which means that they are inevitably bound to be both safer and more efficient than the older primary housing unit.

Owner-occupancy requirements also have another insidious impact on ADUs that is both complicated and not intuitive; it relates to financing. Risk-averse lending institutions would be less prone to loan against properties with such deed restrictions. Since a lending institution or any LLC cannot owner-occupy it, they cannot rent it out. An owner-occupancy requirement limits the value of the property in the eyes of the lending institution.

In terms of appraising a property with an ADU, by overlaying restrictions on how the property can be used, it is difficult to appraise a market value for the ADU improvement to the property that is in alignment with the actual development cost of it.

There are numerous anecdotes in which the appraised contributory value of ADUs was greatly less than the cost to build the ADU. This devaluation is partially due to the restrictions of uses that apply to ADUs in many cities and partially due to old guidance from Fannie Mae and Freddie Mac that limited an appraiser's ability to consider the income-generating value of the ADU in an appraisal. This practice persists despite the fact that the majority of permitted (as well as informal) ADUs have proven to be viably used as income-generating units (see "The Challenge of Financing ADUs" in chapter 7).

The ADU bylaws limiting uses of ADUs that prompt these systemic economic issues must be addressed head-on if a City is seeking to induce more ADU development. The layering on of use restrictions can only serve to retard permitted ADU growth, not foster it. If a City has an underlying goal of fostering ADUs, then any use restriction specifically singling out ADUs is counterproductive.

In a real estate market where both the primary unit and the ADU can be rented out, it is very likely that the highest and best use analysis would indicate that an income-based valuation method would help inform a higher and more accurate opinion of value of the property for an appraiser.[24] If both units on the property cannot be rented out as market-rate rentals, an appraiser's highest and best use analysis of the property might not be able to include an income-based valuation to help determine an opinion of value the way a comparable duplex would be appraised.

Under an owner-occupancy requirement, the appraiser may restrict the valuation of the house to an opinion based solely on sales comparables rather than considering the property's income potential as they would appraise all other single-family homes. However, the "sales comps" approach to valuation is not a reliable methodology for an appraiser to develop an opinion of value for a property with a permitted ADU because there are not sufficient numbers of comparable properties with ADUs being transacted on the marketplace. Until ADUs are very mature in a given market, it will be nearly impossible to find viable sales comps. Finding a recent, geographically relevant sales comp for a property with an ADU would be comparable to the difficulty of finding viable sales comps on a home with eleven bedrooms and one half bathroom. Most properties are unique to some degree, but properties with an ADU are much more singular, even in Portland.

An appraiser's guess for the contributory value of an ADU may vary wildly due to a lack of understanding of the legal uses of an ADU. Appraisers may significantly undervalue the contributory value of the ADU so as to err on the conservative side, attributing similar value to the ADU as they may attribute to a home addition. And with the use restriction, the owner-occupancy restriction could actually decrease the overall pool of potential buyers and thus the value of the property in the eyes of buyers.

Wildly unpredictable appraisals, caused partly by the uncertainty that this owner-occupancy provision conveys, are very problematic for homeowner developers. One of the editors of AccessoryDwellings.org built an ADU for roughly $100,000, and an initial appraisal after construction showed that his property's appraised value increased by only $10,000 of value. Later, a second appraiser said it added $100,000 of value. It's one thing to sink $100,000 into a property improvement and anticipate being able to sell that property for $75,000–$100,000 more as a result of that improvement. It is quite another matter to sink $100,000 into a property and only anticipate being able to sell it for $10,000 more as a result.

In this case, homeowners who are assessing the return on their potential investment options must essentially be willing to forfeit the construction cost of the ADU without hope of seeing a commensurate level of equity added to the property upon future resale value of the property. If the value of a property is only worth $10,000 more after ADU construction, according to appraisers, then a homeowner cannot access after-rehab-value renovation financing. Construction loans and renovation loans, which base their value on expected future value of the property after the improvement, are sometimes the only way to fund ADU development for homeowners who do not have sufficient capital or home equity established.

If a property is only worth $10,000 more after ADU construction, according to appraisers, then homeowners cannot refinance the property afterward to help amortize the cost of any short-term, higher-interest personal construction loans (e.g., personal loans, HELOCs, or credit cards).

The homeowners also cannot expect to accrue enough equity in the property to substantially improve their first mortgage position by the improvement. In my case, I purchased a home in 2010, putting a 5% down payment on the initial home purchase. I then cobbled together cash savings of $115,000 to build my ADU. After completing it and having the contributory value of the ADU add roughly $80,000 of value to the property, I was able to show that I had accrued a 20% equity position in the property in the first year because of the property improvement, which allowed me to refinance my primary mortgage—dropping my second mortgage and mortgage insurance—saving me several hundred dollars a month in ongoing mortgage costs.

Put bluntly, owner-occupancy bylaws can strip the value of the ADU down by 90%. Why would anyone build something when only 10% of the development cost can be captured?

Low appraised opinions of value are based on a misunderstanding of the legal uses of ADUs and may be partially a result of owner-occupancy bylaws that can greatly limit the value and legal uses of an ADU. Fixing appraisals is relatively simple as long as an appraiser can have the flexibility of appraising the property like they would a duplex. This flexibility hinges partially on the use provisions in the zoning code. Owner-occupancy requirements eliminate this flexibility.

While owner-occupancy bylaws largely diminish ADU development at large, if an owner builds an ADU and lives on-site, they theoretically can still rent out one unit and live in the other and make rental income while they do so. In limited situations, even with an owner-occupancy bylaw in effect, it may still make financial sense to develop an ADU if the owner is absolutely certain that they will live on the property for a long time (ten or more years) and can rent out one of the units at market rates to recoup the ADU construction cost. However, they cannot take advantage of refinancing like I did, they cannot access increased home equity lines of credit, and they cannot expect to sell the property at a cost commensurate with the full structural value of the ADU improvement. And if they plan to move, the bylaw effectively coerces them to sell the property altogether.

With an owner-occupancy requirement, if the owner has a need to build an ADU for one reason or another, why would they bother building it legally? Most rational homeowners would simply opt to carve out an informal ADU inside their house instead, saving significant construction cost and regulatory hassle, and maintaining the freedom to do with the property as they please.

A homeowner who simply wanted to improve their property value would certainly opt for any other improvement that would add more predictable appraised values and resale value to the property instead of building an ADU, which greatly limits their flexibility. They may rationally opt to build an addition, which would increase the size of their primary house. This may not serve any laudable civic purpose whatsoever, but at least it would not be a counterproductive way to invest their money. Or maybe they'd just use their extra cash to buy any other residential property in their city and use it as a rental. There's no owner-occupancy requirement on investment properties as long as they do not put an ADU on it.

In summary, an owner-occupancy requirement changes how much value appraisers can add to a property based on the perceived value of the improvement. This perceived value limits how lending institutions can treat these improvements from a financing perspective. This in turn limits how valuable this kind of improvement actually is on the market. The effective market devaluation then undermines a homeowner's motivation and ability to build the ADU in the first place. Therefore, rational homeowners either opt to build without permits to save significant cost, or they opt to build a different type of improvement to circumvent the restriction-of-use penalty associated with the ADU.

And this, dear readers, is one significant reason why so few permitted ADUs are built.

In interviews with city planners from five cities—Portland, Austin, Seattle, Vancouver, and Los Angeles—there was no understanding of why such a provision was currently necessary. For astute observers of the changing nature of cities, housing demographics, financing, economics, housing trends, and real estate, it is clear this code language is antiquated.

In Portland, which no longer requires owner occupancy, city planner Phil Nameny articulated that the bygone bylaw does not recognize a change in social norms: "I don't know if owner-occupancy requirements address the changing nature of how people own and rent property nowadays."[25]

Jake Fry, an ADU builder in Vancouver, said that the owner occupier would be very problematic there.

> What if it was your mom's property and you've inherited it, and you don't want to sell it and run into capital gains and you want to keep the property for your kids? Are you going to not be able to rent it?
>
> I don't see what the benefit is of owner occupation on these. And, I believe the less restrictions you have, the more ADUs you have.[26]

In Austin, Texas, a college town that does not have owner-occupancy requirements for properties with ADUs, Nicole Joslin, the development manager for the Austin Community Design and Development Center, said:

> Most of the owners that come to us are looking to build a unit on their own lot. They live in the front house, or want to live in the back house. The only person that has come to us that has a rental property on which they wish to build an ADU, they're looking at building an ADU on their rental property and their own property. So, they want to build two ADUs. One on a lot they live on, and one that they already rent out.
>
> An owner-occupancy requirement would have a significant impact on the community development corporations that are obviously not owner occupied. They're all rental housing. But, as far as private homeowners, I haven't seen very many people that have rental properties that they're looking at building an ADU on.[27]

I asked whether she had heard any complaints about the lack of owner-occupancy requirements during recent public forums about ADU zoning-code issues. "With the recent ordinance, I don't recall hearing any discussions distinguishing between owner occupied or non-owner occupied lots being able to build ADUs," Joslin answered. "I haven't heard any complaints about that."

Santa Cruz, California, still requires owner occupancy. David Foster, a citizen pioneer of ADUs and executive director of the local Habitat for Humanity chapter, lives in Santa Cruz and owns an ADU. He says,

> The restrictions on owner occupancy seem silly. You can have an ADU in a house that's zoned single family and then next door to it you can have a multifamily place that can have up to ten rental units without any owner occupancy...without any management company having to be there. So, why, all of a sudden, does an ADU have a requirement that's not required of rental properties? Or, if you have a single-family house, you can rent it out. There's no requirement that you have a management company, or that you have to have someone that owns the house live there or live next door or whatever.
>
> I think eventually the city is going to realize it makes it very difficult for people because if someone builds their home and builds their granny unit for their in-laws, and then eventually the house gets sold and a new owner comes in and says, "I can't afford to live here so it's going to be a rental and I guess I have to close up and not use the ADU because I can't legally rent it out." A perfectly good house being told by the city it can't be rented.[28]

When I asked Kevin Casey of New Avenue, an ADU project management company based in Berkeley, California, about owner-occupancy requirements, he said, "Overreach into private property. And it's our duty as Americans to push back on that."[29]

The lack of evidence that owner-occupancy requirements accomplish any positive social goal should be reason alone to drop the poison-pill provision. But for cities that hope to induce more ADU development, the significant economic deterrent and the loss of flexibility resulting from this bylaw should be clear. Owner-occupancy requirements kill permitted ADUs. If a City now wants to foster ADUs instead of actively hinder them, it would be wise to drop this antiquated provision.

Off-Street Parking Requirements

Off-street parking requirements are another widespread zoning-code provision that effectively kills ADUs. Cities that seek more ADU development should not require additional off-street parking for them.

Seattle's ADU code (circa 2016) provides a good example of both of these first two poison-pill bylaws: owner occupancy and off-street parking. (Boldface type is mine for emphasis.)

> You can build these separate living spaces in a single-family or lowrise zone. Our codes limit the size and placement of your accessory or detached unit. The **owner is required to live in either the house or in the additional unit**; we require a signed owner occupancy covenant agreeing to this condition. Attached accessory dwelling unit (ADU) requirements:
>
> **One off-street parking space is required for the ADU** except for a rowhouse or townhouse in designated urban villages and urban centers and in lowrise zones
>
> Detached accessory dwelling unit (DADU) requirements:
>
> **One off-street parking space is required for the DADU**, except in designated urban villages and urban centers and in lowrise zones.[30]

ADU regulations typically state something simple to this effect: "An additional off-street parking spot must be provided when building an ADU." Here's a list of commonly found off-street parking requirements when an ADU is added to a property, from worst to best:

- one to three dedicated, covered, off-street parking spaces
- one or two dedicated, side-by-side, off-street parking spaces
- one or two dedicated parking spaces allowing tandem parking—parking vehicles end to end
- no additional off-street parking if the ADU is near a transit corridor (usually within a quarter to a half mile)
- no additional off-street parking requirement

For many lots where you would want to build an ADU, adding an additional 9-by-18-foot parking space is either impossible, nearly impossible, or highly undesirable. Fitting two or three parking spaces is far harder still.

Adam Peterson, an architect with Muddy River Design in Bend, Oregon, who has designed several ADUs in his town, spoke about his experience with off-street parking requirements.

> Especially lots where we are right here downtown, adding off-street parking is always an issue. Once you add that ADU, you have to add an off-street parking stall. That additional off-street parking space can be a challenge if you're already maxed out on your property and there's nowhere to place it.
>
> I designed one over here on Fresno Street. It's a 2,000 sq. ft. house, and we put an ADU above the attached garage. And it was on an unimproved alleyway, so it was a challenge with the planning department to make all of the parking spaces work. They required two in the garage and then two outside the garage for the house, and then one off to the side for the ADU. So there's no yard because it has to be hardscape for that parking stall.[31]

In case you lost count, Bend's planning department somehow managed to require five off-street parking spaces for one single-family house with an ADU.

Seattle has roughly 1,400 permitted ADUs as of 2016. It has allowed attached ADUs since 1994 and detached ADUs since 2010. In early 2016, Seattle was strongly considering relaxing both their owner-occupancy and off-street parking ordinances and had gone through the public comment period as a part of that ordinance change. In December 2016, a citizen who did not like the proposed changes, backed by some neighborhood groups, brought the City to court over its attempts to relax the regulations. Such is the stymied march of ADU progress in cities across the country.

Seattle's slower rate of ADU development (about a hundred per year) relative to Portland and Vancouver (each now has more than 500 permitted per year) lends convenient counterfactual evidence of the stymieing impact of these two poison-pill regulations. Given that it is one of three major cities in the same cultural, economic, and climatic region as Portland and Vancouver, and has similar housing-affordability challenges and single-family zone dominance, Seattle should theoretically have similar ADU development rates. However, Seattle has these two poison-pill regulations in place, whereas Portland and Vancouver do not, and the relative lack of ADU development in Seattle is the result.

Asked about the impact of parking regulations in the hundred-plus cities where New Avenue has worked in the Bay Area of California, owner Kevin Casey said,

> Our experience has been that for remodels and additions, parking is almost a non-factor. Our experience for accessory dwellings is that parking is always a factor. It varies from a smaller challenge of showing that you could fit two cars in a driveway or an additional car in the driveway [tandem parking],

> which can be relatively minor, to extraordinarily burdensome—like, you must have a three-car covered garage.
>
> We have definitely had instances where people have either not been able to proceed because they couldn't fit the required parking space, or the required covered spaces were so expensive or inappropriate for the lot or unwanted by the homeowner, so they've either killed their project, or modified their project so that it wasn't technically an accessory dwelling.[32]

Casey explained that a majority of homeowners must go through a lengthy and expensive permitting process to ease the permitting requirements for off-street parking. Yet, in these same cities, additional parking is not required if an additional bedroom is added to a house.

Requiring any off-street parking space, regardless of whether the residents need or want it, should not be required by an ordinance. Donald Shoup, the author of *The High Cost of Free Parking*, espouses that parking should be market-based, not based on minimum parking standards.

Off-street parking requirements seem to politically override municipal housing priorities. Shoup puts it this way: "When parking requirements prohibit converting garages into apartments, cities put free parking ahead of affordable housing." He continues, "Families who are willing to convert their garages into second units will find a new way to finance homeownership, and will at the same time provide a supply of decent and affordable rental housing within walking distance of local stores and public transit. Higher urban land prices are not a bad thing if it leads to more housing, but off-street parking requirements prevent higher densities."[33]

Concerns around a lack of street parking should be contextualized within broader policy goals. Otherwise, valiant urban planning initiatives will continually lose out to vocal cries for parking space protection. In this instance, local policy makers may want to consider whether requiring off-street parking for ADUs is actually undermining policy goals regarding housing access and affordability. The subtle

Image 8.1. There are several well-known ways to commute without a car.

and accidental by-product of these unexamined parking ordinances is redirection of owners' interests toward building larger and more expensive primary houses instead of fostering more small and affordable homes. Requiring an off-street parking spot for a studio apartment at the same level as a four-bedroom house is effectively a regressive disincentive for the studio. Dan Parolek, a form-based code expert, framed the issue of off-street parking requirements more broadly for the development of missing-middle housing types this way.

> A system based on density immediately disincentivizes smaller units because a developer can only do a certain number of units. They're almost always going to choose to build the biggest units that they possibly can because the numbers of units are limited. A lot of missing-middle housing types have a foundation of being smaller units to provide that housing choice in communities. Also, if you start to require additional off-street parking, it makes these housing types economically inefficient and unviable for housing developers and builders.[34]

The specter that drives the particular off-street parking requirement for ADUs is that rampant ADU development will suddenly cause inexorable residential street parking congestion. It is common for public discourse about ADUs to trigger visceral reactions that relate to parking, like this reaction to a California's ADU law from Long Beach, California:

> This law has the potential to destroy single-family neighborhoods, cause unmitigated parking problems and destroy quality of life. [35]

The reality is that, even in cities that are leading the ADU movement in North America, like Portland and Vancouver, there is no noticeable impact on the residential street-parking supply. Here are Oregon DEQ's findings on this matter. Notably, this is the only time that the impact of permitted ADUs on residential parking supply has ever been quantitatively researched.

> The effect of ADUs on parking in Portland has been negligible, to date, for a number of reasons. ADUs are associated with a modest number of vehicles per dwelling; some of these cars are parked off the street; ADUs are dispersed throughout neighborhoods; ADUs are generally rare; and other forms of development have far more impact. Until those factors change substantially, the fear that ADUs harm parking conditions will have little rational basis.[36]

Any feasible ADU development rates would not significantly alter the supply of street parking opportunities in single-family residential neighborhoods.

The inevitable outcome of an investigation of many off-street parking requirements for real estate development, including the requirement for off-street parking for ADUs, is that parking requirements prioritize cars over people.

Let us pretend that there was a development ordinance that required that all new houses had to install a 10-foot satellite TV dish antenna in their yard with service to over a thousand channels. Home developers would be frustrated by the additional regulation, but they would add the dish antenna and then pass that cost on to the prospective homebuyer. This cost would impact the homebuyer, whether or not they watched television. It would take up a lot of yard space that they may otherwise wish to use for a garden, fence, hedge, porch, or deck.

In real life, local building ordinances would never dare state that satellite TV antennas are required, let alone a 10-foot satellite dish. Such an ordinance would be viewed as a preposterous overreach of government at best and a conspiracy between satellite TV providers and government to induce more TV addiction and consumerism at worst.

However, off-street parking minimum requirements are not perceived in this same way because American cities and towns treat our vehicles with sacred deference. Off-street parking requirements are obedient to our vehicles' needs and symptomatic of that timorous subservience. This blind obedience is perpetuating automobile dependency.

Ironically and counterintuitively, these onerous parking regulations actually increase traffic and harm pedestrians' urban experience by deteriorating walkability, increasing carbon emissions, and degrading urban air quality. In the case of ADUs, the total parking supply resulting from off-street parking requirements may not increase at all. Rather, the expansion of a curb cut to create an additional off-street parking spot may effectively remove a street parking spot.

As a nation, we love the freedom that we associate with our automobiles if we are lucky enough to own one. And we feel entitled to car parking as a right. Knee-jerk reactions about a deluge of additional concentrated cars stemming from ADU development are not founded in fact and stem from fear that people have when assumed entitlements to ample street parking are threatened. Citizens and cities alike are prioritizing an imagined dystopian future neighborhood blighted by diminished car-parking habitat over a reality of more affordable housing for people.

Image 8.2. A pocket community in Port Townsend, WA, centered around a common green space. (Image from "Third Street Cottages," Ross Chapin Architects, http://rosschapin.com/projects/pocket-neighborhoods/third-street-cottages/.)

The obsession that we seem to have over free parking preservation on our public streets results in dramatic stifling of where ADUs can be legally built. For planners and elected officials, it is worth considering whether the off-street parking ordinance is serving a higher purpose than ADUs could serve. Communities are unflinchingly attached to off-street parking requirements for ADUs because these requirements protect a presumed entitlement. But this entitlement comes at a cost. Given the lack of evidence that ADUs actually diminish parking supply in cities, it is worth calculating whether such fears have any merit whatsoever.

Parking spaces cost money to build: $3,000–$5,000/space, not including any curb cutting that may be needed. This increases the development cost of the ADU, which makes the housing more expensive for the owners and future renters. Donald Shoup said, "Parking requirements bundle the cost of parking spaces into the cost of dwelling units, and therefore shift the cost of parking into the cost of renting or owning a home, making cars more affordable but housing more

Image 8.3. Elfreth's Alley in Philadelphia, PA, is said to be America's oldest residential street. It was originally a cart path through working-class urban housing. (Image from Joanne Danifo, "Elfreth's Alley," Encyclopedia of Greater Philadelphia, 2012, http://philadelphiaencyclopedia.org/archive/elfreths-alley/.)

expensive."[37] Any perceived additional administrative penalties such as this are likely to deter homeowners from building a permitted ADU.

The irony is that the future hypothetical ADU tenant may not have had any need for these additional off-street parking spaces. After all, if parking supply were truly going to be an issue, would not it be in the owner's personal interest, above all others, to seek out a car-free tenant? Interestingly, it turns out that the data from the DEQ study indicates that ADU residents actually have fewer vehicles per capita than a typical resident.

Cities may want to consider allowing experimental residential and mixed-use neighborhoods to be centered around pedestrian activity instead of solely allowing them to be designed around automobile parking. Prioritizing people in urban design requires building civic places where people love to be. Because right now, outside of our personal homes, it seems like while we are out in public spaces, Americans are mostly relegated to being inside their vehicles by design.

Image 8.4. A mixed-use development in Christchurch, New Zealand, that has apartments located directly above retail shops. Trains and pedestrians come through this area, but cars do not.

Conditional Use

A conditional review or conditional-use permit—also known as a type of discretionary review—is a process whereby an applicant submits for permission to use their property a certain way but is not guaranteed the right to build something outright. Rather, they are directed to apply for permission to build something. Depending on a range of factors, the applicant may or may not be granted the permission to do a project.

A conditional review process may involve a neighbor notification, a public hearing, and a written and oral justification. This type of process can be political, opaque, intimidating, and expensive for novice homeowner developers. A preferable permit process is called "by right," "straight to permit," "administrative permit," or "ministerial permit," which ensures transparency and predictability.

One of the requirements of a conditional-use permit may be notification of the neighbors, who may also be given a public opportunity to weigh in. If given the choice, many people may oppose an architectural addition such as an ADU being built next to their property.

> Neighbors will only complain about an existing accessory unit, whether legal or illegal, if its presence is actually causing an annoyance, due, for example, to excess noise or intruding on privacy.
>
> The same neighbors are much quicker to oppose a permit request for a new accessory dwelling next door simply because it means change which, in many instances, triggers fear.[38]

This is an example of a conditional review process from Renton, Washington:

> In what zones are Accessory Dwelling Units allowed and how do I establish one?
>
> Most residential zones in Renton allow you the opportunity to request that City staff review your proposal for a detached accessory dwelling unit. Commercial, Industrial and Residential Multi-Family (RM) Zones, however, do not allow Accessory Dwelling Units. After verifying that your property is zoned RC, R-1, R-4, R-6, R-8, R-10, or R-14 and would potentially allow the unit, the next step would be to request a free preapplication meeting. Then, if the results of the preapplication meeting are favorable, your next step would be to formally apply for an Administrative Conditional Use Permit.
>
> What is a Conditional Use Permit, how much does it cost to apply, and how long does it take to process?
>
> A Conditional Use Permit is a discretionary review process in which the Planning Director may make a decision to approve, conditionally approve, or deny the permit. In general, the Conditional Use Permit process takes approximately 4–6 weeks. The application fee is $1,030.00 and is not refundable should your permit be denied.[39]

In this instance, applying for an ADU permit sounds pretty onerous. To a novice homeowner developer, it would seem like an expensive gamble to make, given that the request for a permit may not be granted. To apply, the planning office would require site plans and section and elevation drawings, a level of design development that could easily cost more than $5,000. Professional developers would be accustomed to this kind of discretionary process and may be reluctant but willing to incur the risk of proceeding without certainty of approval. But for ADU homeowner developers, this type of development uncertainty deters them from initially even pursuing the idea. Indeed, no other residential renovation work in Renton requires a conditional-use permit. Average homeowners who are unfamiliar with an involved city process such as a conditional-use permit may feel intimidated. Maybe this is partially why Renton issued fewer than ten ADU permits in 2017.[40]

In what other circumstances would a homeowner be forced to spend over $1,000 (or more than $6,000) on an application where permission may not be granted? The lack of predictability is a huge hindrance for developers, professional and amateur alike. If a municipality wants to see ADUs built, there should be a transparent, predictable set of codes that, if followed, allows an ADU to be built by right. It should be as easy for a homeowner to get a permit for an ADU as it is to get a permit to build a garage or an addition.

Predictability is requisite if a City wants to induce ADUs. It is far better to have a set of strict ADU development regulations that are totally predictable than to have a flexible set of development regulations that are discretionary.

As it stands, most jurisdictions require a conditional-use permit of some sort. Kevin Casey of New Avenue says that of over a hundred projects in Californian cities, he's only experienced one project in which the ADU was allowed by right. This project was on a very large and expensive property in the Berkeley Hills. Every other project and city have required a conditional-use permit.[41] In eastern Massachusetts,

Image 8.5. An alley unit that was developed on the same DC alley in 1983, but which is now considered a nonconforming use. (Image from Jamal Kadri, "Dwelling in the Urban Alleys of DC (Part II)," Accessory Dwellings, December 11, 2011, https://accessorydwellings.org/2011/12/11/dwelling-in-the-urban-alleys-of-dc-part-ii/.)

84% of the towns surveyed in 2004–2005 required a special-use permit for an accessory apartment.[42]

One colleague in Washington, DC, shared his testimony of trying to get permission from the city to build an ADU on an alley that had many other historic dwellings on it.

> My experience with the Special Exemption process was that it was very costly and time consuming. In my case, my architect urged me to hire a land-use attorney. The professionals who are familiar with the process require tens of thousands of dollars to navigate the unpredictable path to a permit that costs thousands more. The changes required add little value and significant cost.[43]

In the end, permission was not obtained, even though this proposed ADU was in character with the historic alley ADUs on his block.

This process cost him $30,000 in the end and substantially eroded the capital that he had hoped to spend on the development of the ADU.

Discretionary reviews create uncertainty in the development process. As with the anecdote above, a discretionary review process might not align with the potential impacts of the proposal, and the fairness of the process may come into question. Soliciting neighbors to get intimately involved with a project that may impact them, when they are typically uninformed about zoning codes in general, can give them an opportunity to come up with their own worst-case conclusions.

If a City wants to make ADU development approachable, it must create fair development regulations that address the community's design values up front and allow the applicant to obtain a permit without a conditional-use review.

PROHIBITIVELY RESTRICTIVE DEVELOPMENT REGULATIONS

This book does not focus on specific ADU development regulations, design provisions, or building-code regulations, which vary so much from place to place that it is difficult to make generalizations about them. Examples of these development regulations are requirements for certain roof pitch, color, shape, architectural style, height, and so on.

An underlying premise of *Backdoor Revolution* is that making housing development easier and providing more housing choices generally are ways to achieve more market-based affordable housing. Indeed, in the case of ADUs, loosening of these design and building-code restrictions may well be one of the most significant ways to achieve any measurable progress in ADU development. In general, the less restrictive or more flexible the ADU code is, the better the chance is that a homeowner will opt to actually build one.

It would be challenging and possibly pointless to advise a uniform local approach to or standards for ADU development regulations. There is a wide range of development regulations nationally. It is probably good for architectural development regulations to be customized to meet the community's design standards, as there may be a host of local, cultural, and architectural variables that factor into contextualized urban development. Such architectural development regulations can be reasonably applied to ADUs just as they are applied to all other forms of development. Provided ADUs are not being singled out, these development regulations do not seem to have much impact on the rate of ADU development one way or the other. For example, Vancouver homeowners can build ADUs by right, provided they follow planning/zoning and building-code regulations. The development regulations for these units are quite architecturally strict, but they are totally predictable.

However, there is a distinction between development regulations that govern the design and construction of the ADU structure and the zoning regulations that govern the placement and size of the ADU. The regulations regarding placement and size can each be as potent in deterring ADUs as the first three poison-pill regulations, so we'll cover these barriers here, as well as some general advice on how to improve them. These regulations are not typically as controversial to alter as the poison-pill regulations.

A 2015 Urban Institute report to the White House stated that zoning regulations tend to make development more difficult and more expensive by constraining supply. "Zoning gives rise to rents by restricting supply. Zoning restrictions—be they in the form of minimum lot sizes, off-street parking requirements, height limits, prohibitions on multifamily housing, or lengthy permitting processes—are supply constraints."[44]

Property Line Setbacks

A *setback* is the distance that the foundation of a structure must be from a neighboring property line or public right-of-way. In residential zones, these setbacks are established partially to ensure a degree of sun and air protection for neighboring properties.

Some cities have 10- or 20-foot setback requirements for detached accessory structures along adjacent property lines. This requirement makes it nearly impossible to build a detached ADU in the backyard of most standard-sized, central-city residential properties.

In areas where ADUs are most needed—in or near transit-oriented development—residential lots in walkable urban areas are often in the range of 50 × 100 feet. Standard lots in many cities are narrower and deeper than this. For example, standard residential lots in Vancouver are 32 feet wide by 122 feet deep.

A gratuitous 10- to 20-foot setback requirement would make it effectively impossible to place a detached ADU on a lot of this size. Yet, it is in these small-medium 3,000–7,000 sq. ft. lots where ADUs are most needed.

A 20-foot setback requirement is not necessarily a problem if the lot is 100 feet × 200 feet or larger, which might be a standard property size in some suburban or exurban neighborhoods, but on most walkable urban lots, even a 10-foot setback requirement makes ADU placement extremely challenging.

In walkable urban neighborhoods, setback requirements should be kept to a minimum to enable detached ADU development: 3–5 feet is a reasonable setback requirement for such lots.

It is worth evaluating whether ADU setbacks are more restrictive than the setback for other comparable accessory structures, such as garages. Setback regulations for detached accessory structures may also consider tiered standards based on the detached structure's height to protect light and air for adjacent lots. Portland has a 5-foot setback for detached ADUs that are greater than 15 feet in height, and a 0-foot setback requirement for accessory structures that are less than 15 feet in height. To protect neighbors' privacy, no windows or doors are allowed within the sides of the structures that are within 5 feet of the property line. This nuanced, tiered setback approach protects neighboring properties' light, air, and privacy while affording smaller lots the same development entitlements as larger lots. It is the same development standard that applies to garages and other accessory structures.

Size Limits on ADUs

ADUs are generally capped at a given size. Sometimes this size is definitive, sometimes it's tied proportionally to the primary house, and sometimes it's both.

Capping ADUs size is useful because there is a widespread need for the market to increase the supply of more small, affordable housing units in cities. ADUs should be viewed as an effective mechanism to achieve certain small housing goals.

However, if a municipality wants to induce more ADUs, it should:

- have a size cap that would allow for two people to comfortably live in the ADU, and
- the cap should not be tied to the existing floor-area ratio of the primary structure.

Restricting the allowable size of the ADU to be proportional to the primary house (e.g., the ADU can be up to 50% of the size of the main house) could be perceived as economically regressive for people with smaller primary houses, so it makes more sense to state a definitive size cap (e.g., the ADU can be up to 1,000 sq. ft.). However, it is reasonable to cap ADUs to a size that is equal to or smaller than the primary house, as ADUs are intended to be accessory to the primary house.

Kevin Casey of New Avenue felt that this issue was one of the largest barriers to ADU development:

> Make sure that ADUs can be at least up to 600 sq. ft. Many cities have a floor-area ratio between the main house and the ADU that restricts the ADU to 300–400 sq. ft. And that does not work for someone who is fifty-five and has lived in a single-family home for decades. And it doesn't work for a couple who is going to have a kid and going to live a normal life with friends and family that come and visit. A home that is 600 sq. ft. can function as a real home by the standards of what people want in life.[45]

Many cities have codes that require ADUs to be less than 600 sq. ft.—a size cap that works well if the intention is to produce housing for single people, but anything less than this size greatly diminishes the potential appeal of ADUs to work well for two-person households. I generally suggest that 400 sq. ft. per resident is a good size threshold to consider.

In general, if a City wishes to increase housing stock for one- or two-person households, 800–1,000 sq. ft. size caps are reasonable for ADUs. And if a City wishes to foster ADUs as a housing option for small families (e.g., two parents and one child), it makes sense to have a code that allows for ADUs to be up to 1,200 sq. ft.

Minimum Lot Sizes

Many cities have lot size minimums for ADUs, which serve as another example of a cloaked, regressive ordinance that merits examination. Limiting ADUs solely to large lots accidentally provides entitlements to more expensive properties. More importantly, larger lots will tend to be located in areas where there may be less demand for smaller rental housing units than there is in central-city neighborhoods, where lot sizes are smaller.

Ordinances are generally written using a fixed minimum size limit, but sometimes the minimum size limits are prescribed to be tied to the zoning, such as in Hillsborough, North Carolina: "The ordinance currently allows such [accessory] dwellings only when a lot is twice the size of the zoning district's minimum requirement. The lot size requirement was put in place to maintain the density of dwelling units per acres established by the zoning."[46] Hillsborough's limit makes little sense if it was seeking to induce ADUs, as these owners could already legally subdivide their properties if they wished.

Pasadena, California, maintains a 15,000 sq. ft. minimum lot size for ADUs. This, along with the requirement for two additional covered parking spaces, has predictability resulted in a grand total of one permitted ADU in the last decade.[47]

Conversely, Austin, Texas, changed its code in 2015 to reduce the minimum lot size that allows detached ADUs from 7,000 sq. ft. to 5,750 sq. ft. This increased the number of lots that could potentially have an ADU by 8,900, helping to lead to an uptick in recent ADU development.

Structural Forms

Other common design restrictions address the type of structure that can serve as the building for the ADU: basement units (Washington, DC), internal ADUs (eastern Massachusetts), detached ADUs (Renton, Washington), or existing detached structures (San Francisco).

Limiting ADUs to one structural form or another is one more factor that significantly decreases the potential for ADUs to flourish. For cities that are attempting to induce more ADUs, there is a predictable, strategic progression of codes that allow flexibility in building ADUs in an array of structural forms. We'll discuss this more in chapter 11. Appendix 5 contains one model ADU zoning code taken from AccessoryDwellings.org.

Sewer or Water Connections, Development Fee Costs

Connecting to the city's sewer and water systems in a public right-of-way can often be extremely expensive. If a City were to require a designated sewer or water main connection for ADUs, this would present a significant financial barrier to development. New sewer service connected directly from an adjacent right-of-way may cost $20,000, and new water service may cost $5,000–$10,000. These utility service costs alone would financially overwhelm a homeowner who may otherwise wish to build an ADU.

Typically, water and sewer service can simply be extended from the primary house to the ADU, and this type of extension should not trigger any extra utility connection fees. This issue is covered in greater detail in appendix 1. A City's policy on these matters may effectively kill ADUs. Apart from sheer administrative cost, districts sometimes outright deny new development such as ADUs based on municipal infrastructural capacity constraints. This may be a reasonable policy if it was applied to comparably sized remodels and additions. It would not be reasonable if ADUs are selectively scapegoated by a jurisdiction and held to a different standard.

In March 2017, after a valiant municipal effort to spur ADU development in Honolulu, Hawaii, the local sewer authority denied 268 inquiries for ADUs over the previous year based on the municipal sewer systems being unable to handle any additional capacity.[48] However, infrastructural capacity is typically not the barrier. It is the fees that intimidate homeowners and deaden their motivation to build.

Development service fees, also known as residential impact fees, are a one-time fee that a developer of a housing unit must pay to a City to account for the permanent infrastructural burden the new housing unit is adding to the city's water, sewer, parks, and transportation infrastructure. Some municipalities do not have these fees, while other municipalities may charge upward of $30,000 for them.

Waiving the residential impact fee for ADUs has proven to be extremely important in terms of the overall development cost for an ADU. Portland waived its $8,000–$12,000 development service fees for ADUs starting in 2010. Other cities, such as Bend, Oregon, tier the development fees for ADUs to be proportional to the size of the additional unit. If the development service fee for an ADU were the same as the fee for new single-family construction ($25,000–$30,000 in Portland), this would be a deterrent to permitted ADU development.

Typically, cities are responsible for addressing these zoning barriers. However, there have been instances where a state government has opted to intervene to promote better ADU codes statewide. Most notably, California did this in 2017.

The State of California had passed Assembly Bill 1866 in 2003, which made it mandatory for all cities in California to allow ADUs by right—no discretionary reviews or public hearings. The remaining regulatory barriers that cities had in place still prevented much ADU development. Some local governments adopted ordinances to make ADU development regulations more restrictive in reaction to this bill. Other jurisdictions that were neutral toward the new state law adopted the state's default planning- or zoning-code regulations on ADUs. Neither of these two actions induced significant ADU development.

In 2016, California passed a couple of statutes that relate to ADUs: AB-2299 and SB-1069. These are the most assertive pro-ADU state laws to date. AB-2299 goes quite far toward eliminating key ADU barriers; specifically, it deals with reducing most additional off-street parking requirements for ADUs in urban areas and eliminating or significantly reducing utility connection fees.

California faces a perpetual housing crisis. ADUs will be developed in greater numbers throughout many cities in California with the passage of these laws, though there are still ample mechanisms by which cities may opt to restrain ADU development if they wish by using other zoning rules, such as requiring exorbitant minimum lot sizes.

One significant ADU barrier that the State has not yet addressed in any fashion is owner-occupancy requirements. California cities that do not have an owner-occupancy requirement and have the correct real estate market conditions will see the most ADU development traction resulting from the passage of this state law.

As a result of this law, Los Angeles suddenly emerged as a national leader in ADU development with roughly 2,000 ADU permits issued in 2017. The previous 13-year average had been 80 permits per year, so 2017 brought with it a 25-fold increase in permitted ADU activity. The majority of these permits were legalizations of existing unpermitted garage conversions. Nonetheless, this provides evidence that the state law has been effective at reducing regulatory barriers such that homeowners were inclined to legitimize their informal ADUs.

Notably, Los Angeles does not have an owner-occupancy requirement. Due in part to the passage of these laws, other California cities such as Oakland and Santa Barbara are also well-poised for significant surges in ADU development.[49]

Chapter 9

Impacts on a City

THIS CHAPTER WILL FOCUS ON SUPPORTING AND DEBUNKING SOME common myths about the economic and social significance of ADUs on neighborhoods and cities. There have been very few statistically valid studies of how permitted ADUs are used and what the impacts are on those communities. For the purpose of providing real data about impacts of permitted ADUs on a city, I'll continue referencing the Oregon Department of Environmental Quality ADU owners survey.[50] My additional interpretation of the survey's findings is based on my professional observations of hundreds of permitted ADUs and their owners.

The dearth of research on this topic is due largely to a lack of geographically concentrated, permitted ADUs, which stems from the extensive regulatory obstacles for their development in many cities (see chapter 8). Notable surveys have been conducted on informal ADUs. One such study contains some findings that closely support the findings from the Oregon DEQ study.

Geoff Anderson, the president and CEO of Smart Growth America, made a poignant observation about the existence of so many informal ADUs. Their presence, he said, indicates that "these things are actually working fine, without causing the horrible disruptions to communities that sometimes are feared."[51]

The actual impacts of future (hypothetical) permitted ADUs on neighborhoods are likely to be fairly nominal compared to the current impacts caused by the thousands or tens of thousands of informal

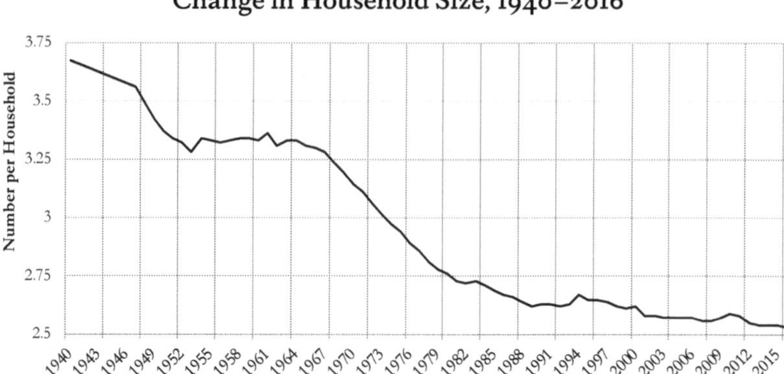

Figure 9.1. Average household size dropped from 3.67 people per household in 1940 to 2.53 in 2016.

ADUs that already exist in neighborhoods in most US cities. In the absence of bountiful research of statistical impacts from formal ADU development, we can instead consider the current impacts of informal ADUs. After all, even in Portland and Vancouver, the most permissive cities in North America for ADUs, the number of existent informal ADUs dwarfs the number of permitted ADUs by three- to fivefold.[52] If the current impacts of the informal ADU supply on neighborhoods are not already noticeable and damaging in a city, then there is a vanishingly small chance the impact of permitted ADUs would be noticeable to neighbors or damaging to neighborhoods either.

MATCHING HOUSING DEMOGRAPHICS WITH HOUSING OPTIONS

Nuclear families are a diminishing housing demographic, while households consisting of one or two adults, adult partners without children, and single parents with children are a surging demographic. Small housing options in residential neighborhoods are in huge demand to meet the needs of this burgeoning housing demographic. (See figure 9.1.)

One- and two-person households now represent 62% of the country's households. Single-person households have themselves become extremely common in major cities. (See figure 9.2.)

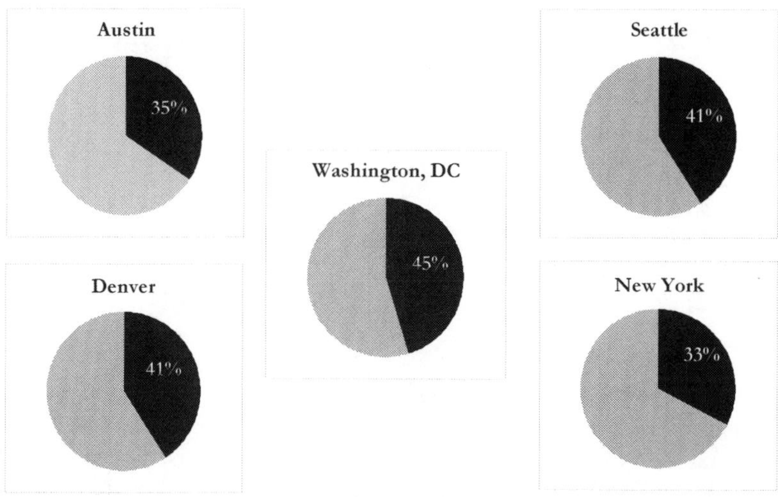

Figure 9.2. The dark sections represent the percentage of one-person households in 2014. (Data from Vicki Been, Benjamin Gross, and John Infranca, "Responding to Changing Households: Regulatory Challenges for Micro-Units and Accessory Dwelling Units," NYU's Furman Center for Real Estate and Urban Policy, January 2014, http://furmancenter.org/files/NYUFurmanCenter_RespondingtoChangingHouseholds_2014_1.pdf.)

The days of five-plus-person families are behind us, and one- and two-person households have been forming in droves. For the many 2,400-plus sq. ft. homes that are being constructed, there are relatively few US households with five or more people in them anymore. Smaller households are a result of a range of factors, including declining birth rates, postponing or forgoing marriage, increased divorce rates, and increased life expectancy. Household sizes have been shrinking from the 1850s into the twenty-first century.[53] Here are some facts and projections that start to draw a startling new picture of future housing demands:[54]

- One-person households increased from 6,917,000 households in 1960 to 35,388,000 households in 2016.
- In 1950, one-person households represented one of every ten households. In 2000, they composed one of every four households.

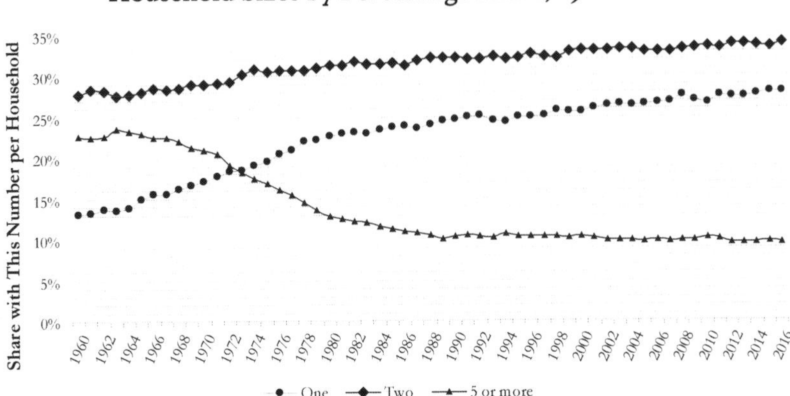

Figure 9.3. One-person households increased from a 13% share to a 28% share from 1960 to 2016. Two-person households increased from a 28% share to a 34% share in the same time frame. Together, one- and two-person households represent 62% of the country's households. Incidentally, five-plus-person households dropped from a 23% share in 1960 to a 10% share in 2016.

- Of the new households formed between 2010 and 2030, 52% will be one-person households.
- Of the new households forming between 2010 and 2030, 87% will not have children.
- Up to 85% of all households by 2025 will not have children.
- The population share of seniors will rise from 13% to 19% by 2030 and stay at that percentage until midcentury. The average household size of seniors is 1.76 compared to the average household size of 2.6.
- Of the new households formed by 2030, 50% will be from the 65-plus-years-old cohort, which will be dramatically swelling in population share. (See figures 9.3 and 9.4.)

Let's focus in on just one of the variables influencing household size: children. The percentage of households without children has increased significantly since 1940, as shown in figure 9.5.

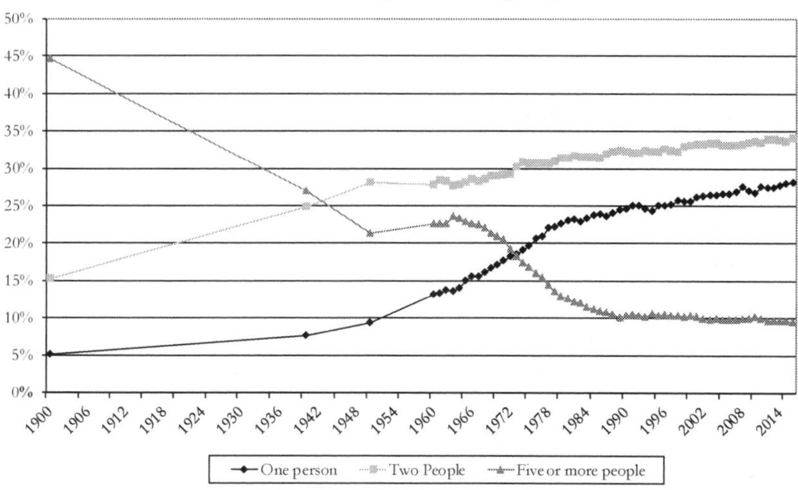

Figure 9.4. When we zoom way back to 1900, these same household size trends are even more pronounced.

Share of Households without Children, 1940–2010

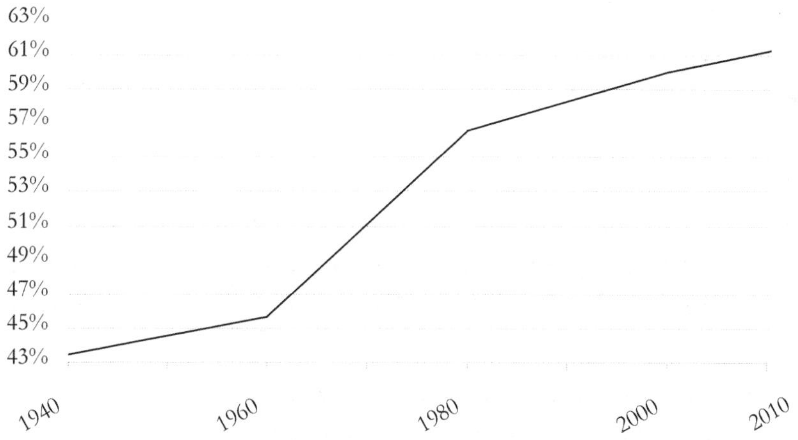

Figure 9.5. Data from Linda A. Jacobsen, Mark Mather, and Genevieve Dupuis, "Household Change in the United States," Population Reference Bureau 67, no. 1, September 2012, http://www.prb.org/pdf12/us-household-change-2012.pdf.

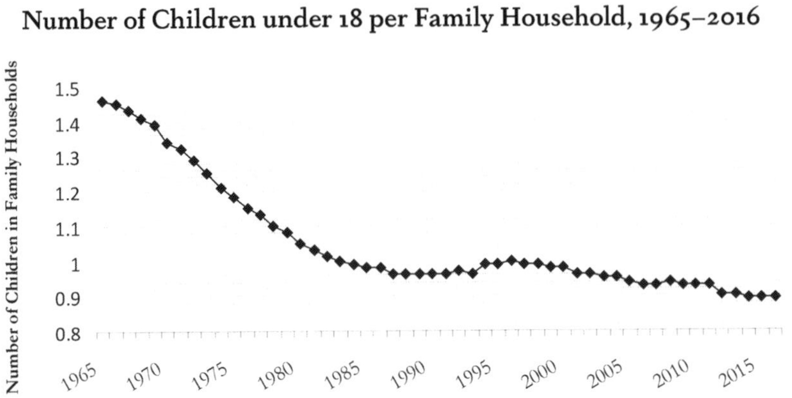

Number of Children under 18 per Family Household, 1965–2016

Figure 9.6. Data from "Average Population per Household and Family: 1940 to Present," United States Census Bureau, https://www.census.gov/population/socdemo/hh-fam/hh6.xls.

Even among the shrinking number of households that have children, the average number of children has declined, as shown in figure 9.6.

And for those with children, single-parent households have become increasingly common, as shown in figure 9.7.

These and other trends spell out a systematic and clear need for an increased number of smaller housing units, particularly ones located in walkable, transit-served areas. Even if 100% of the nation's new housing supplied through 2030 was walkable, small, urban infill housing, we still would not meet the projected 2030 demand for it. We'd still be stuck with an oversupply of conventional, suburban/exurban detached single-family homes from the existing 2015 housing inventory.[55]

Large apartment and condo buildings will play the lead role in the story of how cities and markets will provide additional demographically suitable housing choices this century. These are already being supplied successfully by the marketplace in commercial and multifamily zones. However, they will not be able to provide the desired housing type for a significant portion of the one- and two-person households. Various housing preference surveys indicate that a majority of people prefer living in residential neighborhoods with a yard instead of

Percentage of Household Living Arrangements for Children under 18 with One or Two Adults, 1968–2016

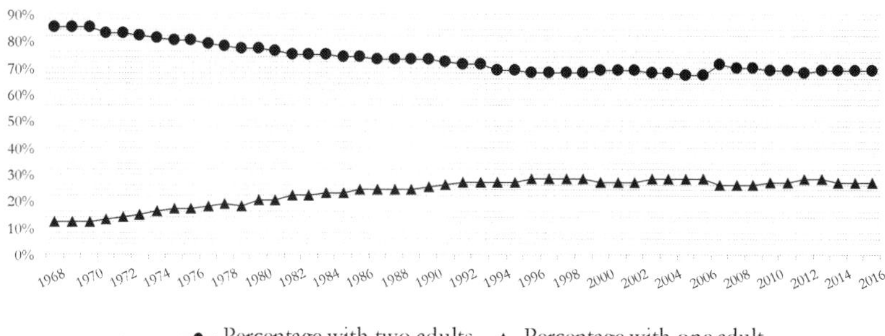

Figure 9.7. Data from the United States Census Bureau, https://www.census.gov/population/socdemo/hh-fam/tabCH-1.pdf.

having to walk through shared common spaces to get to shared common outdoor space.

Also, larger-scale multifamily housing development is not a legal option for geographically partitioned sections of cities where single-family homes dominate. Conversely, ADUs are a housing option that is only applicable on properties with single-family houses in the geographically dominant residential zones where the majority of people wish to reside.

"It's become really obvious that there's a tremendous mismatch between the types of housing we're regulating for and building and the types of housing and walkable communities that more and more people want to live in," Dan Parolek said. "We see the missing-middle housing types as ingredients of vibrant and diverse communities."[56]

ADUs are the best way for an individual homeowner to create a highly desirable and more affordable alternative to single-family housing in our dominant residential zones. They provide a distinctive mechanism to fill in this critical gap in residential housing for small households, for which there is a huge, unsatiated demographic housing demand.

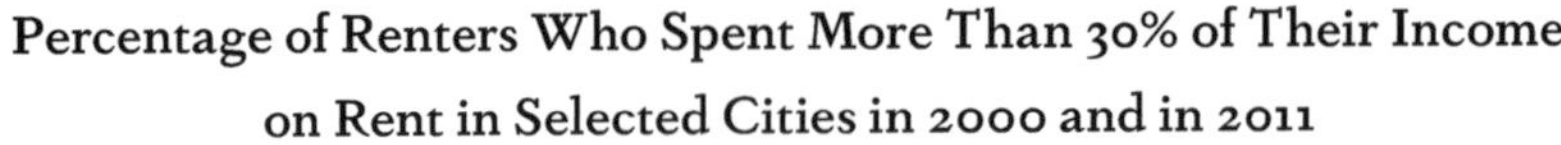

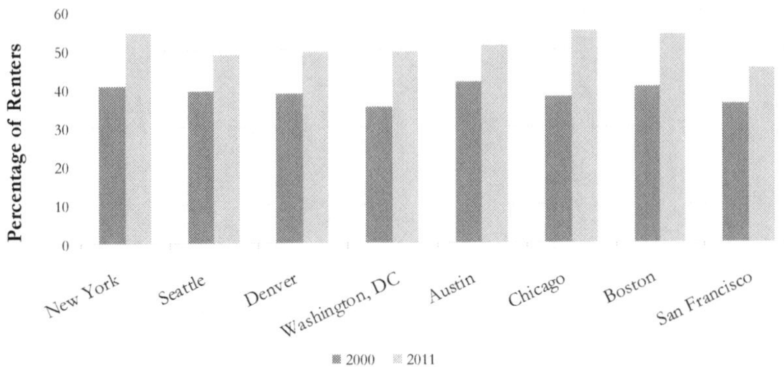

Figure 9.8. Data from Vicki Been, Benjamin Gross, and John Infranca, "Responding to Changing Households: Regulatory Challenges for Micro-Units and Accessory Dwelling Units," NYU's Furman Center for Real Estate and Urban Policy, January 2014, http://furmancenter.org/files/NYUFurmanCenter_RespondingtoChangingHouseholds_2014_1.pdf.

ADUs as Affordable Housing

Given the towering one- and two-person household demographic housing demand that ADUs can naturally and easily serve, it makes sense that the majority of homeowner developers would opt to rent these units and use them to generate passive income. Indeed, most ADUs are used as market-rate long-term housing.

From a City's vantage, ADUs will make increasing sense if the City is facing a housing crisis. One metric of a housing crisis is the rapidly increasing percentage of people who must spend more than 30% of their income on housing costs each year, a common economic benchmark that is called *cost burdened*. Figure 9.8 shows the rapid increase in this trend in a few selected cities.

In 2014, a staggering 49.2% of all renters across the 100 largest metropolitan areas were cost burdened.[57] The number of moderate-income renter households (incomes between $30,000 and $45,000) that were experiencing a cost burden increased by 48% between 2001 and 2014. This trend was largely concentrated in larger metropolitan areas.[58]

As of 2012, more than three-quarters of the 302 largest US cities and towns had a median gross rent that exceeded 30% of the renters' median household income for more than half their renting population.[59] This cost burden indicator and historically low vacancy rates indicate exacerbating housing crisis trends in cities all over the country. The cost burden is experienced most acutely by renters.

For decades, policy analysts, urban planners, and architects have written wistfully of the potential for ADUs to play a more substantial grassroots role in providing more affordable housing to help mitigate these trends. Indeed, permitted ADUs should play a substantial role in providing smaller, desirable, and demographically suitable housing options. Informal ADUs are already filling this gap to some extent.

Jake Wegmann, a professor of housing, real estate development, and planning at the University of Texas at Austin, had this to say about why he researches ADUs:

> I've been intrigued by ADUs for a number of years, because unless I'm missing something, they're the single cheapest way to add housing units to relatively dense, relatively close-in central-city neighborhoods.[60]

Integrating ADUs into single-family neighborhoods is one way to add housing that costs less than single-family houses to develop and own. These units also rent for lower market rates than their neighboring single-family counterparts due to their deliberately restricted size. Furthermore, unlike a standard apartment unit or house, a significant percentage of ADUs are rented at a below-market rate at times—an unregulated form of affordable rental housing.

According to the Oregon DEQ study, 13% of ADUs were rented for no money to parents, siblings, and friends. In addition, roughly 7% were rented out at $500 or less—less than half the market rate ($1,100/month). So in total, 20% were rented out at less than half of their market value. Of that 20%, 85% of the tenants were friends or family of the owner.[61] The 2012 East Bay study of informal ADUs in the Bay Area of California found that 17% of the ADU tenants did not pay rent and were friends or relatives of the owners.[62] A 2017 study in Edmonton, Alberta, Canada, found that 25% of ADUs were rented at under $500.[63]

This irrational economic behavior on the part of a fifth of ADU owners is part of what makes ADUs charming compared to other conventional residential rental housing options. Due partially to the ownership characteristics of ADUs and their proximity as intimately managed rental housing, a significant percentage tend to be used as truly affordable housing even without any regulatory mandates to do so.

Inclusionary zoning laws—tools designed to create affordable housing using development regulations—specify that 10%–30% of developed units are rented out at an affordable rate. So without any enforcement, it appears that ADUs, interestingly, tend to match or exceed the standards that affordable housing programs aim to achieve through laws that sometimes seem contentious.

In addition to providing naturally affordable housing for future renters, ADUs can just as easily be thought of as an affordable housing strategy for homeowners. In Vancouver, ADUs are often colloquially referred to as "mortgage helpers." Vancouver homes without the additional qualifying income from an ADU are simply not possible for many homeowners to afford. In cities where property taxes are escalating beyond what aging homeowners can afford on their fixed income, the additional income from ADUs can help them age in place.

It is not just their size or ownership that makes ADUs a compelling form of unregulated, alternative affordable housing; it's the residentially zoned locations that help distinguish them from conventional apartment complexes and condos. When placed in walkable residential neighborhoods, ADUs have a lower impact on the neighborhood than conventional multifamily structures and help integrate social class demographics in neighborhoods.

Jane Jacobs, a famous architectural critic from New York City in the 1960s, wrote of how affordable housing is best dispersed within the urban fabric of a city instead of centralized:

> One of the unsuitable ideas behind projects is the very notion that they are projects, abstracted out of the ordinary city and set apart. To think of salvaging or improving projects, as projects, is to repeat this root mistake. The aim should be to get that project, that patch upon the city, rewoven back into the fabric—and in the process of doing so, strengthen the surrounding fabric too.[64]

While ADUs should not be regulated or treated as conventional affordable housing projects, they can help play a similar economic role but with fewer acute infrastructural, aesthetic, and community impacts than larger multifamily housing developments may have.

Impact on Neighborhood Character

Sometimes referred to as hidden density or discrete density, formal and informal ADUs provide additional housing without much visual impact on a neighborhood whatsoever. They're typically entirely or mostly hidden from the street.

Often neighbors on the block will not even be aware of the existence of the ADU. Even on certain street blocks that have a highly disproportionate cluster of several ADUs, a pedestrian or driver passing by may not even know they are there.

Detached ADUs tend to be lovely structures due the homeowner's heavily vested interest in their design. But from a neighborhood character perspective, this is only relevant if you can see the ADU from the street—and typically, a passerby can barely tell it's there. Internal ADUs are especially difficult to notice other than hints of their existence, such as additional street addresses and secondary electric or gas meters.

Image 9.1. These two adjacent houses each have detached ADUs behind them, but a passerby would not realize this from the street.

Image 9.2. A basement ADU, with its entryway through the gate shown on the right side. A stairway entry is tucked into the side of the house.

PARKING IMPACTS

The street parking impacts of ADUs in Portland and Vancouver are minimal. This topic was researched in detail in the Oregon DEQ survey and follow-up study because parking requirements play an extremely outsized political role in the delicate fate of permitted ADU development in many jurisdictions compared to the extremely limited impacts that ADUs actually have on parking supply in reality.

For the 800 ADUs in Portland at the time of the survey in 2013, the DEQ survey found that ADUs contributed 0.93 cars per ADU on average, or an additional 744 vehicles.[65] The 2012 East Bay study also found that an ADU contributed 0.9 cars on average.[66]

Relative to multifamily housing, which clusters densely on a single block, ADUs and the vehicles associated with them are widely distributed. As of 2017, Portland has approximately 250,000 total housing units and approximately 1,800 finished ADUs. This means that there is less than one ADU for every 138 housing units. And for Portland's 148,000 total single-family residential units of housing, there's one ADU for every 82 properties. Assuming an average of 20 properties per block, for each 4.1 residential blocks in Portland, there are 0.9 additional vehicles added as a result of ADU development. (See figures 9.9 and 9.10.)

Admittedly, ADUs are not spread out uniformly in practice. There are neighborhoods in Portland where very few permitted ADUs exist and other neighborhoods where there are many. In some cases, there are street blocks with two or three ADUs. Even in these instances, the addition of parked vehicles on the street as a result of ADUs is still not noticeable. (See figure 9.11.)

Furthermore, unlike many cities, Portland does not require an additional off-street parking space to be provided on the property when an ADU is added. Thus, one could assume that the parking impacts of ADUs in Portland would be more severe than cities that required additional off-street parking upon ADU development.

But even in a city that has more ADU development than anywhere in the United States, has no off-street parking requirement, and allows

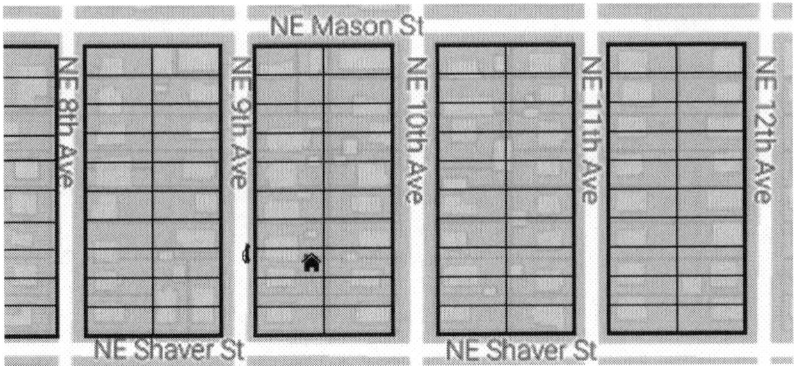

Figure 9. 9. For every 92.5 properties, <1 car is added. This is an accurate representation of the actual parking impacts of ADUs in Portland based on the number of ADUs in Portland.

Figure 9.10. This ADU is representative of the average distribution of ADUs among single-family homes without ADUs in Portland, the leader of ADU development nationally.

ADU development to be clustered, the impact of ADUs on parking supply in residential neighborhoods is effectively nonexistent. In five years of active public policy discussions and interactions with ADU homeowners and neighbors, I've never once heard parking supply raised as a problem. This is not an issue.

Vancouver city planner Heather Burpee described how her city relaxed its off-street parking standards for ADUs. She shared that there

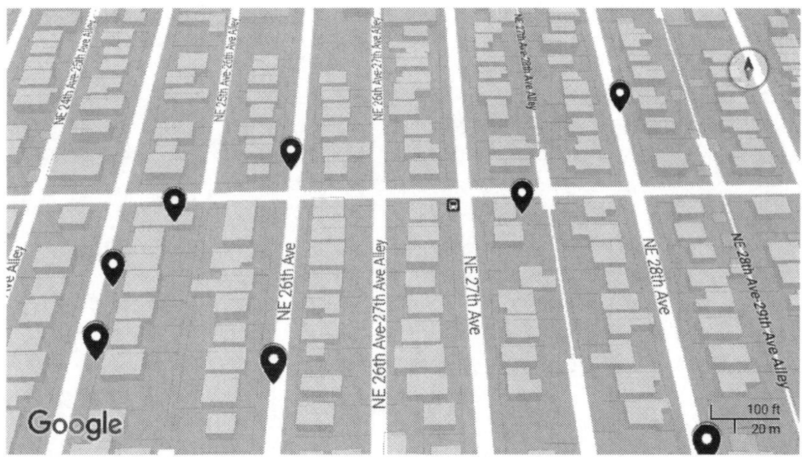

Figure 9.11. Even in neighborhoods like this one in Portland that are relatively densely populated with ADUs, the impact on parking supply is completely unnoticeable.

were no perceptions of street parking supply issues in Vancouver as a result of ADU development. "Most of the concerns were anticipatory concerns," she said. "We did go around and just have a look to see what the situation was, and certainly in areas where they were in proximity to commercial uses or churches or schools, there was a challenge for parking, and it was a preexisting challenge." Heather went on to explain, "On standard residential streets there has not been a significant issue. There is still opportunity on the street for street parking."[67]

When I asked Nicole Joslin, the development manager at the Austin Community Design and Development Center in Texas, the same question about whether ADUs have elicited any street parking problems or complaints, her response was similar. "No, not from ADUs. The places in Austin that people complain the most about the lack of parking on their street are places that are close to corridors that are developing rapidly that aren't able to provide the parking for restaurants, bars, and other retail business. So I haven't heard any complaints connected to ADUs."

In Portland and Vancouver, where there are actually significant numbers of ADUs and liberal parking requirements for ADUs, there

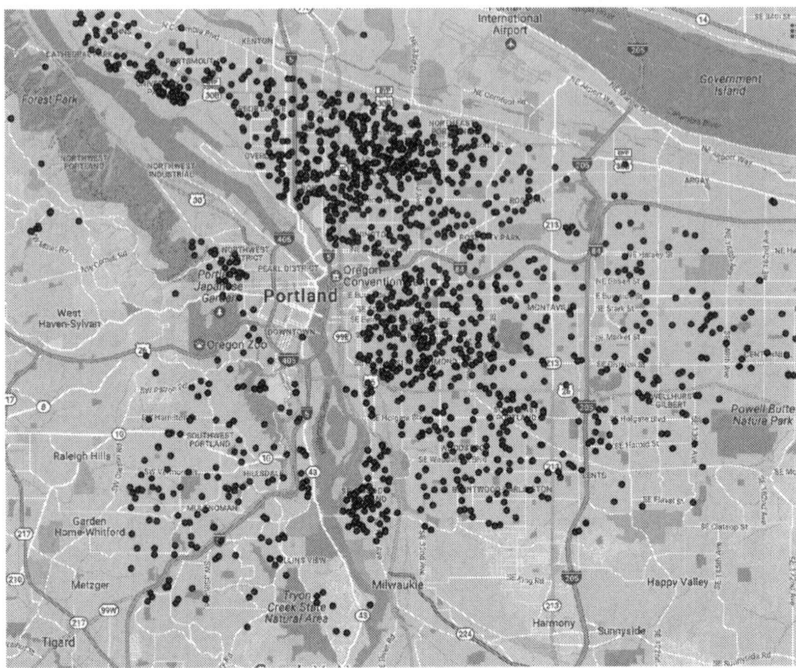

Figure 9.12. Geographic distribution of ADUs in Portland, Oregon, built between 2000 and 2016. ADUs tend to be built in more central and walkable parts of Portland.

is no evidence that ADUs have posed a parking issue. While there may be significant parking supply issues that occur around particular retail corridors in cities, that issue is not related to ADU development.

There is an absence of evidence supporting the fear of parking issues resulting from ADUs. The common anticipatory fear of their impact on residential street parking supply seem to be hypothetical and without statistical merit. Conversely, relaxing or abolishing off-street parking standards has proven to be critical for cities that are attempting to induce ADUs.

Space Efficiency and Location Efficiency

Residential space efficiency and residential location efficiency are arguably the two most significant aspects of an individual's total energy

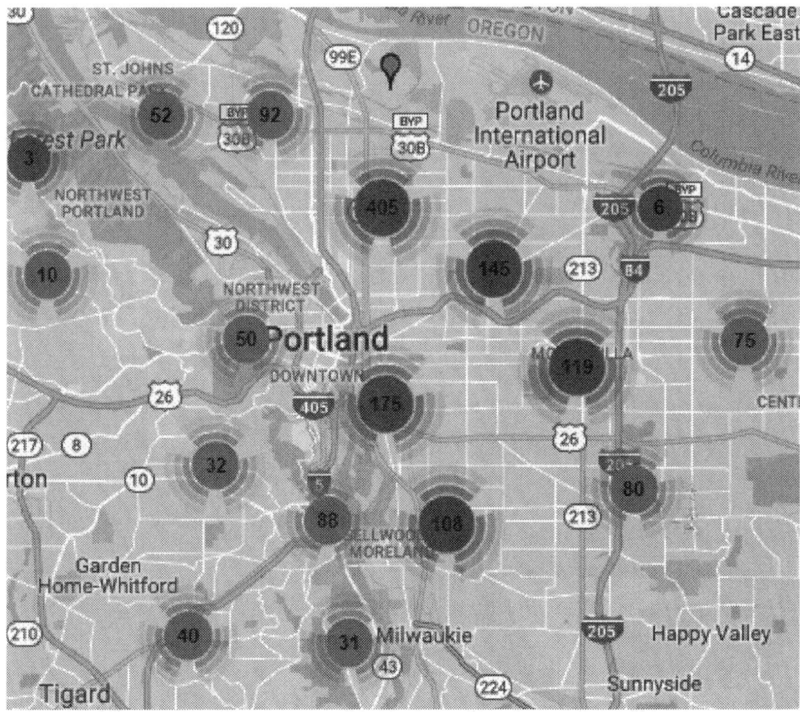

Figure 9.13. A cluster distribution representation of ADUs in Portland, Oregon.

footprint. ADUs tend to be correlated to areas where there is a strong housing rental market. In general, the strongest rental markets are in centrally located neighborhoods that are walkable, bikeable, or transit-oriented. (See figures 9.12 and 9.13.)

Residents in such neighborhoods will tend to have dramatically fewer vehicle miles traveled in a year than US residents living elsewhere. When centrally located residents choose to drive, they generally have shorter distances to travel as a result of their relative proximity to a mixture of work and retail destinations. Due to location efficiency, occupants of ADUs will most likely have lower transportation-related emissions than residents in a typical residential location.

There's a significant market undersupply of smaller housing units in transit-served areas. "Even if all new housing and nonresidential development built between 2010 and 2030 were in locations that one-third to one-half of Americans preferred, the market demand would still not be met."[68]

ADUs are much smaller than the average house and have less embodied energy and less waste built into their construction and habitation than most US homes. Due largely to heating and cooling demands, 21% of the energy used in the United States is in residential buildings. Many American houses are significantly larger than what the residents may want or need. An individual may end up purchasing a 2,400 sq. ft. home whether or not they want to be in a house that size because that is the average size of the houses that are available to them on the market. Small houses in neighborhoods with inflating land values are increasingly rare. At an average of 470 sq. ft. per capita, ADU occupants have residential footprints that are 44% smaller per capita than other single-family residential structures.[69]

As a starting point for conversation about space efficiency, consider residential sizes of 400 sq. ft. per capita, which can be a luxurious amount of space if designed well. Using this simple standard, an 800 sq. ft. house would make sense for two people, while a 2,400 sq. ft. house makes sense for six people. However, there are a large number of one- and two-person households, and not many 400–800 sq. ft. homes in residential zones available in desirable real estate markets. This is because the land values for residentially zoned lots are disproportionately high for such a small home. It is not that there is a lack of demand for small units; it is basic development economics that have eviscerated small houses from desirable neighborhoods and replaced them with large houses.

Since the residential building sector accounts for 21% of energy consumed in this country, and the transportation sector accounts for 28%, ADUs can be viewed as a strategic measure to help curtail municipal carbon emissions due to their location and space efficiency. (See figure 9.14.)

Taking these factors into account, it is possible that building an ADU is one of the single most significant actions a homeowner can take to reduce global carbon emissions. It would be useful to measure how this one action compares in greenhouse gas reductions to other

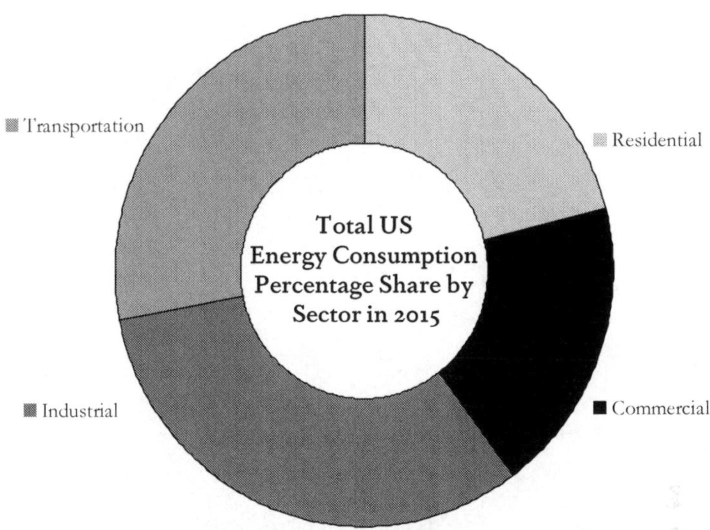

Figure 9.14. Data from the US Energy Information Administration, https://www.eia.gov/todayinenergy/detail.php?id=9250.

homeowner actions, such as changing from fluorescent bulbs to LED light bulbs, recycling waste, growing one's own produce, being vegan, biking to work, using solely renewable energy, not having children, or building net-zero passive houses.

The Presence of Informal ADUs

Until the 2010s, modern permitted ADU development remained rare except in a couple of cities. So while there are some historic and patchy remnants of nonconforming ADUs, there has not been much active permitting ADU development happening in the last sixty years. However, informal ADUs are being built in vast numbers even to this day—a gray-market expression of the demand for this housing type. These are referred to by several names: informal ADUs, unpermitted ADUs, and illegal conversions. These bootleg units are commonly called "in-laws" or "basement apartments" or sometimes vague terms like "studios." In *Backdoor Revolution*, I'm using the term "informal ADUs."

Image 9.3. An informal garage-conversion ADU.

It's difficult to get a definitive understanding of how many informal ADUs exist because there is not any formal tracking of unpermitted work. But a range of academic studies and a patchwork of enforcement surveys and news stories indicate that there are surprising numbers of these informal dwellings in many US cities, greatly dwarfing the number of permitted ADUs. A number of studies and estimates of the number of informal ADUs are summarized in appendix 4.

When and where estimates of informal ADUs have been studied, the numbers are astonishing. Informal ADUs appear to represent roughly 10% of total housing units. The rate of informal ADU development has likely increased since the 1960s as tighter housing markets have arisen, as home values have increased faster than income levels, and as zoning regulations have become more strict. Informal ADUs flourish to this day under, or in spite of, the radar. They will likely continue to persist except when their permitted ADU counterparts are effectively encouraged.

The Cottage Industry Economics of ADUs

Small businesses are well suited to deliver ADU services. Small businesses can align well with intensive, customized, one-off, residential-scale, small house projects. Increasing legal ADU development requires a bona fide cottage industry.

> I've been in business for six years, and ADUs have been in my business plan since the beginning. They're unique in their smallness, so you learn to pay attention to every single inch and look more critically at every single detail.
>
> —Holly Huntley of Environs LLC, a design-build company

The majority of ADU development is done by amateur homeowner developers who hire small design teams, maybe only one or two people, for their custom structure. The site plan and ADU design usually must be customized due to the site constraints and size limitations. This type of boutique and intensive design work is best suited to small design outfits, as opposed to larger design and construction firms that may tend to focus on larger-scale projects.

> I never really marketed it, so I built two or three ADUs per year for many years. With the recent recession and everything changing, I decided to focus on ADUs, and it's now the majority of what we're doing. I was part of the very first SDC waiver and testified to the City Council. I was surprised how fast the word got around about the SDC waiver. That increased my inquiries threefold, and it was the major reason I shifted out of general construction into ADUs.
>
> —Joe Robertson of Shelter Solutions LLC

> What convinced me to do a second ADU? All the people that came knocking after the first one was done. There's been a great response to my work, and I feel really lucky that people continue to come to me for their designs.
>
> —WILLIE DEAN OF GROUND UP DESIGN WORKS

Amateur homeowner developers of ADUs are not conventional housing developers experienced at building and selling single-family homes, housing developments, and multifamily buildings. The money spent on ADU development labor primarily goes to small, boutique construction companies and local subcontractors and labor. An ADU is typically built by a general contractor who farms out much of the work to various subcontractor trades. Accounting for all of the trades, it's not uncommon for dozens of people to be involved in the construction of an ADU, even though it's a small structure. In this way, ADU development tends be a grassroots form of housing development that inherently supports small, local businesses.

Chapter 10

Case Studies of Advancing ADUs in Cities

As of 2017, there were only two North American cities with a very substantial number of recently permitted ADUs and where the rate of ADU development was flourishing: Portland, Oregon, and Vancouver, British Columbia. This chapter relates what steps Portland and Vancouver took to help foster and accelerate ADU development. I'll provide some ADU history and the real estate market context in these cities, as well as some analysis of the ADU policy and regulations used by these cities.

We will also briefly discuss Austin, Texas, and Santa Cruz, California, two other cities with notable ADU development. Their experiences provide valuable lessons that other cities may wish to consider in forming their own programs. Accelerating ADU development is covered in greater detail in the next chapter.

This section will focus primarily on the success of detached ADUs. When including internal ADUs in the standard of a successful municipal ADU development program, there is arguably success in many more cities. But it is very challenging to measure and synthesize this success of internal ADUs for several reasons. Some cities may allow in-law apartments without classifying or tracking them as ADUs, so it is harder to quantify the success. And most large cities already have thousands—or tens of thousands—of existing informal in-law apartments, muddying the conversation about how a City may substantiate its success in permitted ADU development. Besides being more challenging to foster politically, it is easier to cleanly quantify and synthesize the successes of detached ADU development.

PORTLAND, OREGON

With roughly 1,800 permitted ADUs completed as of late 2017, Portland is the leader of modern ADU development in the United States. Not only are there far more permitted ADUs in Portland than in other cities in the United States, but the rate of development grew exponentially since 2010, so the movement's momentum is strong.

ADU History

In the early 1900s, zoning ordinances were much looser than modern zoning ordinances. In 1918 in Portland, if property owners wanted to have certain uses or buildings that were not normally allowed by right, the City Council would grant the request except "wherever it appears that the granting of the same is or may be detrimental to the public health or safety, or detrimental to the welfare and growth of the City."[70]

In Portland's first zoning code in 1924, four types of zoning were established: (1) single family, (2) multifamily, (3) business-manufacturing, and (4) unrestricted. At this time, multifamily zoning encompassed the largest portion of Portland's land area (approximately 33% of the total). In this zone, there was no governance on the number of allowable units. In multifamily zones, you could and still can add multiple dwelling units by right. ADUs were not an applicable concept in this zone.

In 1959, Portland's zoning master plan was revamped to drastically reduce the amount of multifamily zoning and replace it with single-family zoning. Over fourteen square miles of Portland was turned from multifamily to single family, a sixteenfold reduction of multifamily zoned areas.[71] At this time, there were antiquated codes that allowed for guesthouses, servant's houses, and caretaker's quarters in single-family zones.

Modern-day ADUs have been allowed for more than three decades in Portland. In 1981, there was a program that prompted several internal ADUs to be created. Regulations for ADUs were consolidated from across the zoning code in 1991 under the Accessory Rental Unit program.[72] At that time, ADUs were only allowed in the form of basement conversions. It was not until 1998 that Portland started to allow detached ADUs and dropped its owner-occupancy requirement. A trickle of ADUs were developed each year from that point forward, but they did not take off as a substantial type of development until 2010.

Political Support

Portland's City Council is generally a proactive supporter of ADU development. The council typically heeds the advice and recommendations from the City's nationally lauded planning department, which has proposed incremental ADU improvement measures for the City to adopt over the years. Partially as a result of the political support for ADUs, Portland does not have any of the poison-pill zoning regulations: owner-occupancy requirements, additional parking requirements, or conditional reviews.

As the ADU zoning codes were being periodically updated over the last thirty years, Portland has experienced its share of community resistance. Portland city planner Phil Nameny recently researched archived testimony about the allowance of detached ADUs in 1998. The majority of the individual and neighborhood associations testified that they did not want to loosen restrictions when it came to allowing detached ADUs. Typical statements were "Don't commercialize our single-family neighborhood," and "The backyard is our sanctuary," and "We don't want others living next to our backyard." The same types of complaints are heard whenever there are any proposed zoning changes that may facilitate more infill in residential zones. The City Council moved forward with incremental ADU zoning updates despite these objections.

In 2010, following the great recession, the City Commissioners waived System Development Charges (SDCs) as a mechanism to promote ADUs. This move proved to be a tipping point for ADUs in

Portland, though there were a number of contributory variables that caused ADUs to finally materialize en masse at that time, including a tight rental market and various advocacy efforts. Political support from the City Council helped iron out regulatory kinks that have arisen during the rapid acceleration of ADUs that has occurred since 2010.

It is not clear whether it has been the courage of local governmental officials in Portland, or whether it is Portland's Urban Growth Boundary that makes these progressive land-use choices more essential, or perhaps it is partly due to the cultural zeitgeist of Portland, but it is clear that some degree of leadership was required to make some incremental but controversial policy changes to the ADU code to remove prohibitive regulatory barriers over the years.

Economics

Portland's recent ADU development surge is intimately bound to its tight rental market. If the demand for rental housing were flat in Portland, homeowners would not be developing ADUs en masse. Like many US cities, Portland is growing rapidly and has a housing shortage, which is partially a latent result of development slowing down following the Great Recession in 2008.

Portland's low rental vacancy rate—another statistical proxy for rental housing shortages—and rising rental rates have been constant features in local and national news outlets since 2013. In 2015, the City Council declared that Portland was in a bona fide "housing emergency," a regulatory declaration that provided flexibility around zoning-code standards to help address surging homelessness. More generally, Portland was facing a growing housing affordability crisis that was having a significant impact on renters. (See figure 10.1.)

Zoning

Despite the fact that the city is an economic center for a region with 2.3 million people, much of Portland's land is actually zoned for single-family residential use, a form of zoning with an inherently restricted housing carrying capacity.

Average Vacancy Rate in Portland, Oregon

Figure 10.1. Data from Multifamily NW annual fall apartment reports, http://www.multifamilynw.org/apartment-report.html.

In 1927, 33% of Portland's residential zones allowed multifamily dwellings and only 20% was zoned as single-family residential. Through zoning-code updates over the decades following the 1920s, more and more restrictions were overlaid on these zones, until finally the city became dominated by residential zoning that only allowed properties to house a single family. By 2016, 42% of the city was restricted to single-family zoning and only 10% was zoned to allow multifamily dwellings. (See figures 10.2 and 10.3.)

URBAN GROWTH BOUNDARY

There are approximately 148,000 units of housing in single-family zones and a population of approximately 609,000.[73] The greater Portland metropolitan area population is 2.35 million.[74]

The Portland metro area is subject to Oregon's Urban Growth Boundary (UGB), a man-made boundary that restricts development to within a deliberately limited area surrounding each of Oregon's cities and towns. Portland is only indirectly affected by the UGB, as it is bound by geologic features on some sides and abuts suburbs on other sides. (See figure 10.4.)

The cultural and political acceptance regarding population growth within the city limits is largely attributable to Oregon's UGB laws,

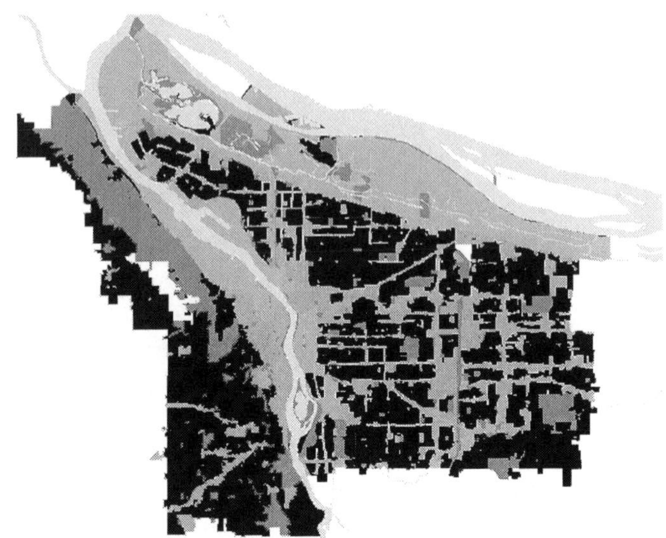

Figure 10.2. Black areas on this map are single-family residential; these areas comprise 42% of the land area of Portland in 2016.

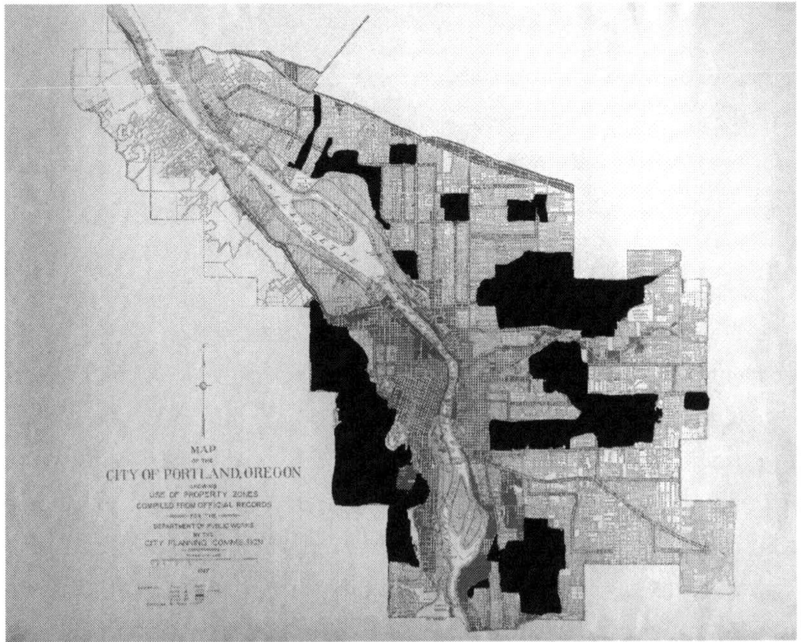

Figure 10.3. A zoning map from 1927. Black areas are single-family residential (20% of the total land area). Multifamily housing was allowable in 33% of Portland's total land area in 1927 and only 10% of the land area in 2016.

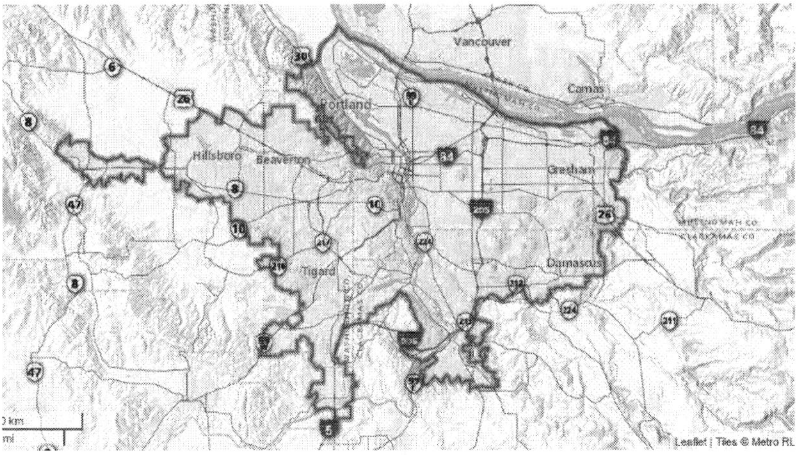

Figure 10.4. Portland Metro's Urban Growth Boundary.

which were passed in 1973. The boundary has helped Oregon's cities and towns establish and foster an understanding, acceptance, and appreciation of increased residential densities as a measure to help conserve natural resources and farmland.

This state law is key to the policy position that the City of Portland has codified about embracing better urban infill development. In the absence of a UGB, Oregon's cities, like all US cities, would simply extend outward at their periphery into agricultural lands. The UGB also sets a backdrop for the City of Portland's general attitude of embracing higher residential densities. Some residents resent rapid urban development, but most seem to have a tacit acceptance that Portland ultimately must grow up or lose its influence as the region grows in population.

ADUs—specifically, detached ADUs—seem to represent a change in norms for cities and citizens who are protective about the character of their single-family neighborhoods. But in Portland, ADUs are now embraced as an acceptable form of urban infill. Now that citizens have had the chance to actually become familiar with ADUs, they are rapidly growing in popularity in Portland.

The UGB plays a role in Portland's acceptance of urban infill, and the support for ADUs is just one manifestation of this policy.

Image 10.1. An aerial view of the urban growth development boundary as defined by the UGB, in Troutdale, Oregon, fifteen miles east of Portland. (Image from Google Maps.)

Regulatory work in 2017 known as the "residential infill project," which among other changes would allow two ADUs on all properties in single-family zones, is another manifestation. These types of housing innovations are needed, as the greater Portland region is projected to increase in population by 38% between 2010 and 2030,[75] or by 856,000 people.

Use Provisions

In 1998, a large swath of North and Northeast Portland called the Albina Overlay District had an owner-occupancy requirement for properties with ADUs, while the requirement was dropped for the rest of Portland. Up to that time, all of Portland had been subject to that bylaw.

When a monitoring study of permitted ADUs was conducted in 2003 in the majority of Portland where owner occupancy was not required, many owners were living on the property nonetheless (55 of 61 of the properties, or 90%). Counterintuitively, in the Albina Overlay District, where owner occupancy was required, a much larger proportion of the owners were not living at the property (5 of 14 were not owner occupied, or 35%).

This disparity indicated to the City that the owner-occupancy provision had no impact. Furthermore, this discovery helped the City realize that there were no complaints about owners not living on the property in the Albina Overlay District. It determined that the owner-occupancy requirement was irrelevant and dropped it at that time. Nameny explained that enforcing owner-occupancy requirements also would have been difficult for Portland, or any major city, to enforce.

For short-term rentals, Portland does not currently treat ADUs any differently than single-family homes are treated. The City allows the owners to rent up to two bedrooms on a given property as a short-term rental. These bedrooms can be in an ADU or in the primary house. The applicant must live on-site and apply for a special by-right permit in order to do short-term rentals.

> The forms in which money is used in city building—or withheld from use—are powerful instruments of city decline today. The forms in which money is used must be converted to instruments of regeneration—from instruments buying violent cataclysms to instruments buying continual, gradual, complex and gentler change.
>
> —Jane Jacobs, *The Death and Life of Great American Cities*

System Development Charge Waiver

When adding new housing units to Portland's infrastructural systems—water, sewer, parks, and transportation—the developers of those units are responsible for paying into the City's coffers to help pay for the infrastructural burden that the housing unit will add to those systems. These fees are known locally as System Development Charges, or SDCs. The SDCs for a new single-family house can be $25,000–$30,000. Note that these SDC fees are not the same as building-permit fees; all cities have administrative permit fees for construction and renovation work.

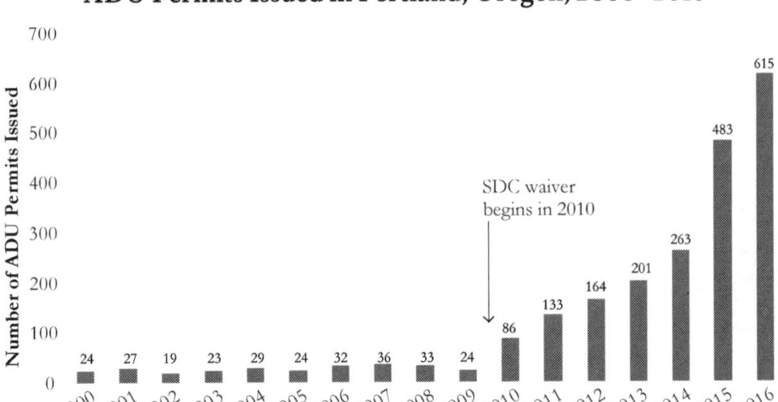

Figure 10.5.

The permit fees for a detached new-construction ADU in Portland are commonly \$5,000–\$7,000 but can be as much as \$10,000.

Following the Great Recession of 2008, the City decided to temporarily waive SDCs on ADUs beginning in 2010. The SDCs for a new ADU at that time were \$8,000–\$12,000. Waiving the SDC fees was a bold political measure that was intended to promote the construction of ADUs, which the City had long philosophically endeared as a mechanism to build affordable housing and create additional housing density. But like other cities, few ADUs were actually built in Portland. Up to 2010, the development rate had been puttering along at roughly thirty ADUs per year for the previous ten years.

The SDC waiver for ADUs proved to be incredibly effective at stimulating their development. The SDC waiver jump-started the development of ADUs, and the rate has been growing dramatically since 2010. In 2016, 615 ADU permits were issued—a twenty-two-fold increase in the rate of ADU development in just six years. (See figure 10.5.)

The SDC waiver was not necessarily instrumental to the development of all of Portland's ADUs, but without a doubt the incentive kick-started their development into high gear. This approach was relatively remarkable in comparison to most other cities, where ADUs are regulated out of existence. The SDC waiver accomplished three things simultaneously:

1. It significantly reduced the capital cost of development. As discussed in chapter 3, the capital cost of financing ADUs is particularly challenging. This additional SDC fee could be the difference between allowing a homeowner to proceed with building an ADU or not.
2. It was used as effective marketing. The psychological carrot that a $12,000 incentive played should not be underestimated. The possibility that a significant incentive might disappear lit a fire under those who had otherwise put building an ADU on hold.
3. It bolstered faith in government. This kind of financial incentive was the City's way of putting its money where its mouth was. It sent a clear signal to citizens that the City wanted more ADUs. In addition to the economic carrot, this kind of signal was perhaps psychologically important in helping average homeowners know that the City supported their development. Given that an amateur homeowner developer may spend $160,000 or more to build an ADU—a huge investment by middle-income homeowner standards—it is invaluable that homeowners trust in the process. A large part of this is trusting that their government actually wants ADUs built, exemplified by the fact that it also has skin in the game. Predictability in the regulatory process is a prerequisite for ADU development, and this incentive proved that the City was serious about its interest in inducing ADU development.

Permitting Office Transparency

The Bureau of Development Services is Portland's retail department that deals directly with customers about development projects, including ADUs. In my experiences as a retail end user, the experience of visiting and receiving assistance from Portland's permitting office has been productive and informative.

Portland's regulations are clear, and the planning and building-code plan reviewers are transparent regarding how a proposed project does or does not meet the standards. The importance of this transparency and predictability through Portland's permitting office is not limited to ADUs, but it is critical to Portland's ADU development.

By-Right Development

Assuming that the regulations are followed correctly, ADUs may be built by right in Portland. There is no conditional-use or discretionary review process. So while a homeowner may not like the regulatory design constraints, if they abide by the rules, they are entitled to build an ADU. However, even with relatively relaxed ADU development codes, many homeowners simply cannot meet the zoning-code standards. By definition, ADUs are compact urban infill development, and they will likely confront setback and size constraints. If an applicant cannot abide by the zoning regulations, they can apply for an adjustment from the zoning code, which is sometimes known as a variance.

In 2015 in Portland, it was observed that approximately 15% of ADU developers applied for an adjustment. Provided that an ADU project met the intent of the zoning principles that the planning officials are charged with protecting, adjustments were routinely approved. In December 2015, Portland passed the Accessory Structures Zoning Code Update, which aimed to reduce the number of adjustment applications for accessory structures. The recommendations were derived from evaluating which regulatory provisions were most frequently causing owners to seek an adjustment. This regulatory update process—and the City Council's political approval of it—is an example of how general policy support by elected officials and city planners results in the City of Portland incrementally removing ADU development obstacles for homeowners.

Flexible Development Regulations

Portland allows homeowners to make an ADU in any number of structural forms, including new construction, garage conversions, additions, basement conversions, and other internal ADUs. This type of flexibility means that all residential properties could theoretically add an ADU one way or another, though certain structural options are more financially or physically realistic than others.

Portland development regulations that cover the setback requirement, height, and size limitations are reasonable: 5-foot property line setbacks in most cases. The 2015 Accessory Structures Zoning Code Update even allowed short and small ADUs to be constructed within the 5-foot setback right up to the property line. This flexible setback standard helps more homeowners entertain the possibility of detached ADU development even if their backyard is fairly small.

Portland has its particular community design standards that inform the scope of allowable architectural ADU details: eaves, siding, roof pitch, and so on. The specific design standards of what Portland allows and does not allow do not seem to have a substantial impact on how many ADUs are developed, but importantly, they do not pose any significant obstacles to development. These standards are reasonable and characteristic of standard zoning and development regulations in Portland. ADUs are not treated with any more or less development regulation vigor than other detached accessory structures, such as garages or art studios.

Advocacy and Educational Entrepreneurship

The City of Portland made ADU development incrementally easier over the years, but the City made no single remarkable effort to popularize them, other than the temporary SDC waiver first established in 2010.

Seizing on the opportunity that the SDC waiver presented, a number of outside stakeholders stepped in to promote ADU development, since Portland appeared to be well poised for an uptick. Seeing ADUs as a way to reduce the material and energy-related impacts of residential homes, Oregon DEQ convened a workgroup of individual advocates,

Image 10.2. AccessoryDwellings.org, a volunteer-run website about ADUs.

organizations, professionals, and government agencies. Over several years, this consortium contributed to and organized a range of educational projects and advocacy endeavors to help increase the supply and demand for ADUs, including small contracts to fund ADU surveys, research, blog posts, conferences, videos, and ADU tours.

In 2012, three ADU advocates—myself; Eli Spevak, a small-house enthusiast and developer in Portland; and Martin John Brown, a researcher and writer who had built his own ADU—started a website called AccessoryDwellings.org. We built the site to be a hub of information for all things ADU related with the intention of primarily providing information about real-life projects. This site developed a strong readership and helped many homeowner developers understand best practices for ADU development.

Personally, I've taught a daylong ADU class to over a thousand Portland residents, and I instruct a half-day course for real estate agents. I provide an ADU Specialist designation for real estate agents who complete the course and pass a test. I have also hosted five citywide self-guided tour of ADUs, and several thousand Portlanders have

Image 10.3. A workshop about ADUs hosted by a neighborhood association.

attended. Other individuals, companies, and organizations around Portland have also created topical ADU events and opportunities. Thanks in part to these events and to ongoing, positive local media coverage of ADU stories and issues, there is now a sense of community and cultural awareness around small housing concepts in Portland. In addition to the growing cadre of design and build professionals who focus on ADUs, these grassroots efforts have successfully helped create an increased supply and demand for ADUs in Portland.

Vancouver, British Columbia

With 2,554 laneway houses and 4,137 secondary suites permitted as of January 2016, Vancouver is the leader in ADU development in North America.

Laneway house (LWH) is the term that is used to describe a detached ADU built along a residential alley, known locally in Vancouver as a "lane." *Secondary suite* is the term that is used to describe a basement ADU. I'll use *ADUs* when writing about both types.

Image 10.4. A laneway house. (Image courtesy of the City of Vancouver, BC.)

History

Vancouver's first laneway homes were built in the 1890s.[76] In the 1920s, the City cracked down and made this type of development more difficult to build.

> The conversion of larger older single-family homes to provide additional units is not new. As housing demand shifted to suburban locations in the 1920s onward, single-family houses in the West End and other inner city areas were split up into suites or rooms. In 1940, the War Measures Act set aside municipal housing bylaws and encouraged the creation of additional suites in single-family neighbourhoods as a way of relieving housing shortages.
>
> With the City's adoption of the Zoning and Development Bylaw in 1956, secondary suites and other multiple-unit buildings in the areas zoned RS-1 (single-family) became illegal. In the late 1950s, Council decided to remove all illegal suites over

a 10-year period, and by 1966, over 2,000 suites had been removed under the program. Between 1966 and 1974, the need for the rental housing provided by suites led to extensions of the timelines for closing suites, and exceptions against enforcement were allowed for family suites or on hardship grounds. In 1981, Council decided to enforce closures only on a complaint basis.[77]

Political Support

As with other cities, Vancouver faced a lot of public fear about what the impact of allowing these secondary units again would be. The City Council took some brave steps to allow both secondary suites and later LWHs, and both changes incrementally reduced the barriers to ADU development.

In 1987, Vancouver had explored the idea of allowing LWHs. The City's planning staff reviewed legislation in Melbourne, Australia, where granny flats were permitted by right. (Incidentally, the state of New South Wales, Australia, where Sydney is located, is another global leader in granny flat development: 4,818 were developed in 2014, 2,867 were developed in 2013, and 1,511 were built in 2010.[78])

According to Vancouver city planner Heather Burpee, in the late 1980s, over two thousand people attended a public meeting to protest against regulatory issues including allowing secondary suites in residential zones.

By the early 2000s, Planning and Housing Centre staff went back to the Council with a proposal to permit secondary suites in all residential areas. Perhaps due to a recognition that prolific numbers of informal secondary suites were not causing the types of conditions feared by neighbors, only a handful of people showed up at this public hearing, and the Council passed the Secondary Suites provision in 2004. Since then, the city has issued 2,154 permits for homes that include secondary suites and an additional 1,983 permits for renovations to existing homes to include secondary suites, for a total of 4,137 secondary-suite permits between 2004 and 2015.

Notably, Census Canada estimates that there are 25,300 secondary suites in Vancouver. Even Vancouver itself reports to have 25,300 secondary suites in its publications, and its neighboring city Surrey is said to have 18,000 secondary suites. However, this number is accounting for both permitted and informal secondary suites. For the purposes of comparing apples to apples in this book, I have chosen to use the count of permitted secondary suites instead. We'll review this nuance more in the next chapter.

When LWHs were brought to the Council's table again for consideration in 2009, political support was there. Perhaps it was recognition of the vast numbers of informal ADUs that helped the Council reconsider this approach.

In the early days of the LWH program, there were complaints about the bulk and massing, loss of privacy for neighbors, and anticipatory concerns about potential impacts on street parking. Asked about how the community reacted to the 2009 changes to allow LWH, Burpee responded,

> The prevalence of Secondary Suites throughout the city—people were already comfortable with that—so it wasn't such a huge change. The NIMBYism was really around the structure in the rear yard and loss of privacy that someone might be overlooking a neighbor's property...as opposed to the number of people, it was really around privacy and change of character at the lanes.[79]

Some small regulatory changes were made in 2013 to address these concerns. Now in 2016, there is public support for LWHs and secondary suites in the city and little objection or complaints about them, according to planning staff.

Burpee said there is "strong political interest in increasing the number of rental units/housing variety in low density residential neighbourhoods." The City Council and planning department are both actively engaged in helping to develop more affordable housing options within

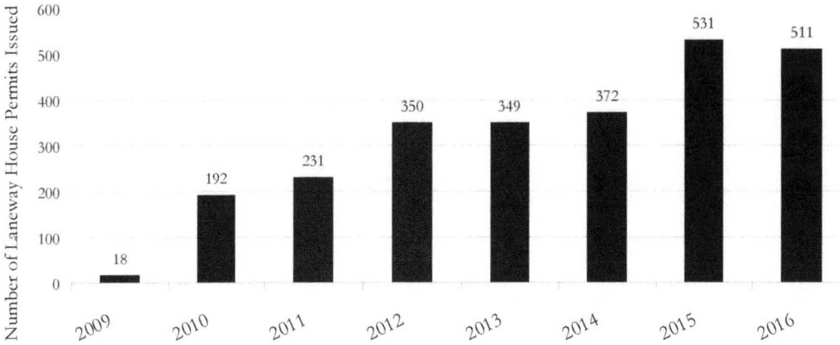

Figure 10.6. A total of 2,554 laneway house permits have been issued since 2009, the year Vancouver started to allow them again.

the city. The City produced a "Laneway House How-to Guide" but did not do anything too special beyond their progressive regulations.

As a result of having an ADU program that works well, the City is not planning on making any changes to their LWHs and secondary suites program; it's moving on to other planning priorities. The lack of apparent drama and tension among citizens, architects, builders, and the planning/zoning department toward LWHs and secondary suites could be seen as a sign of the success of their program. (See figure 10.6.)

Between 2010 and 2015, of the new single-family houses built, 37% also included a secondary suite (1,937 out of 5,202). And approximately a quarter of new single-family dwellings included a LWH.

Economics

This amount of ADU development is due largely to the tremendously high cost of land in Vancouver and the increased demand for rental housing stock. There is a perpetual affordable housing crisis in Vancouver. Vancouver also has extremely low vacancy rates for one-bedroom apartments, a good proxy for ADU demand. (See figure 10.7.)

The astronomical land values are quite specific to Vancouver and are atypical in both the United States and Canada. Due largely to the

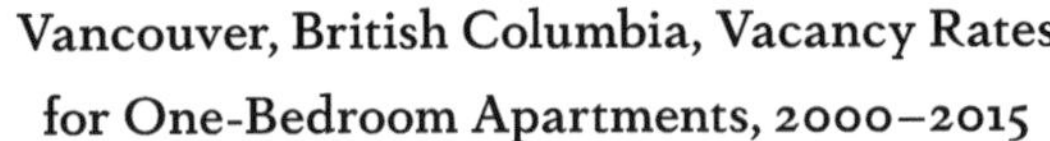

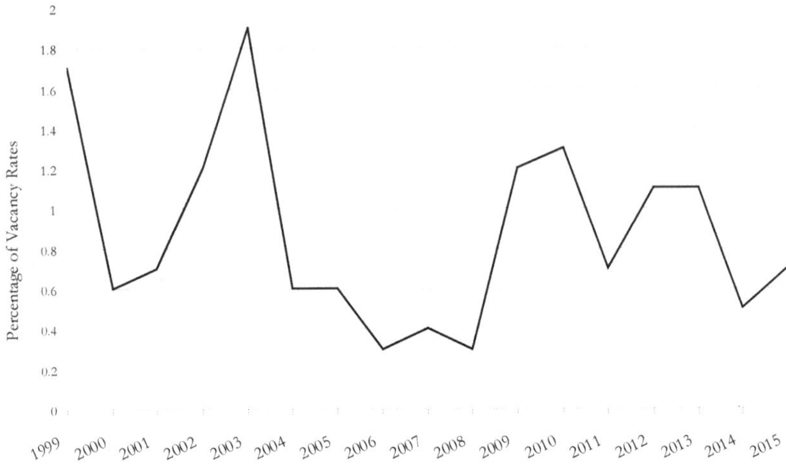

Figure 10.7.

high value and relative security of owning real estate in Vancouver, land ownership is perceived as an international holdings commodity. The average home price in Vancouver was C$1.47 million in 2016.[80]

The City views LWHs and secondary suites as tools to both provide economic support for homeowners and increase the stock of additional rental units in the city. ADUs are not only perceived as a useful urban development tool by the City of Vancouver but also deemed an essential element of affordability for middle-class homeowners.

Urban Growth Boundary

There are roughly 603,000 residents in Vancouver and 2.4 million in the greater metropolitan area. Vancouver is expecting 100,000 new residents in the next ten years, yet there is a total of only 75,000 single-family properties in the city (2011 Census data).[81] It does not have an urban growth boundary, but it is bound on all sides by water and suburbs. Unlike Portland, surrounding suburbs are not compelled by any UGB statute to restrict sprawl. However, in the greater Vancouver metropolitan area, there is a regional planning framework to increase transit around density and employment nodes. The City of Vancouver has a limited land base, and its planning efforts frequently grapple with how to increase the housing stock within its jurisdiction.

Zoning

Of the 75,000 single-family houses in the city, 69,000 properties are located in zones that allow LWH development. Of those, approximately 59,000 properties are actually eligible for a LWH. The other 10,000 single-family properties are not eligible to build LWHs because they do not have laneways or their lots are not large enough to allow LWHs based on Vancouver's code. Interestingly, Vancouver does not actually allow backyard secondary homes unless there is an alley.

Part of the rationale of Vancouver's LWH program was to increase housing opportunities in single-family neighborhoods, which dominated much of Vancouver's limited land base. More than half—58%—of Vancouver's land area is zoned single-family residential. Like Portland and many other cities, this inherently low-density form of zoning dominates the urban core of the region.

What is most notable about Vancouver's ADU regulations is the allowance for both a secondary suite and a LWH on the same property. This is a laudable zoning gesture that speaks to an acceptance of the need for urban infill options, and an underlying institutional understanding of the mismatch that exists between the demographic demands for housing, and the reality of the existing supply.

By-Right Development

Vancouver allows LWHs and secondary suites by right and does not have conditional reviews. Currently, 70% of LWHs are developed when new primary houses are being built on a property and 30% by adding the LWH to a lot with a preexisting house. There is no data about how many of the properties in Vancouver have both LWHs and secondary suites. However, according to Burpee, it is very likely that of the 70%

of the sites that are being entirely redeveloped that include a LWH, the majority of them also have secondary suites.

Of the 30% being added to a lot with a preexisting house, it is primarily families who are seeking to build the unit for a variety of residential purposes: a starter home for young adults, a retiree who wants to be able to retain a smaller home in Vancouver and generate income from the LWH, or an adult homeowner who wants to build the LWH for an aging parent.

Of the 70%, some are speculative developers who are developing the LWH and intending to sell the property to families, with the understanding that most people can only afford to purchase the property if it has a rental unit on it to help offset the mortgage. And some are amateur developers who are holding on to the property. There is no solid data on this breakdown, however.

From the City of Vancouver's perspective, more rental housing is needed, so each new property the housing industry provides that comes with a LWH and a secondary suite helps the City meet its housing goals. The ADU program is doing what the City wants it to do: supply more rental housing.

Use Provisions

There has never been an owner-occupancy requirement in Vancouver. The freedom to use the additional units however the owner needs to use them ties into the relative ease of financing them. For a permitted ADU, 100% of the rental income can be classified as valid income to help homeowners qualify for loans to purchase Vancouver's expensive real estate.

Short-term rentals are only allowed in an actual unit where the owner lives. So in this regard, it is unlikely that the secondary units are (legally) used for short-term rentals; however, this provision would be difficult to enforce, and it has not proven to be a problem for Vancouver. The units are intended to be used as a long-term rental opportunity, and the City would enforce this provision if complaints were called in.

Development Regulations

The development regulations for LWHs and the building-code regulations for secondary suites are fairly strict. For example, for a LWH, properties must be 32 feet wide or greater, there must be 16 feet between the primary structure and the LWH, and the upper limit of a second story must be restricted to 60% of the house footprint. Vancouver's lots are standardized, however, and though their development regulations are fairly strict, the regulations have proven to work well for the standard-sized laneway lots. The size of the LWH does not hinge on the size of the primary house.

Vancouver has a provision that a parking space must be provided adjacent to the LWH, but this parking provision is not an insurmountable burden in this instance, as LWHs can only be built off alleys where there is preexisting parking capacity and access. The laneway placement ensures that there is always direct off-street parking access, and the standard laneway lot dimensions have access and space for a LWH and a parking spot. Additional parking spaces may be provided on-site for the primary house but are not required.

Burpee said that there was no discernible impact on residential parking supply from either secondary suites or from LWHs, though parking had been a common anticipatory concern before ADUs were actually allowed in Vancouver.

Economics and Financing

Families who are adding LWHs to a property for a family member are making a rational choice to build a housing unit that will cost them less each month when rolled into a mortgage than a comparable rental unit would cost for them to rent. Meanwhile, they are also building up equity in the property. A rental unit equivalent to a LWH may cost C$2,200 per month, whereas financing a comparable LWH may cost C$1,500 per month. LWHs are quite expensive to build in Vancouver due to the economic conditions of the city. A LWH added to a property with a house may have commonly cost C$350,000 in 2016.

Image 10.5. A laneway house to the left, with parking on its right, as viewed from the alley. (Image courtesy of Lanefab Design/Build; photo by Colin Perry.)

Credit unions in Vancouver support these property improvements because they understand that ADUs are a safe investment. Jake Fry of Smallworks Studios & Laneway Housing Inc. said, "The credit unions really came on board—especially the major one. They saw the value of it and saw a way to use it as a revenue tool. And they've been doing quite well by it."[82]

Vancity, a Vancouver-based credit union, offers a "Mixer Mortgage" that lets partners, family members, or friends share the cost of home buying, including the deposit, the mortgage, and other ownership expenses. Vancity also counts the future ADU rental income toward calculating what a borrower is allowed to borrow.

Vancouver has a large transitory population of renters, and the rental stock is always in high demand. The income that is generated from its ADU stock tends to be a significant portion of the income that is necessary to pay for the homeowner's monthly mortgage. The passive income plays heavily into the purchasing power of the homeowner. Fry said that as of 2016, secondary suites can rent out at C$800

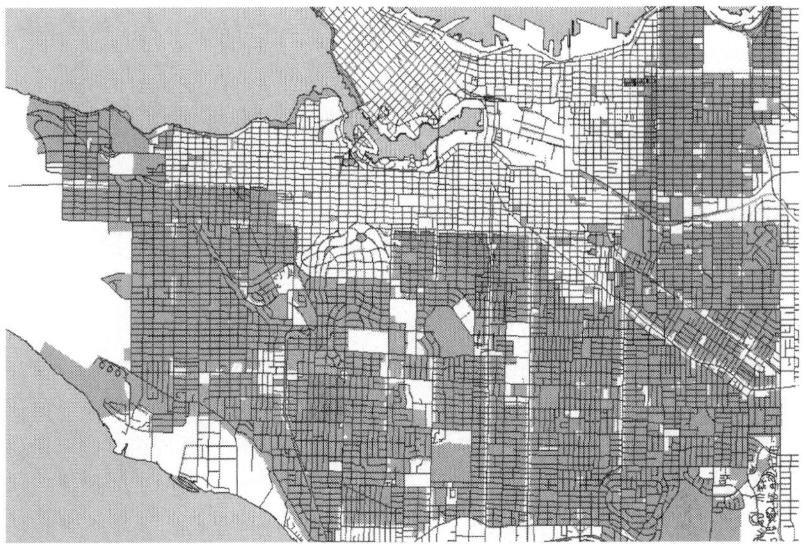

Figure 10.8. A zoning map of Vancouver, BC, that shows in gray the residential zones in which ADUs can be built.

per bedroom or more, and many of the units have two bedrooms. This rental income can translate to an additional C$300,000–C$400,000 of purchasing power for homeowners. (See figure 10.8.)

Austin, Texas

Austin first started allowing ADUs in the mid-1980s, yet very few were developed until 2007. As of January 2017, there were 812 permitted detached ADUs. The city is well poised for significant ADU development, and the number is likely to grow significantly in the coming years. (See figure 10.9.)

Austin does not have basement ADUs or attached ADUs. Austin homes generally don't have basements. And while Austin does not allow attached ADUs, it does allow duplexes by right in its dominant single-family zone, SF-3. So, where an attached ADU would make sense from a design perspective, it would generally be possible to build a duplex instead. Attached duplexes are quite common in Austin.

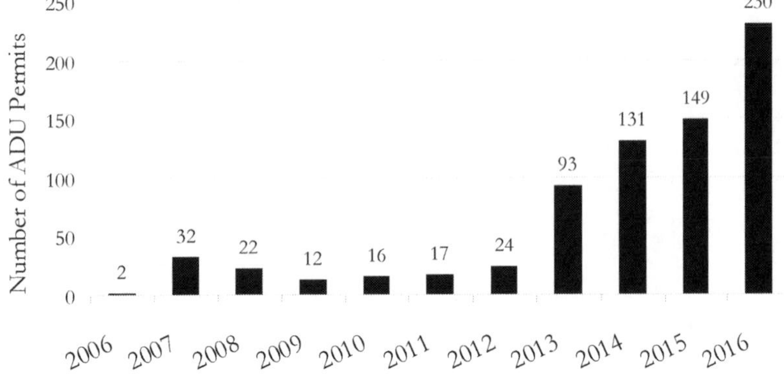

Figure 10.9.

Austin currently has a population of roughly 950,000 and has 162,000 single-family-zoned lots. Of those, 69,400 are zoned SF-3, 10,000 of which have duplexes on them already. Duplexes are akin to an attached ADU in terms of their ownership structure, but unlike ADUs, duplex units do not have small size caps. Duplexes have been allowed since 1980 and seem to be primarily built simultaneously as a single structure in whole site development, as opposed to being added on at a later date after the primary house has been built. Unlike ADUs, duplexes tend to be built by professional developers, and the units are often sold individually as condos.

In 2015, the minimum lot size for ADUs went from 7,000 sq. ft. to 5,750 sq. ft. This number was not arbitrary; it is the minimum lot size for all SF-3-zoned properties. Allowing all SF-3 lots to add ADUs increased the number of lots that could potentially have an ADU by 8,900.

The other common residential zone for single-family properties, SF-2, does not allow ADUs by right, but neighborhood planning districts can opt to allow SF-2-zoned lots to take advantage of the new ADU code if they elect to do so.

Under the 2015 zoning changes, Austin loosened its ADU parking regulations. Formerly, the City required one to three additional parking spaces when an ADU was proposed. Following the change, it required an off-street parking spot for the ADU unless it was located within a quarter mile of an "Imagine Austin" corridor, which is served by frequent transit. Because this geographic swath overlays much of the central portion of Austin, the 2015 rule change greatly loosened the off-street parking requirements for a substantial number of SF-3-zoned properties. This rule effectively relieved a huge number of properties from modifying their site plan to accommodate up to three additional parking spaces, which had often proved to be impossible or cost prohibitive to build.

This incremental relaxation of off-street parking requirements appears to be working for Austin. Nicole Joslin, the development manager for the Austin Community Design and Development Center, works with prospective ADU owner developers. She said in an interview, "I don't think I've had any client come in the door since this ADU ordinance went through that actually needs to build a parking spot for their ADU. They're all within a quarter mile of the Imagine Austin activity corridor."

The new ordinance increased the ADU size allowance to 1,100 sq. ft., which opens up the possibility of using ADUs as family housing instead of limiting them to a size designed mostly for one- to two-person households. This increased size limit puts ADUs on par with duplexes in terms of the type of role an ADU could play in single-family neighborhoods.

Austin does not have an owner-occupancy requirement. I asked whether Joslin had heard any complaints about the lack of owner-occupancy requirements during recent public forums about ADU zoning-code issues. "With the recent ordinance," she answered, "I don't recall hearing any discussions distinguishing between owner occupied or non-owner-occupied lots being able to build ADUs. I haven't heard any complaints about that." Under the new ordinance, short-term rentals are not allowed in ADUs.

There is a coalition of partners involved with the Alley Flat Initiative in Austin, including the Austin Community Design and

Image 10.6. An ADU in Austin built as part of the Alley Flat Initiative.

Development Center, Austinites for Urban Rail Action, HousingWorks Austin, Austin's Housing Coalition organization members such as the Guadalupe Neighborhood Development Corporation, multifamily affordable housing developers such as Foundation Communities, and the University of Texas Center for Sustainable Development. These organizations all collaborate with the City of Austin's Neighborhood Housing and Community Development, which enables members of the group to apply and leverage ADU grant funding opportunities.

The Alley Flat Initiative focuses on building ADUs intended for those who meet certain low-income requirements. This coalition advocates for ADUs because it views them as a housing type that can be added to the housing stock in areas that have access to city amenities, nearby jobs, and transportation options. It aids community development corporations that already own single-family homes and are not easily able to purchase more land in their neighborhoods due to Austin's high land costs. These community development corporations see ADUs as a pathway to creating additional affordable housing on their lots. The coalition also views ADUs as a mechanism to help homeowners who are having a tough time affording increased property taxes, which are inflating rapidly along with real estate prices.

Joslin believes that the code changes will prompt an uptick in ADU development, but she is not sure whether the ADUs will necessarily be affordable, which is the goal of the Alley Flat Initiative. "It opens up a lot more potential for people to consider building them. We've had a lot more interest since the ADU ordinance passed. But," she added, "there's still a big barrier to being able to finance them if you do not have a big pot of money in your bank account that you can just use to build it. The last ADU we put out to bid a month ago, an 850 sq. ft., two-story unit, our lowest bid came out to $155,000." She went on to explain that an ADU the coalition helped to build in 2009 had cost only $85,000. "The housing demand has increased so much that contractors are busy, and this tiny little house isn't a thing that they care to bid on anymore."

Despite the increased market-rate cost of construction, the cost for other site development aspects for ADUs dropped significantly due to the recent ADU ordinance changes. The old parking requirement often required long and expensive driveways to be added to a property. The City also used to require a new water tap to be added for each new ADU. The old requirement was for each ADU to have a dedicated line added to the water main, which involved costly work in the right-of-way (i.e., the street). In this instance, a new water tap added $10,000–$20,000 to ADU construction costs. (Read more about this type of barrier in the section "Keeping Administrative Fees at Bay" in the next chapter.) The 2015 code update removed that requirement.

Austin has no geographical boundary limits for its population growth, so the metropolitan population will inevitably continue to spread out, creating sprawl-like conditions beyond the central city and suburban areas. Because the population could theoretically continue to spread outward, there may not be as much demand to build infill.

Image 10.7. A modern taller ADU behind a short bungalow. Notably, even though this is a large ADU relative to the house, it is nonetheless discrete and innocuous when seen from the street.

But because Austin is recognized as one of the most rapidly changing US cities in terms of affordability, it is likely to continue to experience rapid land-value increases and increases in rent.

The greater Austin area is projected to increase in population by 54% between 2010 and 2030, as compared to the United States as a whole, which is expected to grow by 21%. The city is also projected to have a 75% increase in single-person households during this same period.[83]

To the extent that there is increased demand for housing in the city core itself instead of outlying areas, it is likely that Austin will see a dramatic uptick in ADU development as a result of the regulations that were relaxed in 2015. It is likely that an increasing number of single-family SF-3 homes will add ADUs as the land values continue to soar and demand for rental units increases. Homeowner education, marketing, and outreach about ADUs through events such as ADU tours would likely have a significant impact on the rate of ADU development in Austin.

It seems that adding by-right ADU development to SF-2 zones and relaxing the parking requirements across the board is the next logical, incremental regulatory steps to fostering more ADU development. At the time of writing this book, Austin did not have a web page describing ADU standards and requirements, which would be another simple step the City could take to help foster more ADU development. As ADUs accelerate in Austin, the City could monitor their development to help fine-tune the program and to ensure that the development is helping to accomplish its housing goals.

Santa Cruz, California

Santa Cruz, California, has been recognized for its long-standing ADU program, and it deserves honorable mention as one of the first US cities to actively try to promote the production of detached ADUs. With an overall population of roughly 60,000 people and 18,000 residential lots, Santa Cruz is a small city. It has roughly 400 ADUs, which, when measured against its population size, is a relatively large percentage. Roughly 300 of these ADUs were developed after 2003, though it has had a trickle of detached ADU development since the mid-1980s. This may have helped prompt the City to recognize that there was already ADU potential among its pricey residentially zoned real estate. (See figure 10.10.)

Santa Cruz became an early leader in detached ADUs. In 2003, California started to require that all cities create a by-right set of development rules.[84] Prior to this, Santa Cruz had a pro-ADU program in place, but it was not until the discretionary review process was struck from the local regulation and the City made certain zoning changes that there was significant uptick in ADU development.

Santa Cruz had a strict set of regulations, which included minimum lot size, window placement privacy standards, sprinkler systems, additional off-street parking requirements, floor area limits, and 10-foot setbacks between buildings.

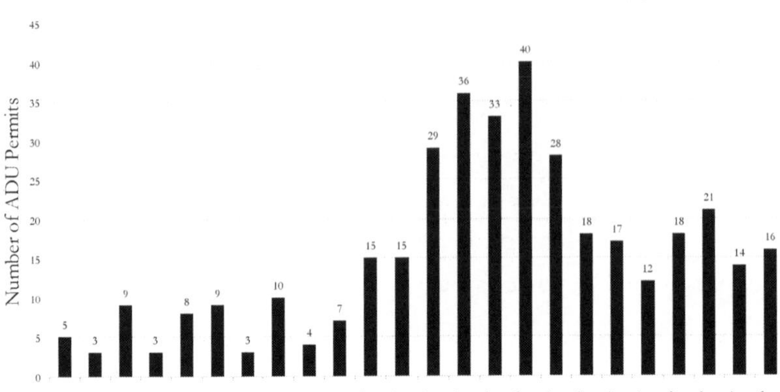

Figure 10.10.

Unlike the other featured cities, Santa Cruz has both owner-occupancy and additional parking requirements in place. In 2015, Santa Cruz opted to eliminate short-term rentals as a use for ADUs. Their ADU regulations are as restrictive as the regulations found in most US cities. This begs the question of why ADUs have been developed in Santa Cruz when they have not been developed in comparable cities.

There are a few market conditions that exist in Santa Cruz that differentiate it from other cities. First and foremost, the rental market is very pinched. Due to being a desirable coastal city and a thriving college town, Santa Cruz has had—and will likely always have—a perpetual housing crisis. It has a low rental vacancy rate, high housing costs, and an expensive rental market relative to average income. As with Portland and Vancouver, Santa Cruz effectively has an urban growth boundary in the form of greenbelts and ocean surrounding the city. The City actively decided that it needed to promote more urban infill instead of growing outward.

Santa Cruz is a university town, so the lack of effective occupancy limits on numbers of tenants in residential properties play into the city's perceived need for an owner-occupancy provision on properties with ADUs. In Austin, another city with an extremely large university, the City put a four-person household occupancy limit in place to address single-family homes being used as "stealth dorms."

Santa Cruz valued having a diverse housing stock with more affordable housing, and the City eagerly engaged in ADU homeowner outreach. With grant funding solicited from the California Pollution Control Financing Authority in 2004, Santa Cruz initiated several innovative programs to help homeowners build ADUs. Collectively, these efforts and tools helped community members shift their perceptions of ADUs as a viable solution to the housing crisis they were facing.

This pro-ADU attitude played a role in fostering ADUs even in light of their restrictive regulatory framework. The following ADU outreach efforts augmented the impact of the zoning changes that were made in 2003 and spurred substantial ADU development.

- Dedicated staff: In 2002–2003, the California Pollution Control Financing Authority gave a grant to the City of Santa Cruz. During this time, a significant amount of one person's staff time was dedicated to developing their ADU program.
- Program to guide homeowners: This seventy-two-page program guide, which is available online, went into great detail to assist homeowners in the design development and project management of ADUs.
- Informational workshops: Normally, public meetings had thirty or so attendees. Unexpectedly, more than one hundred people showed up to the first informational public meeting about ADUs in 2003. This indicated to Santa Cruz that there was a lot of homeowner interest in ADUs.

These are impressive efforts that have received national awards and show that the City of Santa Cruz was ahead of its time in attempting to actively foster ADUs. Its success may be attributable to the degree of institutional support they offered to help homeowners navigate the process, which may have helped the homeowners develop a sense of trust in the development process.

Santa Cruz also attempted several novel approaches to prompt more development. While noble in intent, these efforts appear not to have worked in terms of increasing ADU development.

- ADU Development Program Prototype Plans: Santa Cruz funded the development of seven architectural plans that homeowners could use that meet all of the city's planning/zoning guidelines. These were broadly distributed (roughly 800 copies were purchased), but they were not actually used as prototypes, as Santa Cruz had hoped.
- Fee waivers and loan programs: These programs for affordable housing were not utilized at all, perhaps due to the significant restrictions that were coupled with the programs.
- ADU legalization programs

As is evident from the lack of ADUs in cities with comparably onerous regulations, similar housing crises, and urban growth boundary constraints, Santa Cruz's active ADU program outreach has helped ADUs become a locally endeared and utilized housing product. ADUs will likely continue to be developed in Santa Cruz for as long as the housing crisis continues. That said, the development numbers have tailed off since the Great Recession.

California's 2017 statewide ADU laws forced Santa Cruz to relax its off-street parking requirements, so those changes will likely prompt additional ADU development in Santa Cruz. If the city wished to increase ADU development further, it could do so by eliminating the owner-occupancy requirements. Due in part to the presence of the large university and the stealth dorms that it spawns, the City's concerns about overcrowded properties without owners living on-site may continue to overpower its motivation to eliminate that provision.

Chapter 11

A Pathway for Planners and Advocates toward More Permitted Development

When the going gets weird, the weird turn pro.

—Hunter S. Thompson

What initially prompted me to write this book was an observation that some cities were making valiant attempts to foster more ADUs without much success, while others were making significant strides in developing ADUs. Rather than continue to watch cities and towns flounder and falter in these efforts, it seemed logical to catalog and convey best practices for city planning staff and elected officials in these pursuits. *Backdoor Revolution*—and specifically this chapter—aims to help planning staff, elected officials, and ADU advocates benchmark an existing ADU program within a jurisdiction, improve it, and ultimately induce more permitted ADU development.

Most valiant municipal and state efforts to spur more permitted ADU development have failed at doing so, resulting in few if any ADUs per year being developed in a given jurisdiction. As of 2016, Portland and Austin were likely the only US cities with more than a hundred ADUs being permitted each year. This will undoubtedly change in the coming years with the increasing severity of housing shortages and with ADUs gaining more notice among planners. Most notably with

California's 2017 state law changes, it is likely that many California cities such as Los Angeles, Santa Barbara, and several communities in the Bay Area will see major surges in ADU development.

Based on lessons from the particularly successful ADU programs in Portland and Vancouver, this chapter presents strategies to address common ADU barriers. Though the data is limited, these two cities have highly developed ADU programs, and they provide ample fodder for emulation. These ideas may not be exhaustive, but they are tried and true. More detailed descriptions of these and other approaches are covered in the previous chapter.

In a civic environment where ADUs have full-throated support and little opposition, it makes sense for a City to go big on all of the fronts described below. In the majority of cities, though, there will be significant civic opposition to attempts to facilitate the development of more ADUs. In such cases, the ideas presented in this chapter can be systematically, incrementally, and strategically changed through governmental regulatory processes, partially through applied pressure from nongovernmental coalitions and ADU advocates.

There are a few prerequisites for a successful ADU program, which we will cover first. If a city does not meet these prerequisites, there will not be any substantial permitted ADU development no matter what the regulations are. After the prerequisites, we will dive into the dynamics of what a successful ADU program must include. The success of ADUs likely requires the involvement of nongovernmental actors—namely ADU advocates, urban planners and designers, and building professionals. The second set of recommendations is oriented more toward this set of actors, who may serve as political agitators that help push the regulatory ball forward within their jurisdiction. They may also help address barriers by using some of the suggested market-based approaches. Finally, some cities have attempted initiatives that have repeatedly been unsuccessful. Toward the end of the chapter, those attempts are described so that cities do not spend political capital on efforts that historically have not had much impact.

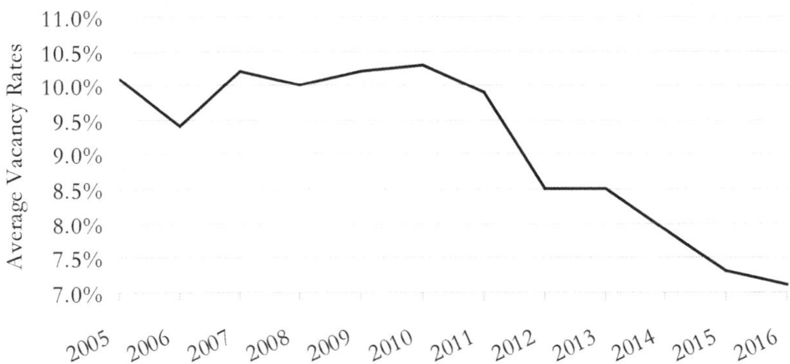

Figure 11.1. Data from "Housing Vacancies and Homeownership," United States Census Bureau, http://www.census.gov/housing/hvs/data/rates.html.

Affordable Rental Housing Crunch

ADUs will only be developed at a larger scale where it makes economic sense for homeowners to develop them. In a tight rental market, ADUs stand a better chance of being developed. If there is not a shortage of housing stock in the rental market, ADUs probably will not be developed at any regionally meaningful scale.

Many medium and large US cities are growing in population, are facing an acute rental housing shortage, and will need more small, affordable rental housing units for the foreseeable future. Low vacancy rates and high rents relative to income levels are economic and market indicators of a gap between the supply and demand for rental housing. This problem is what would motivate a City to consider ADUs as one potential housing solution.

Vacancy rates are another common indicator of rental housing shortages. Regional data on historical vacancy rate trends help tell the story of the current supply and demand for rental housing. Many major metropolitan areas are currently experiencing historically low rental vacancy rates. (See figure 11.1.)

DOMINANCE OF SINGLE-FAMILY RESIDENTIAL ZONING

ADUs can by definition only be built as an accessory unit to a principal single-family house. Since single-family homes are generally built within single-family residential zones, ADUs are only a relevant housing option within those zones. ADUs are a housing strategy to serve the changing demographic demand for housing by providing some flexibility in demographically overrepresented single-family home neighborhoods. These low-density residential zones tend to geographically dominate many cities, even in the central cities of major metropolitan regions.

If a city were already geographically dominated by multifamily zoning, ADUs would be less relevant. However, if a city has a large amount of land that is restricted to single-family residential use compared to land that is allowed for multifamily dwellings, there may be a need for an increased array of allowable housing types within that single-family zoning designation.

Given that roughly one-quarter to one-third of all households are nuclear families, it would be fair to say that a city should have roughly this much of its housing stock designed for nuclear households. But the existing share of large single-family housing in US cities greatly exceeds this percentage. While there is no simple metric to figure out what percentage of the land in major US cities is zoned as strictly single-family residential, it is possible to study what percentage of housing units in cities are single-family residential units. In my analysis of 917 cities with populations of over 10,000 residents, a whopping 68% of the housing stock is single-family residential, more than twice what is required to meet the demand of nuclear families. (See figure 11.2.)

Single-family zones represent 42% of the geographic land area of Portland, and they represent 49% of the geographic land area of Seattle.[85] Based on the chart in figure 11.3, Seattle is actually on the lower end of the spectrum of single-family lot dominance.

Most cities are completely dominated by single-family housing both in total housing units and zoned areas. Zoning laws and financial

Percentage of Single-Family Homes Compared to Other Housing Types in 917 US Cities

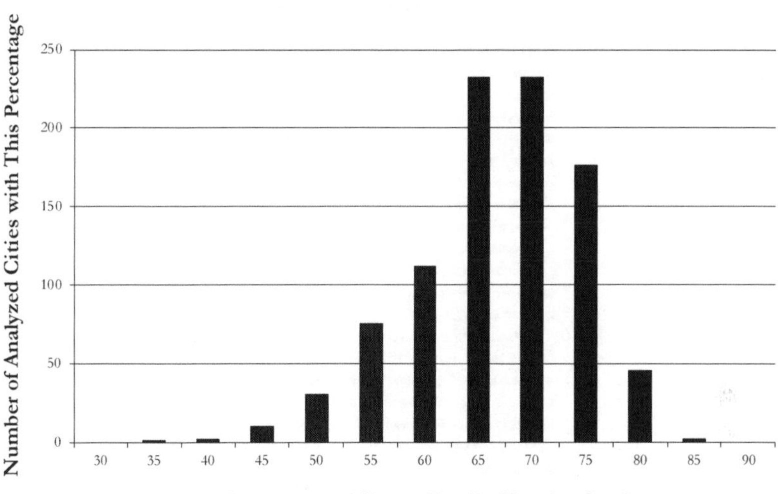

Figure 11.2.

institution policies dramatically skew the housing market toward supplying single-family residential housing. Historically, many of those same residential zones allowed a broader range of housing types, including duplexes, triplexes, fourplexes, and courtyard apartments.

The housing market is supplying what zoning currently allows, developers are building housing that is easiest to finance and sell, and homeowners are buying what banks will allow them to easily purchase with conventional home mortgages.

Political Leadership

Some degree of political will is likely to be required to help fix local ADU regulations initially. Despite their civic benefits and their incredible ROI, ADUs are a rare and precarious form of development. They will only happen with the right set of economic and regulatory preconditions. While a silent majority of citizens may support or be ambivalent

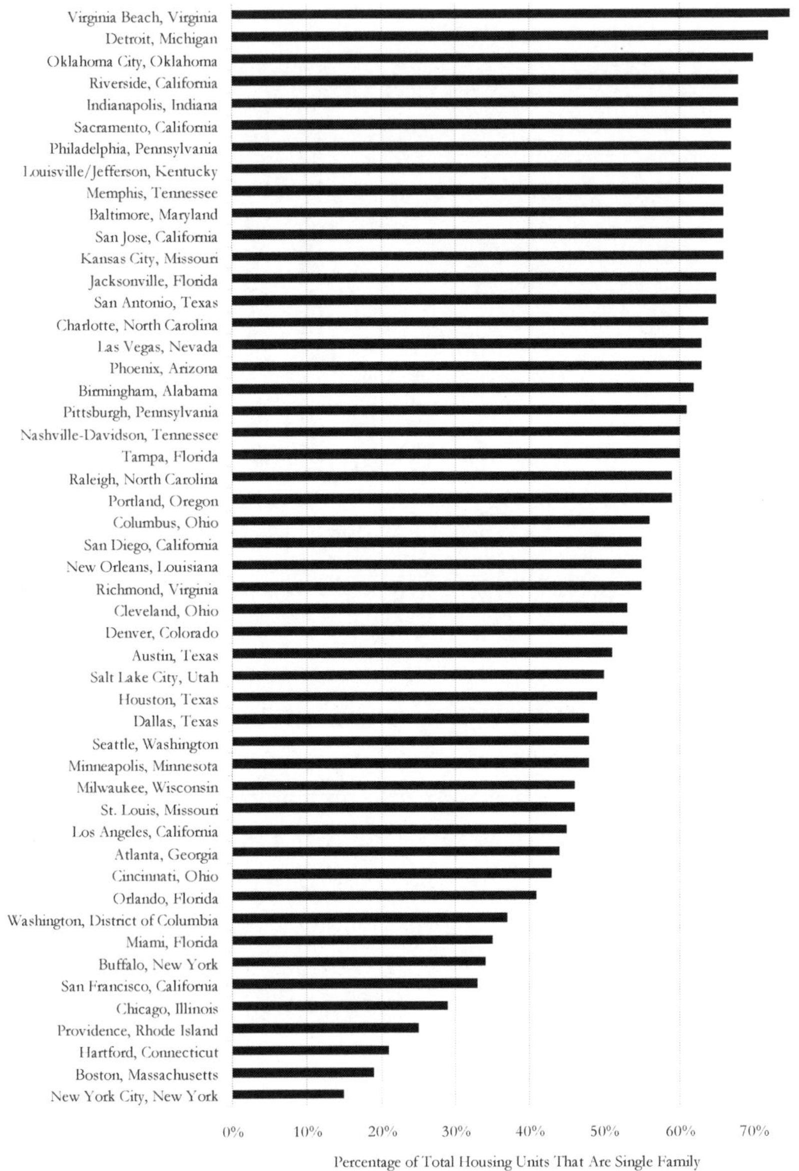
Percentage of City's Total Housing Units That Are Single Family
Virginia Beach, Virginia
Detroit, Michigan
Oklahoma City, Oklahoma
Riverside, California
Indianapolis, Indiana
Sacramento, California
Philadelphia, Pennsylvania
Louisville/Jefferson, Kentucky
Memphis, Tennessee
Baltimore, Maryland
San Jose, California
Kansas City, Missouri
Jacksonville, Florida
San Antonio, Texas
Charlotte, North Carolina
Las Vegas, Nevada
Phoenix, Arizona
Birmingham, Alabama
Pittsburgh, Pennsylvania
Nashville-Davidson, Tennessee
Tampa, Florida
Raleigh, North Carolina
Portland, Oregon
Columbus, Ohio
San Diego, California
New Orleans, Louisiana
Richmond, Virginia
Cleveland, Ohio
Denver, Colorado
Austin, Texas
Salt Lake City, Utah
Houston, Texas
Dallas, Texas
Seattle, Washington
Minneapolis, Minnesota
Milwaukee, Wisconsin
St. Louis, Missouri
Los Angeles, California
Atlanta, Georgia
Cincinnati, Ohio
Orlando, Florida
Washington, District of Columbia
Miami, Florida
Buffalo, New York
San Francisco, California
Chicago, Illinois
Providence, Rhode Island
Hartford, Connecticut
Boston, Massachusetts
New York City, New York
0%
10%
20%
30%
40%
50%
60%
70%
Percentage of Total Housing Units That Are Single Family

Figure 11.3.

about ADUs, small groups of vocal citizens tend to oppose any municipal regulatory changes that encourage them—or any form of infill housing, for that matter. All progressive zoning-code changes require political leadership and strategy, ADUs notwithstanding. Having political support is required if there are corrections needed to any of the poison-pill regulations that commonly hinder ADU development, which are described in chapter 8.

ADUs are literally backyard development, and they serve as a gut-level trigger for the "not in my backyard" preservationists, who fear that ADUs will dramatically alter their neighborhood character for the worse and potentially lower their individual property values in the process. Acquiescing to this baseless overreaction is not a good way for City leadership to adopt regulations that aim to adapt to the changing needs of their city's housing demographics. If stalwart neighborhood character preservationists had their way, codes would never change and ADUs would not advance anywhere. This is all the more ironic because ADU-like development was allowed in many cities prior to 1950; ADUs are much more architecturally "traditional" than the oversized housing that is commonly built today. Opponents of ADUs will not be able to base their fears about them with data, because there is not any data about the social and environmental impacts of permitted ADUs other than the Oregon DEQ survey from 2013, the key impacts of which were discussed in chapter 9.

Apart from a knowledgeable, trained planning staff, it takes courage and leadership on the part of the decision makers (e.g., City Council, mayor, and elected county officials) to recognize that opposition to change may be built into a community's DNA. Sometimes, changes will not seem preferable until the community has a chance to experience what the changes are like in real life. Code change makers should not patiently wait for people to overcome fears, because those fears would never disappear without examples that place reality in front of fear of the unknown.

REGULATORY STEPS TO INDUCE ADUS

The above sections are the three prerequisites I believe that a jurisdiction must possess in order to have any hope of progress with ADU development at any meaningful scale. If the three prerequisites are in order, then the following steps to induce and accelerate ADU development will be effective. These strategies may take time and effort to execute, but by following them, a City can ultimately succeed in inducing ADUs.

ATTACHED FIRST, THEN DETACHED

While the motivations behind ADU construction and functions of ADUs are similar for attached and detached units, they are treated differently in a variety of meaningful ways: permitting, costs, mechanical systems, financing, property taxes, and the planning/zoning code.

Secondary units carved out of existing structures, such as basement ADUs and ADUs above a preexisting garage, already exist in abundance in most cities. And they are already being developed to varying degrees of legality throughout all cities where small, residential infill housing is needed. Where the market needs to supply more housing, additional units will be built on residential properties regardless of what the local rules allow.

Basement ADUs, garage conversions, and other internal ADUs seem to be natural first steps in code development. Sometimes, cities only allow for carve-out ADUs that are within the existing primary-house envelope, as in Newton, Massachusetts. Others, like San Francisco, allow ADU conversions of existing accessory structures such as garages but not in newly built accessory structures. Where detached ADUs initially spark greater community controversy, internal ADU conversions seem to garner less resistance, in part because there are not any visible exterior changes to properties. Perhaps there are legitimate rationales behind these structural-form limitations, but planners should recognize that this type of constraint will greatly limit the number of properties that will ever have permitted ADUs.

Upon examining the benefits of a permitted internal ADU, many homeowners will come to the rational conclusion that it simply makes more sense to create living space that can be essentially rented out as a secondary unit without going so far as to classify it as an ADU. Commonly, homeowners will even accidentally violate a zoning or building-code regulation by adding an unpermitted secondary kitchen sink or stove, crossing into the territory of informal, internal ADU development. From a building-code regulatory perspective, the addition of the kitchen sink and stove would officially require that the improved habitable living space were permitted and designated as an ADU. But from the homeowner's vantage, it is hard to warrant the tremendous cost and effort to create a permitted internal ADU when it seems harmless, hassle-free, and cheaper to develop an informal ADU that performs its function.

Due to the relative ease of creating an internally carved-out, functional, secondary dwelling space without ADU permits, there may not be much apparent grassroots, political, or economic motivation to foster better attached-ADU regulations. The lack of legal attached-ADU development should not be perceived as indicative of the lack of interest in, or need for, these housing units in a community. A jurisdiction may have codes on the books, but the fact that homeowners are not actually building permitted attached ADUs does not mean there is not a significant market for them. Instead of noting interest in ADU development based on pitiful permit numbers, a much better proxy for the demand for ADUs would be the existence of informal ADUs. These numbers dwarf permitted ADU development by orders of magnitude. However, it's difficult to survey and inventory informal ADU development.

Nonetheless, permitted internal ADUs, which will prove to have very little negative impact on neighbors, seem to provide a smooth political stepping-stone for the introduction of detached-ADU regulations. Detached new-construction ADUs are generally the final regulatory chip to fall in terms of what structural forms of ADUs are permissible. This attached-to-detached regulatory chronology may serve as a natural, incremental code-development framework for ADU regulatory liberalization over time.

Liberalizing the code barriers for internal or attached ADUs first by eliminating the poison-pill regulations (see chapter 8) may foster some permitted ADU development. When, after removing those barriers, the development of legal, internal ADUs inevitably causes very little political backlash, the success of such legal ADU development, measured in part by the lack of negative public feedback, can serve as a basis for wading into the waters of legal detached-ADU development regulations. The narrative arc of this process may take longer than ADU advocates might like, but this is how the code successfully evolved for both Portland and Vancouver and how other cities' ADU codes can progress.

Chipping Away at the Poison-Pill Regulations

ADUs will not sprout up in great numbers overnight. Due to the decentralized and amateur nature of their developers, ADU programs will take a while to mature. Knowing that the poison-pill regulations will significantly retard development, it is logical to slowly chip away at the most problematic regulations. As a few legal ADUs are developed, it will be politically easier to stake out those few successes and point to the lack of evidence of any political issues caused (e.g., no evidence of ruining the character of the neighborhood, no evidence of parking supply constraints, no evidence of problematic speculative development trends).

Two key strategies have been used for activating better ADU regulations. These approaches could take years to fully realize if a City is starting from scratch. However, a City that is actively considering how to foster more ADU development will most likely not be starting at ground zero in this ADU development regulation model chronology.

1. First allow attached ADUs, and slowly relax the parking, owner-occupancy, and by-right development standards associated with them. Then, as the internal ADUs are inevitably but rarely built, point to the lack of negative impacts. Then allow ADU conversions of existing accessory structures. Finally, allow the development of new detached-accessory structures. The ADU program is now ripened.
2. If the code already allows detached new-construction ADUs but none are being built, that is likely due to poison-pill regulations or the other restrictive regulatory barriers described. Point to evidence provided by Portland and Vancouver in chapter 10 to help bolster political leadership to take steps toward eliminating the poison pills. In some cases, selected neighborhood districts may adopt more progressive standards. These pilot neighborhoods will inevitably not see harmful ADU development either. Point to the lack of negative impacts as reason enough to allow the more progressive codes to be applied citywide. The ADU program is now ripened. (See figure 11.4.)

With poison-pill regulations in place, so few permitted ADUs will be built that neither architects nor planning officials may have a solid handle on nuances or the best practices for ADU development on a property. Even if architects have not designed ADUs, they will have related design experience that can apply to ADUs. This lack of local experience might make the ADU design and development process more challenging than other development projects, especially when it comes to competence around the handling of relatively obscure ADU zoning or building-code regulations related to utility hookups and building separation. Some motivated and ambitious homeowner developers may be needed to help chart these waters and to help champion ADU development by sharing their personal stories in local media.

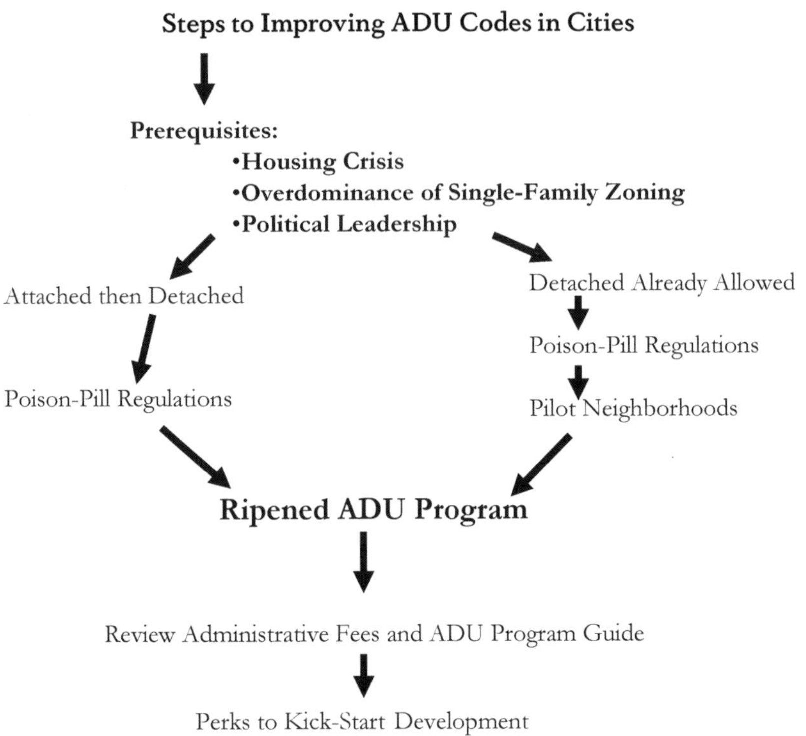

Figure 11.4. A diagram of the steps a municipality could take to improve its ADU program.

Keeping Administrative Fees at Bay

Even if the ADU regulations are flexible, when administrative fees associated with ADU development are disproportionately high, people will not build ADUs.

In some cities, the administrative fees for permits, development, and utility fee connection costs for ADUs can be $40,000 or more. For a standard new house, it is not uncommon for these municipal fees, in aggregate, to exceed $40,000. In such cases, ADUs are likely being treated with development fees equivalent to other new single-family construction.

Treating an ADU with the same administrative costs as a single-family house is a regressive economic disincentive toward this form of small infill development. That $40,000 is a much larger portion of the total design and development cost for an ADU than it is for conventionally sized and financed new single-family home development.

Whereas on a speculative-development single-family home project these $40,000 fees can be absorbed and passed along to the future buyer, who will have access to conventional financing when purchasing a house and land ($40,000 represents only 8% of the total cost of a $500,000 property purchase price), the same $40,000 could easily represent 25% of a total ADU budget.

A conventional speculative developer for a newly developed single-family house may simply have to float the $40,000 in administrative development costs using construction loan bridge financing until the property is resold to a buyer. But the amateur ADU developer will typically have to overcome those costs themselves without the aid of professional construction financing tools. Given the lack of conventional financing options for standard ADU development and the disproportionately large amount that this administrative fee represents, these same $40,000 development fees will most likely stop legal ADU development. That regressive administrative price of admission is perceived by the homeowner as intolerable.

Administrative overhead fees that treat an ADU as any other standard single-family housing unit do not consider several factors that make ADUs different from standard new single-family construction.

1. An ADU is, by definition, a small unit; thus, it should not endure the same administrative flat fees that an average 2,500 sq. ft. new single-family home would trigger.
2. Due to the dispersed nature of ADU development within an existing grid, they do not substantially increase the burden on municipal infrastructural systems.
3. An ADU does not generally increase the number of people who can legally live on a property. In this way, they're more akin to an additional bedroom than a duplex.

The administrative fees should be considered in light of the general policy framework goals that the municipality has for inducing more ADU development. From an infill policy perspective, walkable urban projects should not be paying the same amount in fees as projects that are developed on the fringe of an existing development grid, which have many more costly externalities for a municipality. ADUs add relatively little infrastructural burden to an existing utility grid.

Because ADUs are rare, there are likely to be differences in how ADU fees are levied within a given jurisdiction by various bureaus (e.g., transportation, urban forestry) and utility departments (e.g., sewer, water). Some may simply treat ADUs as a new single-family house instead of scaling them based on their actual impacts. This regressive treatment could ultimately cause the baseline administrative costs of permitting an ADU to be proportionally very expensive. Disparities between bureaus may require internal policy discussions to ensure that bureaus are scaling fees in accordance with ADUs' relatively low impact.

In the best-case scenario, the overall administrative overhead fees associated with permitting an ADU will be roughly equivalent to what would be charged for a similarly sized addition to the primary house.

The common administrative development fees that should be examined to ensure that ADUs are not being regressively disincentivized are as follows:

- permit fees
- sewer service
- storm water management
- water service
- system development charges/development fees
- electrical service
- property tax increases

In Novato, California, the various utility, city, fire, and other ADU permit fees reached $40,000 and included a $17,000 water connection fee, as well as a $9,000 sewer connection fee. Ten permitted ADUs were built in a recent seven-year span.[86]

In 2016, Concord, California, wanted to induce more ADUs. They used a two-year pilot program to reduce the fees. City fees previously were $16,000, and utility connection fees were about $25,000 ($41,000 total). During the pilot program, these fees were reduced to $5,000 and $20,000, respectively. On the one hand, this is a $16,000 reduction in fees, which is great. On the other hand, there's still a $25,000 fee associated with legal development of an ADU. It's not clear what ADU fee range is tolerable to citizens, but most middle-income homeowners would balk at anything approaching a $25,000 administrative overhead fee.[87]

In Sonoma County, California, ADUs were required to have a dedicated sewer connection, which alone costs at least $15,000.[88] The California 2017 ADU legislation addressed this barrier by addressing utility fees directly in the state legislation.

King County in Washington (where Seattle is located) charges all new single-family homes a sewer connection fee. They consider detached ADUs to be new single-family construction and thus charge the same $10,000 side-sewer connection fee for the detached ADU that they charge for new single-family home construction. This fund goes toward maintaining King County's sewer infrastructure. In this instance, the county collects the fee monthly over fifteen years, which comes out to $58 per month, so it does not kill ADUs. If this administrative charge was not effectively financed for the homeowner by allowing it be charged on a monthly basis, it alone would kill detached ADUs.

Note that these jurisdictions are likely not deliberately trying to overcharge for ADU development. But it is evident that these water and sewer connection fees are disproportionately expensive for a relatively small infill house located on an existing sewer grid. The best practice for sewer service would be to not require a new sewer connection tap at all. Instead, once the bureau has ensured that the homeowner's sewer line can handle the additional use, the municipality should allow the property to extend the sewer from the primary house to the ADU. There should not be any new sewer connection fees whatsoever.

Austin used to require a dedicated water tap for each ADU, which added $10,000–$20,000 to construction costs. In recognition of this cost barrier, the City started to allow homeowners to use the existing water service if the water line was sufficiently sized to handle the anticipated water use on the property.

Austin's relaxation of its off-street parking requirements in 2015 also significantly reduced the financial barrier to site development, as the parking space itself was expensive to build, in addition to being difficult or impossible to accommodate in the site design.

Kevin Casey of New Avenue provided his advice on how critical these administrative costs are to the success of ADU development:

> Make the permitting process extraordinarily clear and keep the administrative costs at least below 10% of the construction cost, at maximum. People are terrified of permitting surprises. And, when they get surprised about a hookup fee that's like ten thousand dollars from a utility that they didn't know was coming, they will freak out and it hits a nerve that's like unfair taxation that makes them want to lead a revolution. And they kill their project as a result.
>
> I've seen it, and it's unfortunate. Literally, we had someone who was going to build an ADU for their mother-in-law, and they put her into assisted living and they lost that fee in like three months. Not to mention that she's now in assisted living. So, my advice is to make those fees extremely clear and make it less than 10% of the construction cost.[89]

Fixed governmental administrative fees must be examined. Without examining these baseline ADU development fee structures as an aggregate administrative charge the way a homeowner might experience it when building an ADU, it is likely that the fees end up being collectively economically regressive. They discourage the legal form of discrete urban infill development and further drive homeowners toward informal ADU development.

Once the ADU zoning-code standards and fees are sufficiently relaxed so as not to be a barrier, perks can be added to kick-start a fledgling ADU program.

Program Guides in Plain English

The target audience for an ADU program guide is homeowner developers. Thus, the chronological outline of the steps necessary for a homeowner to pursue ADU development should be spelled out, and links to sample plan sets and other permit documentation should be provided. All of the information should be accessible from a single index page online rather than being scattered and muddled in numerous locations on the website. Providing key information as a downloadable PDF is also useful. The information provided should be extremely clear and direct. Vancouver's laneway house website is a simple and useful example of an ADU program guide page.

There is nothing special to this task—it is just a matter of basic communication written for the intended audience that makes the information more accessible. The information provided on the index page should cover at least the following issues:

- bylaws
- zoning requirements and ordinances
- setbacks, size, height, and architectural characteristics
- special building-code requirements that pertain to allowable ADU types
- ceiling and roof height requirements
- administrative, development, and utility connection fees
- relevant applications, permits, and forms

- chronology of steps and general time frames for each step
- office contact information
- other ADU resources

This simple communications tool should aim to ensure a level of predictability for the development process, to eliminate surprise procedural steps that the homeowner may not know about, and to alleviate commonly asked planning-desk questions.

Incentives to Build ADUs

Municipal incentives to build ADUs are not critical, but they may help jump-start a stagnant program once the regulatory obstacles have been addressed.

There were at least three notable things that were accomplished by the SDC waiver in Portland, and these could be achieved with other incentives to help kick-start a stagnant ADU program.

1. Reduce the capital cost of development.
2. Market ADUs locally through earned media and build in a sense of urgency by placing a deadline on the incentive.
3. Build trust in the municipal ADU permitting process.

While Portland's SDC waiver incentive model may not be a directly transferable idea for another city that does not have SDCs, other incentives could be explored. For example, a City could abstain from charging certain ADU permitting or utility connection fees for a limited period of time. Or a City could subsidize a certain level of architectural services for permitted ADUs for a year, provided the plans would be made public.

Metrics of ADU Development Progress

As an ADU development program is fostered in a municipality, it will be useful for jurisdictions to track metrics to help add to the collective knowledge base. At minimum, cities should track ADU permit numbers, which many cities so far are unable to do.

Beyond this, there are certain monitoring protocols that planners tend to use (address, square footage, structural form, and exterior image), but there are additional fields that would be useful to track. It would help cities understand how ADUs are being used and help them make better-informed decisions about regulatory issues that will foster or dampen ADU development. Here are the most useful metrics:

- number of ADUs by type: basement conversion, other internal conversion, garage conversion, addition, or detached new construction
- what year the permit was issued
- what year the ADU was completed
- complaints by neighbors of permitted ADUs, if any
- primary motivation for development (primary residence, rental, extended family, short term, office, other use)
- ways that ADUs will likely be used in the first year or two (primary residence, rental, extended family, short term, office, other use)
- relationship of likely tenant to property owner
- whether they are providing additional off-street parking (even if not required)

For those jurisdictions that take the initiative to monitor this information, posting and linking to this information on their main ADU web page will assist future research of ADU development trends.

Practical Roles for Advocates

The ADU development industry consists of a decentralized marketplace of services and homeowner developers. Where there are gaps or weaknesses in the market, ADU advocates may wish to try to usher ADU development by using entrepreneurial tactics or educational outreach methods.

First, the obvious regulatory barriers must be addressed. Advocates can reference the ADU program development diagram to see if the primary obstacles have been fully cleared from the ADU development pathway. If not, advocates should continue to be squeaky wheels on these issues, as ADUs will not scale until all of these obstacles are addressed satisfactorily. These obstacles may take a long time to overcome, due to the slow nature of democratic progress, even in a medium-sized jurisdiction.

The next significant development obstacle will likely relate to financing, as the capital cost of ADU development tends to be a major barrier for many owners. Financing options are unlikely to be addressed institutionally until an ADU market matures substantially. Once an ADU market matures, lending practices and loan tools will hopefully improve to meet the needs of the local market. It would be useful for advocates to develop relationships with a local bank or credit union to explore which renovation loan products are available in the area that may work best for aspiring ADU homeowner developers.

Making the ADU market more visible for homeowners is a key to creating a community of practice around ADUs. Professor Jake Wegmann said that getting a few examples built that are eye-catching and can generate some excitement to change the civic discussion from "'ADUs are these nuisances and we have to figure out how to deal with them through regulation,' to 'Hey. These are cool! I want one in my neighborhood. How can I get one?'"[90]

Since ADUs are intrinsically hidden from view, they can go unnoticed unless spotlights bring them to the public's attention. In Portland, we have found that tours of ADUs have been a useful way to fill the demands of homeowners who want to learn about ADUs firsthand. They also help to develop a marketplace to connect ADU services with homeowner developers. Focused ADU workshops, classes, conferences, news media, websites, and videos are all viable methods that shine spotlights on ADUs and raise awareness about them.

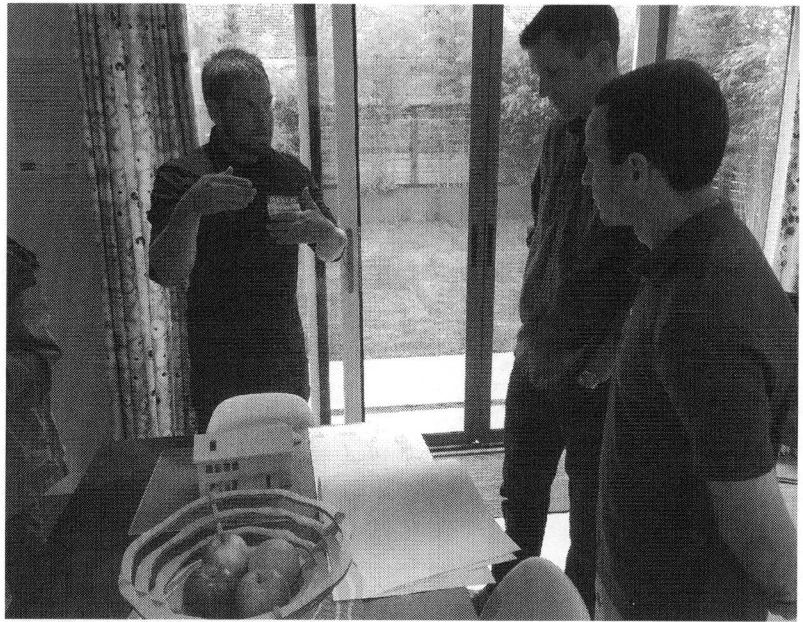

Image 11.1. An architect explaining this ADU's design to attendees on the ADU tour.

When Financing Options Come to Fruition

There is evidence that the demand for building permitted ADUs is colossal relative to the numbers of successfully completed ADUs. Where ADU zoning codes are relatively permissive and flexible, the capital cost of development is the next largest roadblock. There are some unscientific but nonetheless useful indications about the dormant demand to build ADUs.

The existence of informal ADUs is an indicator of demand. It is challenging to determine how many such units exist in a given location, but as described in chapter 9, there is an enormous quantity of informal ADUs in every study, indicating that 10% or more of all housing units are informal ADUs.

A study in the Bay Area found that 21% of homeowners were interested in building an ADU, 7% had tried and failed, and 3% were actively planning to build one. Collectively, that is 31% of homeowners who have past, present, or future interest in building an ADU.[91]

In another study, AARP and a homebuilding company independently found that a third of homebuyers would want a secondary unit if such properties were available.[92]

Homeowner interest in building ADUs trumps the number of ADUs actually being built. Based on calculations comparing Portland's ADU tours and the attendance of the ADU classes I've taught to the ADUs being built, the number of people in Portland who aspire to build an ADU appears to be 30–45 times greater than the number who actually do so.

The City of Portland conducted a survey about general residential infill issues in a voluntary survey in December 2015 and had 7,257 respondents. The survey was not explicitly about ADUs but asked respondents about their five-year plans relating to housing. In this survey, 13.5% of homeowners wished to build ADUs for friends and family, and 10.9% wished to build ADUs for market-rate rent. (See figure 11.5.)

In reality, there are roughly 1,800 permitted ADUs built on Portland's 148,000 eligible single-family residential properties, a 1.2% share of single-family properties. Comparing the current numbers of permitted ADUs against those who expect to build ADUs in the next five years (13.5%) provides a stark numeric contrast.

This survey indicates that at least 13.5% plan to build an ADU. Only one ADU has ever been completed in Portland for every 12 people who plan to build one on their property in Portland today. Even if only 10% of Portland's homeowners want to build an ADU, that means that over 14,000 residents currently wish to build an ADU.

In a city with very flexible development standards and bylaws, there is one obvious roadblock for these 14,000 residents: the capital cost of developing an ADU. The tendency for national lending institutions to not provide loans for ADU development likely relates to the inability of loan originators and private appraisers to accurately determine the value of ADUs. And loan originators' and private appraisers' confusion relates to confusion about the legitimacy of ADUs.

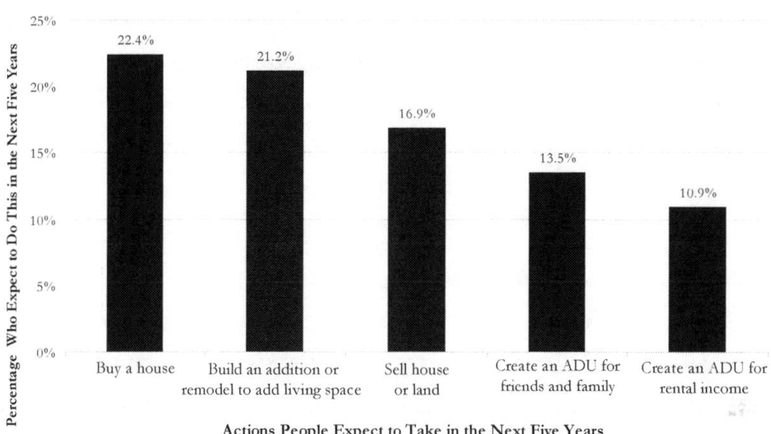

Figure 11.5.

Fannie Mae's 2011 lending guidance actually implied that ADUs were marginally valuable at best, if not illegal.

> For appraisals of one-unit properties and units in PUDs (including those that have an illegal second unit or accessory apartment) based on interior and exterior property inspections. Form 1004 also may be used for two-unit properties, if each of the units is occupied by one of the co-borrowers as his or her principal residence or if the value of the legal second unit is relatively insignificant in relation to the total value of the property (as might be the case for a basement unit or a unit over a garage).[93]

As recently as 2011, the official guidance stated that ADUs must have insignificant value, which undermined the economic viability of ADUs. In contradictory evidence to Fannie Mae's stated guidance, the only study on the contributory value of permitted ADUs found that they contribute an average of 34% of a property's value.[94]

The fact that regulatory text like this still existed in a 2011 Fannie Mae lending guidance publication is a sign of how newly resurgent ADUs are nationally. The updated Selling Guide in 2016 explicitly allows ADUs and does not expressly undermine the contributory value of ADUs.

> Fannie Mae will purchase a one-unit property with an accessory dwelling unit. An accessory dwelling unit is typically an additional living area independent of the primary dwelling unit, and includes a fully functioning kitchen and bathroom. Some examples may include a living area over a garage and basement units. Whether a property is a one-unit property with an accessory unit or a two-unit property will be based on the characteristics of the property, which may include, but are not limited to, the existence of separate utilities, a unique postal address, and whether the unit is rented. The appraiser is required to provide a description of the accessory unit, and analyze any effect it has on the value or marketability of the subject property.[95]

With such recent federal guidance like the 2011 Fannie Mae publication implying that ADUs are marginally valuable at best, it is not surprising that most banks have not started to get into the ADU construction capital lending market. Until better loan options come online, owner developers must use a patchwork of funds and often invest substantial sweat equity to overcome the formidable cost of building an ADU. Over time, more streamlined and competitive loan products may be developed to help bridge the capital financing gap for ADU development. For private financing entrepreneurs, business opportunities may exist here until banks step into this market.

There are some signs of progress on the lending front for the ADU marketplace. In 2015, Fannie Mae released a financing product called "HomeReady Mortgages" that allows preexisting secondary unit rental income to be counted as an income source for buyers of residential properties. This should help some homeowners qualify to purchase properties that have preexisting ADUs that are being rented out at the time of purchase. This market is currently quite limited.

Lenders will not currently allow for future rental income on planned ADUs to be considered an income source for mortgage applicants who are hoping to develop an ADU. The speculative marketplace for ADU development is not institutionally supported by lending institutions.

Challenging the Flawed History of Single-Family Zoning

Single-family zones should no longer be perceived as being designed solely for nuclear families. Such a view may have been tolerable in the 1950s, but the name hides its antiquated bias in plain sight: nuclear families welcome here; others are not invited.

It seems that the restrictiveness of single-family zones may actually be an accident of history dating back to 1926. The social construct of single-family residential zoning was popularized by an interpretation of the term *detached dwelling* mentioned in the Supreme Court case of *Village of Euclid v. Ambler Realty Co.* in 1926. The case provided language that called out "apartments" being classified as a "nuisance" in residential zones. But missing-middle housing types, specifically "two-family dwellings," were not the focus or target of the legal case.

The foundational Euclidian zoning case dealt with assigning zoning use authority to jurisdictions to prevent neighboring "nuisances" near houses—namely, separating industrial, commercial, and large-scale apartment buildings from residential zones consisting of detached residential structures. At this time, detached residential structures were commonly duplexes, triplexes, and fourplexes. The case did not include prohibitions against other missing-middle housing types in residential zones. In fact, *Village of Euclid v. Ambler Realty Co.* explicitly mentions two-family dwellings and provides no constitutional authority or justification for distinguishing two-family dwellings from single-family dwellings within residential dwelling zones.

The primitive language of the case critiques apartment buildings by stating,

> With particular reference to apartment houses, it is pointed out that the development of detached house sections is greatly retarded by the coming of apartment houses, which has sometimes resulted in destroying the entire section for private house purposes; that, in such sections, very often the apartment house is a mere parasite, constructed in order to take advantage of the open spaces and attractive surroundings created by the residential character of the district.[96]

Though I find this language objectionable, it is notably focused on the separation of "detached house sections" from "apartment houses." In other words, the case was primarily focused on the aesthetic separation of much larger structures from discrete residential structures. In 1926, the dominant residentially zoned areas allowed for a variety of missing-middle housing types. This residentially mixed development pattern was common, and this mixture was not the focus of the case.

The opinion further spells out its distaste for apartment buildings mixed in among smaller houses:

> Moreover, the coming of one apartment house is followed by others, interfering by their height and bulk with the free circulation of air and monopolizing the rays of the sun which otherwise would fall upon the smaller homes, and bringing, as their necessary accompaniments, the disturbing noises incident to increased traffic and business, and the occupation, by means of moving and parked automobiles, of larger portions of the streets, thus detracting from their safety and depriving

> children of the privilege of quiet and open spaces for play, enjoyed by those in more favored localities—until, finally, the residential character of the neighborhood and its desirability as a place of detached residences are utterly destroyed.[97]

The ruling goes on to describe that it is explicitly not wading into whether local jurisdictions must or should disallow mixed-use zones:

> The serious question in the case arises over the provisions of the ordinance excluding from residential districts, apartment houses, business houses, retail stores and shops, and other like establishments. This question involves the validity of what is really the crux of the more recent zoning legislation, namely, the creation and maintenance of residential districts, from which business and trade of every sort, including hotels and apartment houses, are excluded. Upon that question, this Court has not thus far spoken.[98]

It was only decades after the landmark 1926 Supreme Court case that local jurisdictions and local and state courts overlaid interpretations and misinterpretations of the case. It came to be considered a basis for excluding duplexes, triplexes, and fourplexes from residential zones. But it was not the scope or intent of this case to provide broad policy directive to foster exclusive single-family home districts. Indeed, zones designated solely for single-family residences were very rare until the 1940s; they were only found in exclusive estate districts for very wealthy homeowners.[99]

In his book *Accessory Apartments in Single-Family Housing*, Martin Gellen describes this phenomenon:

> The Euclid decision began not only the gradual disengagement of zoning from nuisance doctrine but also from serious judicial review.... In the period after Euclid, the court increasingly gave

> to legislative enactments under the police power a 'presumption of validity.' The burden of proof as to the arbitrariness or irrationality of legislative enactment was henceforth shifted to affected parties.... Once this shift had occurred, the rationale for the exclusive single-family districts was taken to be self-evident.[100]

Ironically, this American land-use separation regime separating single-family zones from multifamily zones and retail zones is one that many well-versed land-use planners, architectural critics, and health practitioners of the twenty-first century would now astutely deem a "nuisance" to public health in its own right.

ADUs can be understood as the free market's unconscious hack of antiquated single-family zoning, a hack that plays within the confines of single-family zoning but that does not dogmatically concede to the calcified interpretations of antiquated policies that characterized renters as threats to civil society.

Informal and permitted ADUs in single-family zones are the free market's response to the changing market and housing demography. From the 1920s to the 1960s, many cities went through a period in which zones that allowed multifamily dwellings were rezoned to allow only single-family residences. This effectively fixed and capped the housing development opportunities on available land within city boundaries.

"Conventional zoning has been ineffective in acknowledging the existence of this missing-middle mix of housing types—this blending of densities and blending of housing types that exist," according to Dan Parolek, Opticos Design principal. "So, a lot of those types are nonconforming and are in zones that are single-family zoned. That's a big problem in every community we've worked in.... Any town or city of any size has that issue of the mismatch between single-family zoning and the existence of these pre-1940 missing-middle housing that got built prior to the time the zoning got put in place."[101]

Image 11.2. A traffic jam on I-95 northbound in Miami, FL. (Image from Wikimedia Commons under a Creative Commons license, https://commons.wikimedia.org/wiki/File:Miami_traffic_jam,_I-95_North_rush_hour.jpg.)

ADUs can be viewed strategically as the lowest-hanging policy fruit among missing-middle housing form development types. They are a tool for testing the waters of creating a residential zone that is more conducive and appropriate for the evolving housing demand demographic.

In *Accessory Apartments in Single-Family Housing*, Gellen wrote, "The earlier and more elastic definition of 'home' represents an ignored tradition that deserves greater investigation and research. Its revival could help legitimize current efforts at improving the use of our existing housing stock."[102]

Many of our current zoning laws were developed in the mid-1900s and were based partially upon institutionally racist and sexist ideologies. Originally, single-family zoning was imagined to provide a pure, social environment for young children and designed to enable mothers to protect them from "adult life." This type of protected residential zone was lusted after by elite social classes of the 1920s.

Image 11.3. Here is a single-family residential neighborhood in which residents are forced to drive from residential roads to arterial roads in order to get to the collector roads that take them to retail services. The trip lengths from a house to a store are typically long and automobile dependent in this type of land-use pattern. (Aerial image of Gainesville, VA, from Google Maps.)

At that time, there was also a perhaps historically defensible perception that single-family properties were deemed to be vulnerable to industrialization and needed protection from that nuisance, since *Euclid v. Ambler* had not yet established protocols for how to deal with the health and safety issues stemming from the mixing of heavy industrial areas and residential areas.

It was perceived that single-family housing needed to be financially and socially protected from multifamily and industrial up-zoning lest it be developed for more profitable uses. By assigning uses to particular lots, the worth of a parcel would be established, which brought economic stability with it, allowing the Federal Housing Administration to establish more accessible forms of single-family home purchase financing.

Single-family zones have since become a monocropped land use in many cases, with attendant byproducts such as congestion and obesity that run directly counter to American civic, economic, and health values. In light of the blunt land-use assignments broadly deployed through zoning since the 1940s and the evisceration of desirable land-use mixtures they have caused, US cities and towns must

Image 11.4. Here is a mixed-use traditional development, where residential zones are mixed in with retail services in a traditional grid pattern. The trip lengths from a house to a shop are typically shorter in this type of pattern. (Aerial image of Brookline, MA, from Google Maps.)

now, ironically, fight to mix in vibrant retail uses with residential neighborhoods. (See images 11.3 and 11.4 and figure 11.6.)

Urban life was not envisioned to be so sterile as what has been accidentally created at the regional scale as a by-product of Euclidian zoning. The mindless regulatory enforcement of layers of entrenched rules whose original purposes are no longer relevant have now evolved and calcified the stale geographic separation of civic functions within much of America's land-use development since the 1950s. Private developments, such as homeowners' associations (HOAs), are legally entitled to enact private ordinances, such as owner-occupancy rules and housing types, to help meet the market's demand for that type of land use. But it is not clear why governments should be arbitrarily separating single-family homes from duplexes and triplexes, particularly when there appears to be no obvious basis in *Village of Euclid v. Ambler Realty Co.* for such superficial distinctions.

As for other underlying legal questions regarding zoning, it is not entirely clear that there is legal authority for Cities to require owner occupancy on properties with ADUs. Legal challenges to this overreaching bylaw have won.[103]

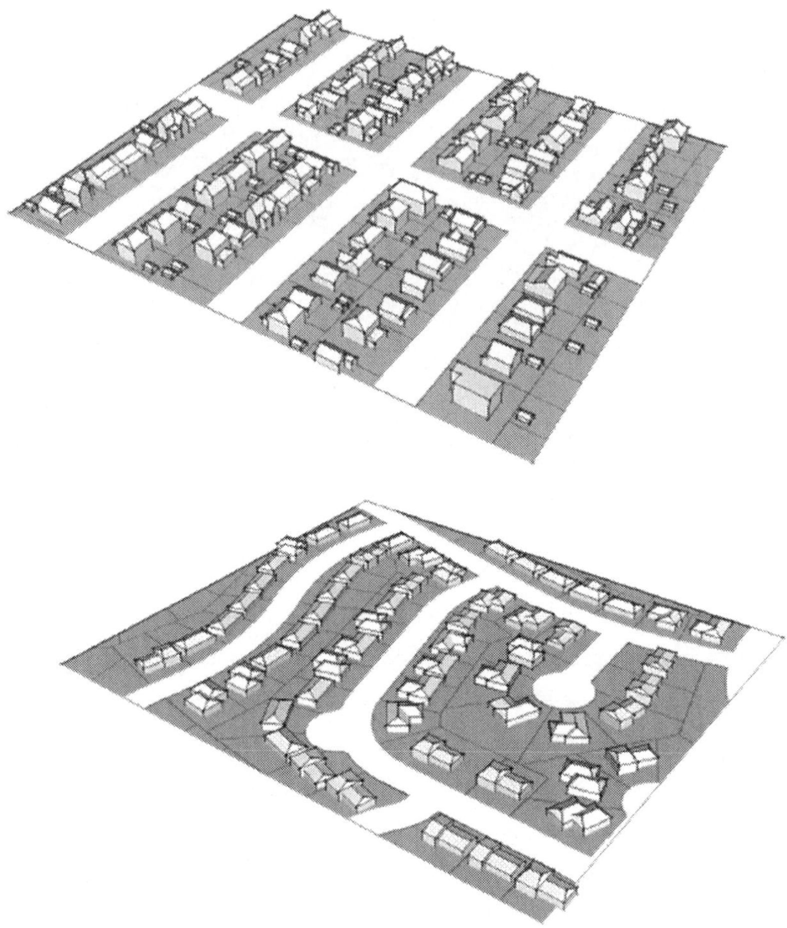

Figure 11.6. Traditional neighborhood patterns (top) and postwar suburban neighborhood patterns (bottom). (Image from "Urban Form," Portland Plan Background Report, Fall 2009, July 12, 2011, https://www.portlandoregon.gov/bps/article/545883.)

PROGRAMS THAT HAVE NOT WORKED

Well-intentioned cities may wish to spur ADU development, but they may in the process end up spending political capital or funds on ADU programs that historically have not fostered greater ADU adoption. ADU legalization programs, also called ADU amnesty programs, and municipal education programs surprisingly seem to be relatively ineffective at scaling ADUs at a meaningful level. Other altruistic programs intended to explicitly tie ADUs to affordable and senior housing have failed.

There have been a few laudable, fledgling, public-private initiatives to build ADUs as a form of subsidized affordable housing, two of which were described in chapter 10. To date, there also have not been any successful attempts to institutionally scale ADUs through any public-private partnerships.

Legalizing Informal ADUs

A municipality must draw the line somewhere as to what is classified as a habitable dwelling. Enforcement, however, is discretionary. The level to which unpermitted work is condoned or condemned varies by municipality and by individual inspector.

Though informal ADUs are far more pervasive than permitted ADUs, this book explicitly provides a framework for developing and accelerating permitted ADUs. It makes sense for a City to have a regulatory pathway to ensure that additional housing units are safe and add to the city's formal housing stock. The focus of *Backdoor Revolution* is on fostering a regulatory environment in which permitted ADUs would actually be built. For better or worse, informal ADU-like units are going to continue to be the dominant form of ADU-like development for the foreseeable future. In the final chapter, I'll review common homeowner considerations about developing informal accessory dwellings on a property.

While City planning and building officials may not be in a good position to publicly condone informal ADUs, there is also political recognition that this unpermitted form of housing is playing an important role in filling a need for providing low-income housing. Many cities and towns have allowed some forms of internal ADUs but not detached ADUs. These internal units are rarely built due to onerous zoning ordinances and use restrictions, and due to the fact that many people simply build informal internal ADU units that meet their needs, thereby avoiding the regulatory hassle and expense of permitting.

This informal development is playing a key role in keeping some rental housing affordable. Well-respected planner Paul Davidoff said of informal accessory apartments, “It’s beautiful. These apartments are a magnificent answer to the tremendous shortage of less expensive housing in the region. They are to everybody’s advantage.”[104]

Some cities have attempted to conduct ADU amnesty programs to legalize the significant stock of existing informal ADUs. In general, these attempts have not actually induced many informal ADUs to “come out of the closet.” Homeowners fear that their space would not meet zoning or building-code standards, and the amount of administrative and physical work involved in upgrading the unit to comply with building codes would prove cost prohibitive. By outing themselves to their City, they have bound themselves into compliance, no matter the cost.

For this reason, laudable initiatives such as one in 2015–2016 in Encinitas, California, failed to induce many unpermitted-to-permitted ADU conversions. As the president of the Encinitas Taxpayers Association said, “There is absolutely no incentive for anyone in their right mind to sign up for it. It was filled with onerous requirements, that if people signed up for it, they would regret it for the rest of their lives.”[105]

In 2015 alone, San Francisco and Sierra Madre, California, and Durango, Colorado, have all had very limited success with ADU amnesty attempts.

There is a relatively minor difference in rental income potential between an informal ADU and a permitted ADU built to the same standard. There is a high perceived economic risk for a homeowner to expose unpermitted work and then be required to bring it into compliance with current zoning and building codes. The risk is substantially greater than the potential economic upside to legalizing the work. When balancing their options, homeowners do not seem to see enough upside to ADU legalization to make it a worthwhile pursuit.

There were discussions of an ADU amnesty program in the 1980s in Los Angeles for its tens of thousands of informal garage-conversion ADUs:

> Lee, the Center for Law and Poverty lawyer, is among the housing specialists who say occupied garages should simply be legalized. That would provide inexpensive housing and avoid concentrations of poor people in public housing projects, she said. There would be "sprinkles of low-income people living in small efficiency apartments in garages."[106]

Later in that same 1987 *Los Angeles Times* article, possible resolutions were discussed. But Los Angeles's resolution was ultimately to kick the can down the road. Among other things, enforcement seemed challenging. "Even a landlord whose case is ultimately turned over to prosecutors can have a misdemeanor charge of maintaining an illegal occupancy dropped by complying right up to the time the case gets to a judge," said the inspector. He attributed the city's reluctance to prosecute to an "incredible workload."[107]

A 1981 American Planning Association publication insinuated a similar undemanding kick-the-can policy approach toward the issue of unpermitted ADUs.

> The lack of complaints may indicate that, at least in the short run and on a small scale, accessory apartments are the planners' equivalent of a victimless crime....
>
> The opportunity provided by accessory apartments will be limited to those willing to disregard the law. In the long run, it is likely that local acceptance will occur more rapidly as the practice of converting houses continues to be publicized and accepted nationally.[108]

While ADU amnesty programs sound admirable, such programs don't seem to get results. In fact, there does not appear to be a silver bullet strategy to dealing with the existing informal ADU inventory.

In Vancouver, unpermitted secondary suites are very common, and governmental agencies do not differentiate them from permitted suites in their overall housing-stock portfolio of ADUs. Official local and federal governmental sources count them as housing units, even though they have not gone through a formal permitting process. The agencies accept that the adverse consequences of enforcement would greatly outweigh the benefits. The fact that the City opts to count and not to just disregard these informal units is confusing but subtly points to a larger perspective their government has apparently come to terms with: the extreme housing market in Vancouver compels this situation.

To afford homeownership in Vancouver, it is evident that income from secondary suites, permitted or not, is necessary additional income for many homeowners. To cope with high rental prices in Vancouver, secondary suites offer a more affordable form of rental housing. The City recognizes that the benefits of removing this rental-housing stock would have a more adverse impact than allowing them to persist.[109] In a dissertation on this issue at the University of British Columbia in Vancouver, Pablo Mendez wrote, "Agencies and actors at various levels of government—including the federal tax agency and the provincial tenant-landlord arbitration system—do not distinguish between illegal and legal secondary suites when dealing with the residents or owners of such apartments. And while it is their own local regulations that make suites illegal, officials in both cities tolerate unauthorized units by choosing not to enforce proactively their own rules; in the city of Vancouver, authorities only act in response to complaints from negatively affected tenants or neighbors."[110]

Meanwhile, partially in reaction to demand, Vancouver has a robust ADU program. Over time, with reasonable regulations in place, it is likely that more owners will opt to build permitted secondary suites rather than informal secondary suites.

While accepting informal ADUs as a bona fide portion of the housing stock is a very counterintuitive approach for bureaucracies, perhaps cities should take a cue from Vancouver. It has accepted the forms of housing that currently exist when considering its housing policies and uses this reality as an indicator of what their future zoning regulations should aim to funnel into the safety net of code compliance.

Promoting ADUs without Creating Suitable Development Conditions

A City can opt to spend effort promoting the benefits of ADUs if it believes ADUs would be a good thing for the community. However, ADUs will only be developed at scale in a city where the regulatory barriers have been removed and where the correct market conditions exist. No amount of a City's efforts extolling the benefits will adequately motivate rational people to build an ADU if the zoning codes and bylaws are perceived as too restrictive to make it worth their while.

When Portland was trying to figure out ways to induce more ADU development, the City considered promoting them using staff resources but did not end up doing this. Perhaps it is counterintuitive, given that it has the most permitted ADUs in the country, but the City is fairly silent when it comes to promoting ADUs. While there is general political support for them, the development permitting staff do not treat ADUs programmatically different than other forms of allowable by-right development.

In an interview with Nameny, a Portland city planner, I asked, "What advice would you offer to other cities that wish to foster more ADUs?" Nameny responded, "I don't think we've done any real advertising.... I don't know if it's us being silent on them or essentially being complicit in allowing them where so many other jurisdictions actually disallow them and even probably have programs that stamp them out a little bit.... Maybe it's just by not being so anti them that by default we got to be good on them."

Similarly, neither Vancouver nor Austin has invested effort in promoting ADUs. Conversely, Santa Cruz, California, offered a disproportionate amount of service to help citizens design and permit ADUs. This had some impact on the numbers of ADUs built after 2003, but there may be a limited threshold on the rate of permitted ADUs that will ever be permitted there as long as it retains the owner-occupancy requirement.

So while basic, simple, and clear communication of the ADU regulations is fantastic, and making the permitting process more manageable for amateur homeowners developers is important, it is not evident that a City actually needs to invest much effort in promoting ADUs once it has removed the regulatory barriers.

Indeed, if a City simply removes obstacles to ADU development, as covered in chapter 8, ADUs may ultimately scale on their own through a combination of ADU advocacy and the private market. In Portland and Vancouver, ADUs now seem to be an organic, market-based outcome of their ADU programs.

That said, as novice homeowner developers venture through the development process for the first time, they do not always understand the basics of zoning laws, let alone the particulars of property-line setbacks, firewalls, energy, storm water management, radon mitigation, or the requirements of the requisite drawings necessary for development. It is helpful for homeowners to use professional designers as representative agents to go through the ADU permitting process, but it is not required.

Tethering ADUs to Affordable or Senior Housing Programs

Efforts to legislatively tie ADUs to affordable housing have not succeeded in spurring more affordable housing nor more ADU development.

An ADU financial assistance program in Santa Cruz, a state legislative attempt in Florida, and numerous local regulatory attempts to limit ADUs solely to conventional affordable housing definitions have all failed at spurring permitted ADU development.

The US Department of Housing and Urban Development's efforts to spur ADUs as a tool to create elder cottage housing opportunities in the 1990s in various rural jurisdictions were also unsuccessful. The initiative was abandoned in the late 1990s after the pilot program attempt, when the mobile-home accessory units appeared to have little lasting impact in the pilot jurisdictions.

In 2000, the AARP and the American Planning Association issued a white paper on model ADU ordinances that was an attempt to help municipalities write better ADU codes with an emphasis on creating more senior housing. There were negligible outcomes from this effort.

Interventions that proactively tie governments into either the development or the management of ADUs have been unsuccessful thus far. While ADUs may incidentally achieve certain desirable policy outcomes by virtue of their small size and infill locations, it appears that efforts to legislatively restrict or constrain the use of ADUs are entirely counterproductive in terms of fostering their development. Instead, it is explicitly when governments have liberalized their regulatory stranglehold over the development or management of them that ADUs have been developed at a meaningful scale in municipalities.

Chapter 12

Civil Disobedience and Accessory Dwellings

> When people can't find affordable housing solutions, they make their own affordable housing solutions.
>
> —Jake Wegmann, PhD, University of Texas at Austin School of Architecture

Informal ADUs are a desire path; the proliferation of informal ADUs is the gray-market expression of the market demand for ADU-like development. If informal ADUs are being developed, it is a signal that the zoning code or building code is a barrier to permitted ADU development.

This chapter will cover development alternatives to ADUs, both permitted options and common extralegal development approaches. In some cases, unpermitted secondary units may not meet all the same structural standards, zoning-code standards, or quality-of-life standards that permitted ADUs would meet. These alternatives to ADUs are not necessarily equivalent to ADUs. Some may not have key building elements that permitted, habitable units must necessarily contain. Nonetheless, while formidable regulatory obstacles exist, these secondary dwelling alternatives play a significant, albeit informal, role in affordable housing and urban development.

THE HOMEOWNER'S PERSPECTIVE

As described in the first chapter, ADUs naturally provide a beneficial housing solution. Developing an ADU is one of the most energy-efficient things that an urban homeowner can do on their property, whether or not they know it. ADUs are likely to be found in cities that have a high proportion of centrally located residential zones where many people desire to live and where there is inadequate housing or rental supply. ADUs also provide a smaller and more affordable dwelling unit than is otherwise readily available in those centrally located areas.

However, if residential real estate market conditions require more small infill units to meet housing demands, ADU-like development will happen with or without a formal ADU program to support their development. When Cities do not allow permitted ADUs or make them unenticing to develop, informal ADU development flourishes. Indeed, this is precisely what has been happening in cities for decades. Sometimes, an incremental urban development phenomenon takes place right under our own noses, unnoticed until it is identified and named. Then, upon being correctly labeled, the phenomenon at play seems so intuitive that it seems obvious.

Jane Jacobs, the architectural critic, famously lambasted the abstract land-use separation ideals promulgated by professionally trained planners as being totally out of touch with the very people they were ostensibly working to serve. Much academic, policy, and health-related research conducted since her book *The Death and Life of Great American Cities* was published in 1961 has proven Jacobs to be a bellwether of contemporary urban planning criticism. Many now argue that modern planning and zoning ideas and policy have eroded the very fabric of what historically made our beloved traditional cities most livable.

Related critiques evolved and were popularized in the decades to follow; now, her ideas are accepted as foundational by many urban planning practitioners. Proactive alternative planning approaches partially informed by Jacobs are now embodied within an urban planning framework commonly called Smart Growth and practiced by an edgy architectural movement called New Urbanism. These movements are framed as land-use planning alternatives to the dominant planning paradigm of the latter half of the twentieth century that resulted in suburban- and exurban-sprawl architectural typologies.

It was this separation of land-use typologies that Jacobs was critiquing in her famous book, and erratic urbanism was the heroine. She provided prosaic descriptions of conditions that enriched cities or deadened them. To generate "exuberant diversity" in a neighborhood, the following traits are required:

- It must serve more than one primary function.
- It must have short, dynamic blocks.
- It must have a varying architecture.
- It must be densely settled.

ADUs are also an incremental form of development that can slowly improve neighborhoods and cities. Indeed, it seems ADUs enable parallel principles on a residential property scale:

- They provide a type of housing flexibility that ensures the long-term value and utilization of the property.
- They create housing and land-use efficiencies at residential, neighborhood, and regional scales.
- They add architectural value and social dynamism to a neighborhood.
- They increase housing supply in single-family neighborhoods.

Building a permitted ADU in a city is a wonderful thing. ADUs are a way to discretely and effectively hack our antiquated yet dominant single-family residential zones. *Backdoor Revolution* is primarily oriented to helping people build permitted ADUs where it is possible and desirable to do so. But permitted ADUs must adhere to both zoning and building-code regulations. And unfortunately, most cities have code barriers that make it undesirable or impossible to build a permitted ADU. This is precisely why permitted ADUs are so rare and why informal ADUs are so pervasive.

The strict ADU regulation frameworks that homeowners circumvent out of perceived necessity are why independent research efforts in Los Angeles, San Francisco and the Bay Area, Boston, Portland, Long Island, Queens, and Vancouver have each found that there are tens of thousands—or hundreds of thousands—of informal accessory units in their cities, as detailed in appendix 4. Based on the smattering of independent research efforts conducted on this topic, it appears that roughly one of every ten housing units in the United States is an informal ADU-type development. If you are in a centrally located residential area where small units are needed, informal ADU development likely exists in your neighborhood or most certainly in your community, if not in your own home.

Professional small housing developer Eli Spevak of Orange Splot LLC put it this way: "The code should be written so that people do not build them under the radar."[111] Citizens will not build permitted ADUs in the face of what they perceive as severe bureaucratic, administrative, or financial penalties for doing so. Here is a partial list of why owners may create accessory units without permits:

- Local bylaws and zoning ordinances prohibit the owner from doing so legally.
- The property owner does not wish to comply with the planning and building codes.
- The permitting process would cause significant expense and delay.
- Owners wish to avoid property tax increases.
- Conversion of space was thought of as being only temporary.[112]

A 1995 *New York Times* article paraphrased the APA's findings this way: "The American Planning Association reports that studies show that the presence of an ordinance legalizing accessory-apartments does not encourage single-family homeowners to create an accessory unit, and that the absence of such a law does not discourage them."[113] Until the regulations are aligned with their interests, my research, as well as my professional and personal experience, suggests that many homeowners will continue to build informal units. Meanwhile, any regulations that can lure some of this inevitable ADU development toward permitted development are in the interests of a City as well as the homeowner.

I'll review alternative dwelling types below that accomplish some of the same basic homeowner goals as ADUs, though these alternatives are not permitted as ADUs.

Work-Arounds and Loopholes

For those who are planning to build an informal accessory dwelling, it is wise to build the accessory unit as legally as possible. Homeowners should at least seriously inquire about what they can permit and build legally before opting to build accessory units entirely without permits. Earlier chapters of this book introduce homeowner developers to standardized language, terms, concepts, and development advice they can use to pursue developing a permitted ADU. Understanding the local zoning-code vernacular is key to applying these ideas in a given jurisdiction. By understanding the code language, it is possible that the homeowner will be able to pursue projects that they were aspiring to build. Even if the proposed project seemed to be dogmatically banned upon a cursory review of municipal code, they may be able to proceed in the disguise of different regulatory garb.

For example, ADUs may not be allowed in a jurisdiction, but "guesthouses" are allowed. Perhaps by inquiring with their City's planning department, a homeowner will learn that the City does not call the guesthouse an "ADU" because it is not intended for "full-time occupancy." But no one in the planning department has ever bothered to determine what is classified as "'full-time occupancy," so a homeowner

Image 12.1. Though the architectural massing of this house gives it the appearance of being two independent structures, the two buildings are attached by a breezeway. This type of structural attachment can be used to create an "attached ADU" where detached ADUs are not permissible.

can proceed with their project under a different habitable classification, since they only intend to rent out their secondary unit eleven months of the year.

Or perhaps the desired detached ADU is not allowed in their city, but attached ADUs are allowed. And it turns out that an overhead breezeway structurally connecting the ADU to the primary house would be sufficient to classify the ADU as "attached."

Perhaps a new-construction detached ADU is not allowed in a jurisdiction, but the conversion of an existing accessory structure to an ADU is allowed. While the dilapidated garage on-site would not make for a good ADU, it turns out that as far as the dogmatic regulations are concerned, "converting" an existing structure only requires that a single foundation wall of the garage must be reused. Thus the homeowner can effectively build a new-construction ADU, provided they reuse a portion of that old foundation.

This type of architectural loophole or work-around can be used to overcome the detritus that sometimes lingers in regulatory language. Knowledgeable local architects may be able to help homeowners design requisite features to sidestep regulatory roadblocks and pass through such loopholes. Incorrect terminology could cause regulatory headaches if used with the wrong individuals at the planning department, so homeowners should solicit early input from local, professional residential designers and architects and use some of the information from this book to hone their project goals and better understand their local by-right development options.

When a homeowner is seeking information about an unpermitted secondary dwelling concept, there is no clear line of advice to follow. Licensed professionals (e.g., architects, builders, lawyers, electricians, and plumbers) are unlikely to openly encourage homeowners to break rules, but they may be able to offer professional advice on what level of risk may be associated with certain development choices. Homeowners commonly use the rule of thumb that they would only build something that they would live in. Indeed, perhaps they should live in the unpermitted unit. This would not only ensure that the unit was built to their quality-of-life standards but would limit legal exposure compared to the legal exposure of renting out the unit to others. Furthermore, if they rented out the primary house instead of the unpermitted unit, it would likely prove to be a far more profitable approach.

I have consulted with several homeowners about their existing informal ADUs when they were planning to sell their property or have it appraised. Options moving forward can be challenging and often fraught with expensive choices or varying degrees of stressful uncertainty.

If the owner's unit is discovered by a City building-code official on duty, it may prove impossible for the homeowner to convince the building inspector to allow nonconforming uses (like habitation) in unpermitted structures. In more severe building-code violation cases, accessory structures built without permits may have to be removed altogether.

Image 12.2. A stop work order, or a Do Not Occupy notification, placed on a dwelling that had not received proper permissions.

All of these caveats aside, homeowners may choose to deliberately dance around the regulations as they need to, driven by the notion that the value that they are creating for their community by way of the informal accessory dwelling is greater in moral purpose than a planners' adherence to arbitrary or baseless ordinances.

By exploring and pushing the edges of regulations that seem to be causing as much civic harm as good, citizens may even begin to think of building an unpermitted habitable accessory unit as a form of non-violent civil disobedience. Jamal Kadri, a believer in ADUs, described the act of building informal ADUs this way:

Civil disobedience is the intentional act of disobeying a civil law or authority because of a conviction that one has a higher responsibility. For a believer, those higher responsibilities are often found in their faith. Civil disobedience is to follow a higher calling despite the rule of an ungodly authority.

Exclusionary zoning has a history of suppressing choices and segregating communities. For some people who have religion about creating more choices for where and how people live, laws that prohibit the conversion of garages into apartments, or off-street parking into ADUs—laws that prevent us from transforming habitat for cars into habitat for people—are simply wrong.

When obeying the law of humans would put us in direct disobedience to the clear command of our higher power, then civil disobedience is not only warranted—it is required. This means we do what we can in accordance with the law and what we must outside of it.[114]

Alternatives to ADUs

What follows is a list of alternative dwelling types that are not ADUs but are related in the sense that they are small dwellings that are sometimes placed and inhabited on residential lots. Unlike ADUs, none of these options are intended for full-time occupancy independent from the primary house.

Here are some options in order of most permittable and habitable to least permittable. The best resources to view and learn about inspiring examples of these types of informal dwelling options are Lloyd Kahn's books *Tiny Homes, Simple Shelter* and *Tiny Homes on the Move*. Searching for examples of these dwelling types online will also prove fruitful.

Detached Bedrooms and Other Accessory Structures

Accessory structures are outside and detached from the primary house. Common examples of permitted accessory structures are garages, sheds, gazebos, offices, pool houses, or art studios. If the accessory structure is permitted as living space, all of the core elements of a house can legally exist in it except for some kitchen elements.

It may be possible to build a detached bedroom and a bathroom as an accessory structure. A detached bedroom may be a fully permitted accessory structure and is a fully legitimate option if the person sleeping in the bedroom shares the kitchen facilities with the occupants of the primary house. It is quite possible that a given jurisdiction that does not allow detached ADUs, or has extremely onerous ADU regulations, may not have any regulations that preclude or discourage detached bedrooms. Detached bedrooms are fairly rare, but they can serve as a simple regulatory work-around where detached ADUs are not allowed.

Detached bedrooms can look much like an ADU from the outside. Some homeowners develop fully permitted detached bedrooms with a bathroom. Then, once they have received their certificate of occupancy from the city, they may add an unpermitted kitchen sink and stove. These are the only two building elements that detached bedrooms cannot legally add, as they are the building elements that differentiate a detached bedroom from an ADU.

It is highly unlikely that someone would be caught for cooking or washing a dish in their unpermitted detached bedroom sink. But since everything was permitted except for the kitchen sink and stove, those are the only two building elements that would have to be theoretically removed if full-time habitation was cited as a nonconforming use of the detached bedroom. This is a far less risky development approach than building an unpermitted accessory structure that is intended for habitation without any permits whatsoever.

Image 12.3. A finished and well-appointed attic in-law unit.

Basement Living Space and Other Carve-Out In-Law Suites

The lines between separate units quickly get fuzzy as one starts to think about what is necessary and is not necessary for an occupant to have an independent, functional living unit in the basement or in another carved-out portion of the primary house, such as a finished attic.

As with detached bedrooms, the only elements a homeowner may not be able to legally permit are a kitchen sink and a stove connection. Otherwise, it is possible to legally renovate very comfortable accessory living quarters within portions of preexisting permitted living space within the primary house without classifying it as an ADU.

The degree of separation between the in-law suite and the primary unit is totally up to the homeowner. The in-law suite can have a separate dedicated entrance, and it can have insulation and layers of drywall to deaden any sound between it and the primary unit. The space can have independently operable heat sources such as in-wall cadet heaters. All of those elements can be done legally with permits. It can even have its own fridge, toaster, microwave oven, convection oven, and washer/dryer, none of which require permits.

In Washington, DC, my first house had a finished basement with a separate entrance off the alley. It had an unpermitted kitchen sink and a 24-inch-wide electric stove. The house's heat was controlled by the thermostat upstairs, and it shared all its utilities with the upstairs portion of the house, both of which differentiated it from a true permitted ADU. Apart from this, it had its own fridge, microwave, full bathroom, closet, and built-in storage spaces. It functioned like an independent unit during some periods and as just another bedroom within the house during other times. An interior stairway connected it to the upstairs, but at times we used deadbolts on both sides of the door to create a sense of separation and privacy between the two portions of the house. Officially, it was what code officials would classify as a finished basement—habitable living space. Colloquially, one may refer to it as an in-law suite.

The ADU-like features that gave it independence from the primary unit helped it to fetch a better rental price even though it was a basement bedroom. Renting a bedroom in a finished basement was not breaking any rules. Doing so also achieved the same environmental benchmarks and social and economic goals that a homeowner would wish to achieve in developing a permitted basement ADU.

If desired, the connecting stairway to the upstairs could have been legitimately removed so that the basement was functionally isolated from the upstairs living space. Cadet heaters could have been added so it had its own independent heat source. It still would not have to be legally classified as an ADU at that stage, but it would functionally accomplish all of the same goals as far as creating an income-generating, fully independent accessory living space on a single-family residential lot. The only accessories the basement could not legally have in it were the kitchen sink and stove.

I spent my entire childhood and adolescence in a house with a 100 sq. ft. carved-out, informal attic unit. The tenants, who were graduate

Image 12.4. An entry to what is likely an informal daylit basement unit.

students from a nearby law school, paid a modest rent. They had to walk up the primary house's interior stairs in order to access the affordable attic unit. Over the years that each of them lived there, the tenants became like parts of our family. This space would be legally classified as a bedroom or finished attic living space, but with its informal kitchenette, it was effectively utilized as an independent unit.

My parents were separated. My father, who lived nearby in the same town, split his single-family house into two units and created an informal ADU that served as a rental unit. Each unit had its own kitchen, but the house actually only had a single main entry, and it shared electric and gas utilities.

Informal ADUs were everywhere in my life. Like many people, my parents never sought permission to alter their own homes to their liking. They just did it because it was the smartest way to use their property.

It is significantly less expensive to create an informal basement apartment or attic unit than to create a permitted ADU (see "Basement Conversions" in chapter 4). Independent but not fully legal in-law suites like these may rent for marginally less than a completely independent unit would and may not add as much resale value to the property as a fully permitted ADU. But once a homeowner factors in the regulatory roadblocks, additional hassle, and significant costs associated with making a basement into a legal secondary unit, it becomes apparent why there are so many informal in-law units being developed in desirable but unaffordable cities throughout the country.

These types of informal accessory apartments are very commonplace. It is impossible to know for sure, but it is likely that hundreds of thousands of these types of informal apartments are created every year, and many can fluidly transform back into functioning as a single, larger unit with the primary house if needed.

Nonhabitable Accessory Structures

Stand-alone accessory structures are built to be independent from the primary house. Many jurisdictions allow for nonhabitable accessory structures up to a certain size (commonly 200 sq. ft.), such as storage sheds, playhouses, HVAC condenser boxes, or chicken coops, to be built or placed on a property without permits. This kind of structure is extremely common; the majority of residential properties probably have an accessory structure or two.

These types of small structures were never legally intended for habitation. But the relic purposes of these accessory structures, such as workshop sheds, may eventually fade from institutional memory, and they may change in use over time.

Sometimes, people who wish to build a nonhabitable accessory structure refer to this type of structure as a "studio." Because this term has such an ambiguous meaning, they may build their tiny accessory structure without permits and have people stay in it at times, never even questioning whether that is an allowable use of the space. They may just assume that it is on their property, they own it, and they can do with it as they wish. New property owners may never investigate whether it is legal to have someone residing in such a structure. They

Image 12.5. A better-than-average shed that could could eventually become a functional dwelling space. (Image by Seth Vidal, Flickr, licensed by creativecommons.org, https://flic.kr/p/aj1fWq.)

may assume that if structure looks nice enough, it is probably fine to spruce it up a bit and use it for housing. And who would call them foolish for not waking the sleeping regulatory dragon?

Unpermitted accessory structures can be as simple as an off-the-shelf storage shed bought at Home Depot or as thoughtful and deliberate as a cob-built structure with gorgeous curved benches and live-edge countertops.

When accessory structures are used for habitation, it is more common that they are used as studios or bedrooms than as fully independent units, as they typically do not have a sewer connection. Adding a sewer connection without a permit is a more blatant building-code violation, and homeowners will only do this when they are more willing to run afoul of building codes.

There are many inspiring natural building examples of off-the-grid structures that are functionally self-contained units and use

Image 12.6. An accessory structure (left) made of straw-clay and cob, located in front of an ADU (right).

Image 12.7. A cob bedroom in Vancouver, BC. (Image by Mahfuz Ahmed, Flickr, https://flic.kr/p/c96g1A.)

composting toilets instead of a connecting illicitly to a sewer. This type of structure is more commonly found on working farms than in residential zones in cities.

Camping in Temporary Dwellings

The following are examples of dwellings that cannot be permitted for habitation because they do not meet International Residential Code standards. In some cities and towns, it may be permissible to "camp" in these types of dwellings on residential properties. Camping code regulations on residential properties vary by jurisdiction, so if one is considering how to legally reside in unpermitted dwellings on residential properties, it is worth exploring the fine print on camping regulations in their municipality.

Much more commonly, though, people opt to live in these unpermitted dwellings without much in-depth knowledge of local zoning and building regulations. Many cities operate under a complaint-based policy, wherein citations or violations are only given if a neighbor complains that someone is violating a zoning or building code. One would be wise to ascertain the tolerance level of adjacent neighbors toward the planned informal dwelling before investing significant efforts and resources in its development, placement, and habitation.

When cities prohibit camping on residential properties, they have actually eliminated some creative affordable housing options that merit further policy exploration. Residential camping bans have caused some citizens on the lower end of the economic spectrum to be without a viable housing option in any residential zones. Tent camping underneath an interstate overpass is not as safe as camping in a campervan on a residential property. Yet camping of any sort on residential properties is often not allowed in cities.

It is legal to "boondock" (stay overnight) in mobile dwellings in "dispersed camping sites" alongside maintained roads almost anywhere on Bureau of Land Management land and in national forests, which compose roughly 30% of the land base of the United States. This may be an option when traveling but not for full-time residence if basic services, infrastructure, jobs, or community are sought by the resident.

Tiny Houses on Wheels

Tiny houses on wheels are generally stick-frame construction homes built on flatbed trailers. They are typically under 200 sq. ft., but there is no standard size limit for being classified as a tiny house on wheels. To be legally towed on streets and highways without special wide-load permits, they must generally be under 13 feet, 6 inches in height and under 8 feet, 6 inches in width. If they are (illicitly) connected to the utilities of the residential property on which they are placed, they can be fully functional dwellings. They are commonly artisan, cozy, customized spaces, designed for one or two people, and are relatively inexpensive—$30,000–$80,000.

Tiny houses on wheels have become prominent due to a media frenzy about them that began around 2014. As of 2016, several HGTV shows began featuring tiny houses on wheels, indicating how much consumer fascination there was for them. Despite all of the media hype, though, very few people actually live in one. Most tiny-house enthusiasts are intrigued about the tiny-house phenomenon but not very serious about building or living in one.

I'd guess that as of January 2016, 1,000–5,000 people live in home-made tiny houses on wheels full-time globally. This is a wild guess, though, as no one has solid data on this, largely due to the fact, at the time of writing, that tiny houses on wheels are not legal to live in in residential zones almost anywhere in the United States. In late 2015, Fresno, California, passed the first tiny-house-on-wheels code to legitimize the habitation of them as an alternative form of an ADU. In 2017, Portland temporarily deprioritized enforcement of laws against people sleeping in RVs or tiny houses on residential properties. Other jurisdictions are taking advantage of mobile dwellings as housing options during the recovery period following a natural disaster. Outside of a couple of places that have made such regulatory attempts, however, tiny houses on wheels are not currently legal to live in full-time in the United States except in some RV parks.

There has been some progress in 2017 in adopting sleeping-loft codes into an International Residential Code appendix, which will help the cause of legitimizing tiny houses on wheels. Perhaps in the years to follow, more towns will have established bona fide zoning codes for tiny houses on wheels. But until there is a broad zoning shift toward making tiny houses on wheels permissible for dwelling in in residential zones, it will be impossible for tiny houses to realize their potential as a viable, popular form of housing.

Many people who aspire to live in a tiny house on wheels also aspire to build their own. Building one is not a small undertaking. Despite its small size, it requires a significant baseline of construction know-how, skills, and tools. Even though they are small, almost every facet of building a stick-built house is involved during the construction of a tiny house on wheels. Those who endeavor to build and actually complete building and living in their own tiny house on wheels are admirable.

Based on the tiny-house dwelling lifestyle I've observed, tiny houses on wheels have great potential if they are permitted for habitation in residential zones, at least as a temporary housing option.

In some ways, tiny houses on wheels share commonalities with ADUs when they are placed and used in the backyards of larger homes. But there are some observable differences. Tiny houses on wheels oftentimes are not fully independent units; they may not have a shower, for example. The tiny-house occupants must share resources outside their homes more than occupants of ADUs, which by code must have every standard element of an independent house (for cooking, bathing, and sleeping). This means that tiny-house dwellers often have a closer day-to-day living and social arrangement with the occupants of the primary house than an ADU tenant might.

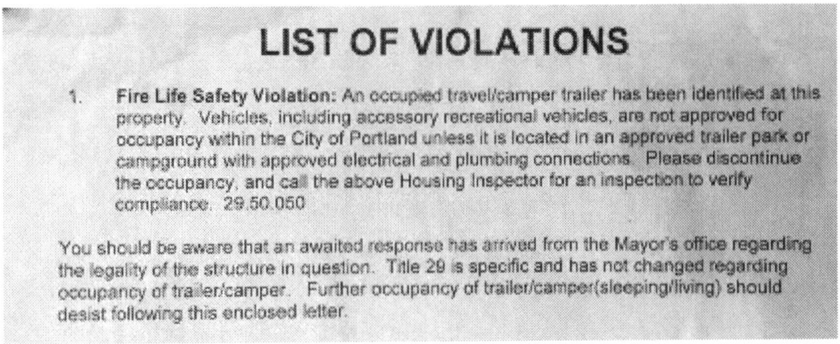

LIST OF VIOLATIONS

1. **Fire Life Safety Violation:** An occupied travel/camper trailer has been identified at this property. Vehicles, including accessory recreational vehicles, are not approved for occupancy within the City of Portland unless it is located in an approved trailer park or campground with approved electrical and plumbing connections. Please discontinue the occupancy, and call the above Housing Inspector for an inspection to verify compliance. 29.50.050

You should be aware that an awaited response has arrived from the Mayor's office regarding the legality of the structure in question. Title 29 is specific and has not changed regarding occupancy of trailer/camper. Further occupancy of trailer/camper(sleeping/living) should desist following this enclosed letter.

Image 12.8. A citation for habitation of a tiny house on wheels in Portland.

Tiny houses on wheels are typically owned independently from the property on which they are placed. Unlike an accessory structure or ADU, a tiny house on wheels can be moved and can be sold independently from the property. Conversely, permitted ADUs are considered legal property improvements that add permanent value to the property. ADUs can play a role in adding a contributory value to the property that facilitates refinancing the property to capture the after-improvement value, which rationalizes the more significant upfront capital cost of ADU development.

While tiny houses on wheels are mobile, they are typically heavy and challenging to move. They are typically parked for long periods of time, sometimes for a year or more. The owner of the tiny house on wheels typically pays a modest but monthly rent for parking and living in it somewhere. In Portland in 2015, the parking space rent on residential properties was typically \$300–\$400 per month. As a point of reference, an average room in a group house in Portland in 2015 was roughly \$800 per month.

Tiny houses on wheels have an interesting historic relationship to ADUs. Jay Shafer, the figurative father of the modern tiny-house movement, developed the idea of tiny houses on wheels as a regulatory workaround to the fact that small houses (on foundations) were not allowed in his jurisdiction. He placed the house on wheels largely to avoid regulatory oversight from the building codes. For him, building and living in a tiny space was a form of civil disobedience, a reactionary political and artistic statement that showcased the value proposition of living in a radically smaller space.

Since tiny houses on wheels are treated as trailers or RVs, they can sometimes be parked legally on residential properties. In such cases, it is the act of actually residing in the tiny house on wheels that is not allowed by code.

Fortunately for the occupants, if the habitation of a tiny house on wheels is cited as a nonconforming use by a building violation inspector due to a neighbor complaint, the occupants can relocate it to the site of another willing and suitable host property. Due to the regulations that commonly outlaw full-time camping on residential property, finding a location to park and live in a tiny house on wheels remains among the most challenging aspects of dwelling in one.

Mobile Dwellings: RVs, Vans, House Trucks, and Travel Trailers

RVs, vans, house trucks, and travel trailers fall into the same legal category as tiny houses on wheels in terms of their habitation in residential zones. One difference is stylistic: these options are not primarily designed to look like a quintessential stick-built home. Rather, they were built for road travel first and habitation secondarily.

RVs, vans, and house trucks are self-motorized. The self-motorized dwelling options may be preferred by people who need to move around—people with nomadic lifestyle needs.

A travel trailer is a nonmotorized mobile dwelling. Travel trailers are lighter and easier to tow than a custom-built tiny house on wheels, and they are often less expensive.

Yurts and Tents

Yurts are attractive, sturdy, large, round canvas tents. They are occasionally used on residential properties as living quarters, as flex space, or for guests. They can cost as little as $10,000. They require a wood

Image 12.9.

Image 12.10.

Image 12.11. Image from treehouses.com, http://treehouses.com/treehouse/treesort/forestreeint.htm.

platform and can be assembled and disassembled in a day or two. They are often heated with woodstoves or plug-in heaters.

Camping tents are rarely used for full-time habitation in residential properties, but they are sometimes used for guests on a temporary basis if the primary house does not have guest quarters.

Tree Houses

Tree houses likely run afoul of many codes, but that does not stop people from building them. Some are built with habitable functions in mind. It is rare for people to live in tree houses full-time. But, when built well, they sometimes serve as guest rooms.

Other Types of Small Housing

Outside of residential zones, there are a number of small, habitable, alternative dwelling environments. It is outside the scope of

Image 12.12. A pocket neighborhood, or cottage cluster, developed by Ross Chapin in Port Townsend, Washington.

this book to cover these, but they include tent encampments (read *Tent City Urbanism* by Andrew Heben for more information about this niche topic), conventional multifamily developments, pocket neighborhoods, micro apartments with shared kitchens, and housing cooperatives.

BUILDING BEAUTIFUL IS ILLEGAL

Building beautiful and alternative forms of construction to standard building code is challenging and sometimes impossible. Some of America's most pleasing cities and wonderful homes could never be built within the regime of today's zoning and building-code standards. Zoning regulations make mixed-use streets we enjoy, collective housing options we want, and tent cities that we need nearly impossible to create legally.

Image 12.13. Cave artist Ra Paulette. (Image courtesy Jeffrey Karoff, *CaveDigger* documentary.)

Some modern-day masters of dwelling craftsmanship must effectively avoid the codes or dance around them in order to build their craft. Unpermitted work is free of regulatory oversight, and its renegade approach to design and development has more potential to be unique and artistic. Dwellings that are ingenuously conceived and built outside the box are inherently charming and at times inspirational.

Standards and regulations are necessary to both streamline the work of construction and oversee the quality of the construction, but artistic craftspeople who build beyond what rules can reasonably regulate are artisans who often raise the bar of our design potential.

Permitted ADUs may not be an option in every city, but there are creative alternatives to meet similar objectives without developing a permitted ADU. Informal dwellings can be both safe and beautiful. If a City is making it impossible to do a permitted ADU, then it is advisable to investigate alternatives.

ADUs represent a pragmatic form of highly desirable urban infill housing. They can be an efficient, free-market investment vehicle for middle-class households while simultaneously serving as a housing form that meets many municipal social, economic, and environmental

Image 12.14. A tiny house on wheels by builder Abel Zimmerman of Zyl Vardos, a tiny-house building company. (Image from JeffreyFreeman.com.)

Image 12.15. A tree house by natural builder SunRay Kelly. (Image from Eric McCool.)

policy objectives. Because ADUs are a distributed form of homeowner development, they do not involve any single decision maker, political body, or company. ADU development is something that will ultimately happen on its own accord, primarily driven by the energetic propulsion of capitalism. It is a matter of whether the ADUs will be built formally or informally, which will be largely determined by the relative restrictiveness and permitting costs associated with a City's ADU regulations. This housing revolution is happening one way or another, whether it's through the front door or the Backdoor.

Conclusion

I WROTE *BACKDOOR REVOLUTION* AT THE PRECIPICE OF WHAT I BELIEVE will be an ADU revolution. My intention was to provide an authoritative snapshot of what ADUs are and what regulations induce or hinder them and to document some best practices related to their development.

As I have studied the history of ADUs and rapid progress that has transpired in Portland and Vancouver in particular, I've realized that the state of ADUs is ephemeral and it will continue to evolve with time. A future reader in forty years may cringe at some of the outdated language about ADUs captured within these pages, just as I have found myself smirking at the assumptions and antiquated language about ADUs from the 1980s.

The field of ADU development will change, evolve, improve, and grow. Indeed, the term *ADU* may one day be replaced, but the concepts of what defines an ADU will persist for the foreseeable future, especially wherever zoning codes hold a strict stance and tight grip on allowing a range of dwelling options in single-family residential zones. In light of changing uses, needs, and housing demands in these residential zones, there will likely be significant and broad zoning changes that span far beyond the confines of ADU development and into legacy housing forms such as duplexes, triplexes, and fourplexes.

The information I have gathered and streamlined in this book was hard-earned and was not easily discovered. This information will help contextualize future research, best practices, and literature related to ADU development. My hope is that *Backdoor Revolution* will serve as a baseline compendium for a host of more detailed literature and digital information on topics related to the issues that were raised here. Like other baseline works, one day this book may be obsolete, which will signal that significant progress has been made for ADU development. I look forward to that day.

Appendix 1

Administrative Aspects of Ownership: How Utilities, Insurance, Appraisals, and Property Taxation Work

THE FOLLOWING ADMINISTRATIVE INFORMATION IS BASED ON HOW ADUs are administered and how they function throughout Portland, Oregon. These administrative approaches are straightforward, so the appendix will explain how they work. This may help other cities benchmark their own administrative practices. City officials and ADU advocates can use this information to develop fair administrative protocols as their ADU programs develop. It will also help homeowners understand the granular details of how they should anticipate their ADU to be treated administratively.

This will not represent an exhaustive list of the ways that ADUs could be treated by a jurisdiction. I'll provide some anecdotal commentary of other administrative approaches and interpretations, as well as the impacts of these alternative approaches.

Utilities for ADUs

How the ADU is connected to utilities is a common question raised by homeowners as they wrap their heads around the scope of ADU development. There are four main utilities covered in this section: water, sewer, gas, and electric.

Utilities and systems for ADUs follow a guiding building-code principle. The occupant of unit A should not have to enter unit B in order to turn on or off their own utilities. The safety principle is that if the electricity, gas, or water go out or get shut off in unit B, the occupant of unit B must be able to turn these utilities back on without the presence or consent of the occupant of unit A. This principle applies to detached and attached ADUs. I'll allude to this concept as we discuss the four utilities.

When an ADU is being inspected by a city inspector during construction, the inspector should not need to enter the primary house. The only time an inspector may need to enter the primary house is to view where the utility connections from the ADU tie into the utility connections in the primary house, and sometimes these connect in the basement of the primary house. If the utility connections take place outside the primary house, the inspector should not need to gain access to the primary house. This understanding may alleviate homeowner concerns about City inspectors potentially seeing unrelated, unpermitted work in the primary house (for related information, read the "Faith in Government" section in chapter 7).

Water and Sewer

Water and sewer are extended from the same utility lines that service the primary house. There is no dedicated or separated service from the City or utility company for either the water or sewage service.

For water service, the water comes from the street's water main to the property's water meter. From the water meter, a main water line comes into the primary house. At some point beyond the water meter, there must be a Y added to the water line. This Y could occur before the water main enters the primary house, or it could occur in the basement or crawl space of the primary house. The new water line from the Y that is added to the water main runs to a detached ADU via a trench. The ADU's new water main feeder line must have its own shutoff valve accessible to the occupant of the ADU without having to enter the primary house.

Image A1.1. Though the water service from the meter may be shared, an ADU water shutoff must be accessible to the occupant of the ADU.

The old water line to the primary house is left intact just as it was prior to the addition of the ADU. Water line service capacity must be considered for ADU development as water service capacity is an issue. Depending on the size of the water meter and the total number of fixtures that the property has after the addition of the ADU, the water meter line size may need to be increased. This can involve work in the right-of-way (the sidewalk, the median, and/or the street), and it is costly. In Portland, this work can cost $7,000. In Austin, this work could cost up to $10,000. Whether the property's water line or water meter will need to be upsized is up to the water department to determine based on a count of the number of water fixtures on the property.

Sewer service is also simply extended from the primary house to the ADU, regardless of whether the ADU is attached or detached. There are labor and plumbing costs for trenching and running the sewer pipe from the sewer stack under the first floor of the primary house to the

Image A1.2. New water service being added to a property in the street. It is labor intensive and costly to add new water service lines. In many cases, ADUs should not trigger this type of work.

ADU. The ongoing use fees associated with the additional sewer and water usage are proportional to the additional water, sewer, and storm water added to the property, based on standard usage rates or standard impervious cover calculations. In Portland, there is no additional administrative or permit cost associated with extending the sewer to the ADU.

Adding a new sewer service all the way to the street is very expensive ($10,000–$20,000), so it is important for a City to consider how to avoid requiring a dedicated sewer if it is trying to reduce cost barriers to ADU development. Citizens in both Seattle and Vancouver have struggled with the costs associated with a new sewer (and storm water) connection fee when adding ADUs.

Electric Service

Electric service receives varying treatments depending on specific site conditions and the policies of the electric utility service provider. We'll discuss the panel and the electric service itself.

In general, the ADU will have a dedicated panel. The panel can be situated inside the ADU or in another place accessible to its occupant, such as outside the ADU, outside the primary house, or even inside a partitioned portion of the primary house, referred to as "common space."

Depending on the current electric service level provided to the property and local codes, it is possible that a new dedicated electric service meter will need to be added to the property for the second unit. In Portland, roughly two-thirds of ADUs end up using a new dedicated electric service line. In this instance, the utility company will come out to the property and add an upgraded service drop from the utility lines to the property. A two-pack meter head is installed to replace the old single meter head.

New, dedicated electric meter service costs $2,000 to add, and each new service has a monthly administrative cost associated with it. Thus, some people may be inclined to avoid having a dedicated electric meter service provided for the ADU. They would rather redirect some (maybe 100 amps) of the existing residential service capacity if they're allowed to do so. The ADU tenant would still have to be able to access the electric panel without entering the primary residence. The advantage of having two meters is a clean, administrative break between the two bills. It is easy to assign responsibility for the electric

Image A1.3. Two meters and two addresses serve the primary house and the ADU.

bill to the respective occupants of each unit. Ultimately, whether the ADU needs new dedicated service or not is a decision typically made by the City, the utility provider, and/or the electrician.

In Portland, electrical and plumbing are the two portions of the construction that must be conducted by licensed subcontractors. The bulk of the construction work can be legally done by a homeowner; however; it's rare and generally unadvisable for a homeowner to do the majority of the ADU construction (see chapter 4). This may vary by jurisdiction. Some may require a licensed general contractor to manage all permitted construction projects.

Gas Service

Gas service is not required for residential construction; however, many homeowners opt to bring natural gas to the ADU because it offers some conveniences and creature comforts. Natural gas service allows the unit to have a fire-burning range and stove for cooking, a gas fireplace, a gas-powered water heater, and a gas-powered dryer if desired. Each

Image A1.4. Typically, if the ADU has gas, it will get its own meter, though there will still be one line coming onto the property from the public right-of-way.

of these gas-powered functions can also be accomplished with electric service if desired. The drawback of using gas is that each application of the gas utility must be vented along an exterior wall.

Running a gas line to the ADU is not very expensive if the primary house already has natural gas service. However, the utility company may require there to be a second meter head for the gas. It would then have its own administrative account. If the property already has gas service, the utility company may cover the cost and labor of installing the second meter, depending on the number of gas-based fixtures that will be in the second unit. Extending the gas service to the ADU may only cost an additional $1,000 in plumbing costs.

Separate Address

An ADU is assigned a separate street address. This address will typically append the letter *B* to the primary house address. If the primary house is 1010 Cherry Street, the ADU's street address would be 1010B

Cherry Street. However, if the ADU is on a corner lot and the entrance for the ADU is located on a different street from the primary house, then it may be assigned a street address on that adjacent street. The address must be posted and visible from the street, as it is used as an emergency-response wayfinding sign in the case of a house fire. The homeowner does not necessarily need to install a second mailbox. All mail for both units can be delivered to a single mailbox. Either approach is acceptable.

Insurance

Insurance can be obtained fairly easily for ADUs. It adds on some marginal additional cost per year ($200–$500) to cover the additional structural replacement and liability costs, but it is fairly straightforward to execute this extended provision of the insurance already established for the primary house.

Appraisals

Appraisals for ADUs are critical to their viability. More academic and professional work is needed to develop working standards. (Read more in the sections "The Challenge of Financing ADUs" in chapter 7 and "Practical Roles for Advocates" in chapter 11, and read about the possible effects of owner-occupancy requirements on the development of permitted ADUs in chapter 8).

If properties with permitted ADUs are appraised incorrectly, as they commonly are, the ADU may only appear to be "worth" a small percentage of its construction cost. A low appraised "opinion of value" has very damaging impacts on the economics of ADU development, including financing them (see chapter 3).

Poorly appraised ADUs present some very problematic scenarios for ADUs in terms of their viability in the marketplace. Here are three ways that low appraisals adversely impact ADU development:

1. Some homeowners wish to build an ADU using conventional renovation financing. Financing institutions such as local credit unions and banks must consider the future value of the property after renovations have been completed when determining how much to loan to a customer for the renovation. If the proposed $100,000 ADU only adds $10,000 of value to a property according to an appraiser, the bank will not easily be able to provide an adequate renovation loan to that customer.
2. If a homeowner wished to refinance their property after adding an ADU, in order to get better loan terms or in order to pay off private (e.g., family) loan debts using a cash-out refinancing option or to eliminate their mortgage insurance, then it is important for the ADU to have added value to the property commensurate with its construction cost.
3. Suppose a homebuyer wishes to purchase a home with a preexisting ADU that has considerable and substantial real value. To them, the anticipated additional rental income from the extra unit will greatly offset their future monthly mortgage costs. The value of the property with the ADU is worth far more to them (and to the current owner) than an equivalent property without an ADU for sale next door. However, if an appraiser does not attribute sufficient value for the contributory value of the ADU, then the buyer will be unable to obtain a mortgage loan that is commensurate with their sense of the property's value. Therefore, the buyer may then have to make up that difference in cash. If the appraiser added only $10,000 of value for the $100,000 ADU, this difference between the sale cost and what the buyer can establish to finance the purchase may be $90,000. Thus, the buyer may have to come up with an additional $90,000 in cash in order to purchase this property at its market value.

There has been some peer-reviewed research on appraising ADUs.[115] Depending on the highest and best use of the property, it makes sense for appraisers to heavily weigh the income-based valuation method into their opinion of value. This differs from standard residential appraising, which tends to lean most strongly on sales comparables to derive an opinion of value. The sales comparison approach does not work well with ADUs because there are so few permitted ADUs transacted in a given real estate market; thus, finding viable comparable sales proves very challenging. Using the income-based valuation approach, the property's value can be partially modeled based on the potential income from both units. This is the same method that is used to appraise duplexes, so it is not an uncommon method to use when evaluating investment properties.

This appraisal methodology largely hinges on the allowable uses of the property in terms of how the two units can be used. Specifically, if there is an owner-occupancy requirement or if neither unit can be rented out, then the income-based valuation method carries less weight.

This facet of ADUs is partially why owner-occupancy requirements are among the most problematic regulatory constraints that commonly exist for ADUs. Cities with this provision in place will generally not see a substantial amount of permitted ADU development.

Property Taxation

Property taxation methods vary by state, county, and city, so it is not possible to make unilateral statements about how property taxes would increase after development of a permitted ADU. However, in general, the property taxes should go up in a manner that is proportional to the real market value of the property. Therefore, it would be important to ensure that the assessed value and the appraised values were in alignment with one another, or at least that the assessed value is not grossly higher than the appraised value.

ADUs are a different and rare type of housing development for many regulators. There may be administrative kinks to work out in the system to ensure that the assessor's methods are fair and accurate and that ADUs are not triggering disproportionate tax increases.

One such county ADU taxation debacle occurred in Portland, Oregon, in 2015–2016 that threatened to undermine the viability of ADUs in the market. The sudden policy change in assessment methods for ADUs in Multnomah County arose from a misunderstanding of what ADUs are, due to their rarity. The county tax assessor unilaterally and incorrectly determined that building an ADU was equivalent to building a duplex and that adding an ADU was equivalent to a property rezoning. The assessor claimed that adding an ADU changed the zoning from single family to multifamily, and therefore the assessed value had to be totally changed to match the new zoning designation. Outcries from owners and advocates triggered a statewide rulemaking by the parent agency, the Oregon Department of Revenue, to ultimately resolve the issue by reversing Multnomah County's position in the spring of 2016. The vigilance of community ADU stakeholders in Portland helped catch and resolve this issue.

Income Taxes

Calculating income taxes with an ADU is akin to property tax impacts from a duplex. If either of the two units will be used as a rental unit (business purposes), the rental income is included as income for income tax purposes. The owner must also establish and apply a depreciation deduction based on the structural value of the rental unit. The portion of the property that is used for personal use is treated differently.[116]

The potential federal and state income tax, property tax, use tax, and a host of other tax ramifications of building and/or owning the ADU are varied and dependent upon each owner's unique situation. In order to more fully understand these ramifications and plan for them in advance, the owner should consult with a qualified tax specialist to understand their options and reporting responsibilities.

Appendix 2

History of ADUs

THIS APPENDIX GIVES A SKETCH OF SOME OF THE ROOTS OF THE ANcestral history of ADUs in the United States as well as a picture of its more recent history.

ADUs have been defined differently over time, have gone by a host of names, and have had varying uses, definitions, and ownership statuses. Multiple dwellings located adjacent to one another in order to house multiple generations have been common...well... since at least the beginning of mankind, and probably earlier than that.

The definitions of *housing unit* and *property ownership* are two large areas of philosophical import that, to this day, vary tremendously with global geography. Even in the United States today, the definition of a housing unit will vary by municipality to a certain degree.

While attempting to illustrate a unified history of ADUs would be impossible, I will share a little history on how secondary dwellings on single-family lots have been built and used over time in North American cities.

PESTILENCE

Servant quarters, guest quarters, and starter homes on properties are all legacy versions of what we would now call an ADU. For example, Thomas Jefferson's south pavilion at Monticello, constructed in 1769

Image A2.1. My wife and I visited a village in Flores, Indonesia, that consisted of small and larger multigenerational family housing units. The smaller of these huts may be "accessory" to the larger huts, but it would not be accurate to characterize them as ADUs, due to the different definitions of a "dwelling unit," property ownership, and land use structures that exist in Flores.

and later dubbed the Honeymoon Cottage, was his starter home while the primary house was being built.

Urban ADUs can be traced back to a form of housing development in London in the 1830s called *mews*, which consisted of workers' living quarters located above horse stables. The first common ADU-like developments in the US cities were found in the mid-1800s. These were sometimes called "carriage houses," "alley dwellings," or "alley homes," and they could be found in major cities of the time: Philadelphia; Pittsburgh; Baltimore; Detroit; St. Louis; Milwaukee; Chicago; Kansas City; Washington, DC; Boston; New Orleans; Los Angeles; and New York. In other American cities, speculators and developers also subdivided the backs of large lots and built working-class tiny homes facing the alleys. These alley homes initially served as housing for servants and renters, but over time they largely became extensions of tenement housing. Limited historic information exists about accessory units, so we'll focus on DC and Philadelphia, two cities for which a written record of this housing form does exist.

By 1774 in Philadelphia, the density of housing land division methods led to the "practice of subdividing blocks with alleys and jamming tiny homes on vacant rear yards."[117] This practice continued unabated for nearly ninety years, and "by 1860 the density of population in Philadelphia's inner wards reached its all-time peak."[118] By 1860, however, major cities were experiencing rapid population growth, and eventually tenements replaced alley houses and covered the entire property. Here's a graphic description of what Philadelphia's tenement housing was like by the late 1800s:

> The rooms are rented by the week at prices ranging from $1.50 to $2.50 per room. They have the scantiest possible equipment of old and dilapidated furniture. They are dirty and unventilated; the beds and bedding indescribable....
>
> In most cases there is but one [bathroom] closet in the yard for all the tenants of the house.
>
> The yards, as a rule, are filthy. There is no apparent effort at cleanliness or supervision. One room is the ordinary rule for one family, with frequent boarders in addition. In some cases the large rooms have been divided by flimsy partitions, and each half is occupied by a family.[119]

In the rear of the tenement housing, there were commonly alley dwellings. Here is another description of the physical conditions of these alley dwellings:

> The third class of houses to which we would draw special attention is that of the rear dwelling, a small two- or three-story house, built sometimes singly and sometimes in rows of from two to eight or ten houses on the rear of the front house. This

> plan of building has been characterized as the horizontal rather than the vertical tenement. The entrance to the row is by a narrow passageway from the street or court. This passageway is also frequently the means by which the surface drainage is carried to the street or to an open sewer-connection at its entrance. The space in front of the houses is the only yard. Sometimes this space widens at the end of the entrance-way and there is a double row of dwellings facing each other and covering the rears of two or three front lots. Sometimes again the open space forms a square with houses on three sides.
>
> Thus one comes unexpectedly on a little community whose existence one has not imagined. More often, however, the narrow passage-way runs the whole length of the row and in many cases the brick wall of an adjoining lot shuts away all air and sunshine and makes a prison of the little court.[120]

One article describes Philadelphia's alleys this way: "The streets and alleys reeked of garbage, manure."[121]

In Washington, DC, developers provided housing in the mid-1800s for incoming population growth by simultaneously developing housing on streets and on their alleys. The assumption was "that the middle classes would live on the streets, while the working-class people would reside in the alleys."[122] The alley dwellings were also used for live-in servants.

In the 1860s, substantial population growth spurred more alley housing in DC. Most trips around the city were made by foot at this time, so this form of infill housing was desirable.

> While alley housing was largely a response to the constraints of the pedestrian city, it was also the result of many individual decisions by landowners, builders, and others to an apparently inexhaustible demand for low-cost housing. This potential for profit, and the efforts to realize it, profoundly affected the nature and character of the alley communities that developed.[123]

Image A2.2. Alley dwelling near Union Station, Washington, DC. (Image from the Library of Congress, http://www.loc.gov/pictures/resource/fsa.8a00173/.)

Some of the alley homes were developed by the homeowners themselves who subdivided their properties and used the small alley houses for housing unskilled workers. The great majority of alley dwellers were laborers.

Increased rents in the 1870s resulted in severe overcrowding in DC's alley homes. This also resulted in accessory buildings that had originally been built for other purposes being converted to alley dwellings. In some cases, stables were converted to dwellings. This perpetuated and caused alleys lined with dwellings that appeared as "dilapidated shanties, patched and filthy."

Over the following decade, DC's building practices matured. More construction used brick and increasingly substantial framing techniques. Matured construction techniques translated into alley dwelling construction as well.

Initially, the alley dwellings were developed piecemeal. But as residential lots were subdivided to allow separate ownership of the alley dwelling properties, more and more of the dwellings were

Image A2.3. Yard, Jersey Street Tenement, c. 1888. (Image by Jacob Riis.)

professionally developed en masse. (This separate ownership status brings these units out of the same category of housing that today is integral to the definition of an ADU.) At its peak in the late 1800s, there were 3,201 alley dwellings found in DC.[124]

In 1892, regulations were passed in DC that made alley-dwelling construction cease on alleys that were less than 30 feet wide and that did not have sewer, water, and lights. In the early 1900s, with the advent of streetcars and popularization of personal automobiles, there was increasingly less pressure for pedestrian-oriented development in the city core. Many remaining alley dwellings were converted to other uses, namely garages. DC's "alley ghettos" were slowly wiped out through attrition and changing housing and development norms around order and segregation of functions. By 1927, 40% of original alley dwelling stock was wiped out or converted to a different use. There was a governmental attempt to ban their use as dwellings altogether in the 1940s. Several pockets of DC's original alley dwellings managed to survive in DC, even to this day.

Image A2.4. Washington, DC, tenement-housing alley dwellings in 1935. (Image from the Library of Congress, http://www.loc.gov/pictures/item/2017758821/.)

World War II

By 1930, more than five hundred cities in thirty-nine states had zoning ordinances that enshrined single-family zones to stabilize property values and "protect" neighborhoods.[125] Up until this point, many cities were dominated by residential zones that allowed multifamily development. ADUs were fairly common until the post–World War II building boom that began in the late 1940s, when many people started to move away from cities into suburbs. Euclidian single-use zoning became a more dominant American land-use pattern during this time.

During the early 1900s, in many US cities, most new and existing accessory units were built without permits, possibly because zoning codes had not been well established. Building-code regulations are now more strict than they used to be. For example, according to the Census American Housing Survey, in 1940 half of all dwellings in the United States lacked plumbing. By 1980, only 2.4% of housing units lacked plumbing.[126]

The use of accessory units changed from being a housing form for low-wage workers to becoming a more standard rental opportunity, or a functional independent dwelling for elderly parents. This may be when the terms *granny flats* or *in-law units* were first commonly used. These units were allowed because they were not explicitly banned, and it was only through the more restrictive zoning regulations that these accessory units became nonconforming in the context of new zoning code.[127]

Euclidian zoning laws separating residential from commercial zones became dominant, beginning with a Supreme Court case in 1926:

> Since *Euclid v. Ambler* in 1926...ADUs have traditionally been labeled in planning and land use documents as nonconforming structures or have been confined to the conditional use status, both of which are traditionally linked to a web of various stricter or altogether insurmountable regulations and limitations.
>
> ADUs were still fairly common up until World War II.
>
> The post-war suburban expansion and related tightening of zoning regulations narrowed cultural norms around single family homes, and eliminated accessory units from new construction. It became increasingly difficult to create discrete accessory units. Regulations restricted the habitation of secondary units through narrow definitions of family and uses accessory to them on single family lots. If ADUs were allowed, it was through a conditional use of a non-conforming structure that was grandfathered in.[128]

Late 20th Century ADU History

Since the 1950s, ADU development has consisted largely of informal ADU development. New ADUs were generally banned outright or heavily discouraged through onerous regulations in the latter half of the twentieth century. These legacy policies are what cities must actively unfurl in order to induce ADU development. Nonconforming ADU-like dwellings sprinkled throughout traditional US cities are a modern artifact of traditional American housing development from the early 1900s. These are ADUs that wouldn't be permittable today, but they were built before they were effectively banned through by-laws. In many places, the only existent legal ADUs in such places are nonconforming. Marin County, California, has 600 such accessory apartments.[129]

In the 1980s, there was a surge of interest in using ADUs as a form of housing for elderly people. A range of governmental initiatives were tested and failed. It is only in recent years, since the early 2000s, that we have begun to witness an active resurgence in permitted ADU development in some cities and towns that have actively worked to induce them, and whose attempts that have been featured in this book.

Appendix 3

Synonyms for ADUs

I'VE SIMPLIFIED *BACKDOOR REVOLUTION* BY STICKING TO MOSTLY ONE term, the most appropriate for the structures discussed here: *accessory dwelling unit*, or *ADU*. But there are dozens of terms for this type of housing, including the popular *granny flat* or *in-law apartment*. This list was partially derived from a list compiled on AccessoryDwellings.org and expanded upon in the research for this book.

1. accessory apartment
2. accessory cottage
3. accessory dwelling
4. accessory dwelling unit
5. accessory housing unit
6. accessory living quarters
7. accessory suite
8. accessory unit
9. ADU
10. alley dwelling
11. alley flat
12. alley house
13. ancillary dwelling unit
14. ancillary unit
15. back house
16. backyard cottage

17. basement apartment
18. bungalow
19. carriage house
20. casita
21. coach house
22. companion unit
23. dawdy house
24. dependent person's unit
25. echo home
26. elder cottage
27. English basement
28. family apartment
29. family dwelling unit
30. garage apartment
31. garage suite
32. garden cottage
33. garden house
34. garden suite
35. Grand Retreat
36. granny cottage
37. granny flat
38. granny unit
39. guest cottage
40. guesthouse
41. infill housing
42. in-law
43. in-law suite
44. in-law unit
45. JADU, or junior accessory dwelling unit—a small, internal ADU
46. Jaffe-gram
47. laneway house
48. limited second dwelling
49. mother-in-law

50. mother-daughter or mother/daughter house
51. multigenerational home
52. Ohana unit
53. personal accessory dwelling
54. residential second unit
55. SDU
56. second dwelling unit
57. second unit
58. secondary apartment
59. secondary dwelling unit
60. secondary suite
61. secondary unit
62. second family residential unit
63. sidekick
64. tiny home
65. two-family house

Appendix 4

Informal ADU Studies

- In San Francisco in 1960, the Bureau of Building Inspection (as it was known then) estimated that there were between 20,000 and 30,000 secondary units in San Francisco, and 90% of these had been built without the proper permits.[130]
- A 1982 estimate suggested that 10% of single-family homes in San Francisco had unpermitted accessory apartments.[131]
- A 2014 study of the Excelsior district in San Francisco found "nearly 70 percent of the people living in that neighborhood of single-family homes were tenants and half of them lived in homes with, typically, illegal secondary units. More than 80 percent of the families in those in-law units were either Asian or Latino, and 86 percent of the households were very low-income, earning no more than half San Francisco's median income of about $73,000."[132]
- Wegmann and Chapple's 2011 study of five towns in the Bay Area found 16% had unpermitted secondary unit development.[133]
- In New York in 1995, "In Nassau and Suffolk Counties alone, the Long Island Regional Planning Board has found at least 100,000 illegal accessory units in areas zoned for single-family houses."[134]
- According to one 2008 study in New York City, there were approximately 114,000 unpermitted ADUs in the form of basement apartments.[135]
- In Los Angeles in 1987, the *Los Angeles Times* reported 42,000 unpermitted ADUs. In three neighborhoods, it was estimated that

34%–80% of the homes had informal ADUs. In Los Angeles's case, these unpermitted units were built in garages.[136]

- In the Boston metropolitan area, 38,000 of all new housing units between 1970 and 1981, which represents 20% of new housing units during that time frame, were estimated to be accessory apartment conversions from within residential structures, mostly informal ADUs.[137]
- In 2011, Jacob Mendez estimated that roughly 8% of Vancouver's total housing stock consisted of unpermitted secondary suites.[138]
- In 1985, Martin Gellen reported the number of annually built informal ADUs as being between 60,000 and 300,000 units nationwide.[139]
- In 1983, the National Association of Home Builders estimated that there were 300,000 unpermitted accessory apartments built each year.[140] The US Census and NAHB estimated that there were 2.5 million such units in the early 1980s.[141] Using NAHB's estimates, there would be 13.7 million such units today, accounting for greater than 10% of the total housing units in the United States in 2015.

Appendix 5

ADU Model Code

THE FOLLOWING MODEL ADU ORDINANCE WAS WRITTEN BY ELI Spevak, a small housing developer in Portland, Oregon, and is posted on AccessoryDwellings.org as an editable MS Word document.* Commentary is provided in italics, along with some alternative clauses that could be helpful for particular circumstances.

ACCESSORY DWELLING UNIT MODEL CODE

1. **Purpose.** Accessory dwelling units are allowed in certain situations to
   a. create new housing units while respecting the look and scale of single-dwelling development;
   b. support more efficient use of existing housing stock and infrastructure;
   c. offer environmentally friendly housing choices with less average space per person and smaller associated carbon footprints;
   d. provide housing that responds to changing family needs, smaller households, and increasing housing costs; and
   e. provide accessible housing for seniors and persons with disabilities.

* This ADU Model Code was prepared by Eli Spevak, with assistance from Martin Brown, Kol Peterson, Jordan Palmeri, and Ben Schonberger.

2. **Definition.** An accessory dwelling unit (ADU) is a smaller, secondary home on the same lot as a primary dwelling. ADUs are independently habitable and provide the basic requirements of shelter, heating, cooking, and sanitation. There are two types of ADUs:
    a. Garden cottages are detached structures. Examples include converted garages or new construction.
    b. Accessory suites are attached to or part of the primary dwelling. Examples include converted living spaces, attached garages, basements or attics, additions, or a combination thereof.

Comment: Alternative name possibilities are listed in appendix 3.

3. **Eligibility.** An ADU may be added to a house on any residentially zoned lot.

Comment: Some codes restrict ADUs to certain zoning designations, lot sizes, and/or geographic areas within the jurisdiction. Such restrictions significantly constrain the number of eligible properties and suppress the number of ADUs that can (legally) get built under the code.

4. **Number.** One ADU is permitted per residentially zoned lot.

Comment: Vancouver, British Columbia, allows both a garden cottage and an accessory suite on a residentially zoned lot. This has not been tested to our knowledge in the United States but seems like a promising idea.

Possible additional language: "Where more than one house is allowed on a single lot through a planned development process at the same or similar density as would be allowed by subdivision, one ADU is permitted per house."

5. **Creation.** An ADU may be created through new construction, conversion of an existing structure, addition to an existing structure, or conversion of a qualifying existing house to a garden cottage while simultaneously constructing a new primary dwelling on the site.

Comment: It's not uncommon for jurisdictions to limit ADUs to certain types (e.g., internal or detached) or to properties where the primary dwelling is of a certain age. Such restrictions constrain ADU development, since property-specific conditions (e.g., existence of basement, size of lot) often limit the type of ADU that can be created.

6. **Density.** ADUs are exempt from the residential density standards of this code.
7. **Approval.** Applications for ADUs must meet the following criteria. Requests to adjust these standards are handled through a ministerial approval process.
   a. The applicant must demonstrate that the ADU complies with all development and design standards of this section.
   b. The applicant must demonstrate that the proposed modifications comply with applicable building and fire safety codes.

Comment: It's appropriate to require a land-use process for adjustments to code standards. But when discretionary land-use processes or conditional-use permits are required for every ADU, this becomes a significant barrier to ADU development. Land-use fees and process time, neighbor notification requirements, and approval unpredictability make an already expensive and challenging project even less accessible to homeowner developers. In practice, many prospective ADU builders never take the first step if the code doesn't support as-of-right development.

8. **Occupancy and use.** Occupancy and use standards for an ADU shall be the same as those applicable to a primary dwelling on the same site.

Comment: ADU codes that place more restrictions on tenure (ownership vs. rental), short-term rental, affordability, and/or home business than would apply to a primary dwelling on the same lot result in less ADU construction. Owner-occupancy requirements make properties with ADUs unsuitable for income-based valuation by appraisers, constraining their value and making them more difficult to finance. Affordable housing restrictions on ADUs sound appealing, except that deed restrictions and tenant income screenings are (unsurprisingly) obstacles for mom-and-pop landlords (fortunately, ADUs provide a surprising amount of market-based affordable housing without subsidy or use restriction).

9. **Design.** Design standards for ADUs are stated in this section. If not addressed in this section, base zone-development standards apply.
   a. **All ADUs (accessory suites and garden cottages)** must meet the following requirements:
      i. **Size.** An ADU may be no more than 800 sq. ft. or the size of the primary dwelling, whichever is less.

Comment: In addition to a total size cap (typically 600–1,000 sq. ft.), some codes also cap ADUs to a certain percentage of the size of the primary dwelling. Note that such constraints effectively act as a small house penalty: limiting the size of ADUs on lots where the primary dwelling is already fairly small, but having no impact when the primary dwelling is big.

Possible additional language: "The size of a basement accessory suite occupying the entire footprint of a home built prior to ____ may be up to [1,000–1,200] sq. ft."

ii. **Parking.** No additional parking is required for an ADU. Existing required parking for the primary dwelling must be maintained or replaced on-site.

Comment: Parking requirements for ADUs can significantly increase costs and remove lots from consideration where it is impractical to add a parking space. A major survey of Oregon ADUs revealed no evidence that ADUs contribute to neighborhood parking problems.

b. **Accessory suites** must meet the following additional requirements:

i. **Location of entrances.** Only one entrance may be located on the facade of the primary dwelling facing the street, unless the primary dwelling contained additional entrances before the accessory suite was created. An exception to this regulation is entrances that do not have access from the ground, such as entrances from balconies or decks.

ii. **Exterior stairs.** Fire escapes or exterior stairs for access to an upper-level accessory suite shall not be located on the front of the primary dwelling.

c. **Garden cottages** must meet the following additional requirements:

i. **Height.** The maximum height allowed for a garden cottage is the lesser of [20–25] feet or the height of the primary dwelling.

Comment: Definitions of height vary from code to code. If they go to the peak of the roof, consider a higher height limit. If they go to the average height of the roof, consider a lower height limit.

ii. **Building setbacks.** Garden cottages must be located at least 6 feet behind the primary dwelling, unless the garden cottage is in an existing detached structure that does not meet this standard.

iii. **Building coverage.** The building coverage of a garden cottage may not be larger than the building coverage of the primary dwelling.

iv. **Yard setbacks.** No portion of an existing building that encroaches within a required yard setback may be converted to or used as a garden cottage unless the building complies with setback exemptions (e.g., for garages or properties abutting alleys) available elsewhere in the code.

Miscellaneous Topics

Design Compatibility

Some cities, including Seattle, Washington; Vancouver, British Columbia; and Eugene, Oregon, don't have any special requirements that ADUs match the exterior appearance of the primary dwelling. There's a good case for this, especially since ADUs represent a sizable investment and builders have plenty of market incentive to make them look appealing and appropriate for the neighborhood. Design compatibility requirements often single out ADUs while offering no such constraints on other types of accessory structures (e.g., garages, art studios). For these reasons, compatibility guidelines are not included in this model code.

However, since design compatibility requirements are quite common and sometimes help build public acceptance for ADUs, what follows is some implementing language that could be appended to sections 9.a and 9.c:

(Add to Section 9.a—All ADUs)

iii. **Exterior finish materials.** Exterior finish materials must visually match in type, size, and placement the exterior finish materials of the primary dwelling.

iv. **Roof pitch.** The roof pitch must be the same as the predominant roof pitch of the primary dwelling.

v. **Windows.** If the street-facing facade of the ADU is visible from the street, its windows must match, in proportion and orientation, the windows of the primary dwelling.

vi. **Eaves.** If the primary dwelling has eaves, the ADU must have eaves that project the same distance from the building. If the primary dwelling does not have eaves, no eaves are required for the ADU.

(Add to Section 9.c—Garden cottages)

v. Exemptions. Garden cottages are eligible for either of the following exemptions:

  a). **Design compatibility.** Exceptions to Sections 9.a.iii–vi are granted for garden cottages that

    i). are under 500 sq. ft. and under 18 ft. average height, or

    ii). meet community design standards, defined elsewhere in the code.

Comment: These exceptions provide design latitude for smaller garden cottages and an alternative path in cases where the primary dwelling is ugly and/or out of character with neighboring homes.

b). **Alteration.** If a garden cottage is proposed for an existing detached accessory structure that does not meet one or more of the standards of sections 9.a.iii–vi, the structure is exempt from the standard(s) it does not meet. Alterations that would move the structure out of conformance with standards it does meet are not allowed. If any floor area is added to a detached accessory structure, the entire structure must meet the standards of sections 9.a.iii–vi.

Impact Fees

Although not typically included in zoning-code language, the way building permits and impact fees (sometimes called "system development charges") are calculated for ADUs can have a big effect on how many get built. This is especially true if such fees represent a significant percentage of the total project cost (particularly likely with relatively inexpensive ADU conversions). Finally, high fees can steer ADU development "under the radar screen" where there's no permitting or inspection at all—and a greater likelihood of dangerous life/safety conditions for residents.

It's common for jurisdictions to charge reduced impact fees for ADUs. Portland's decision in 2010 to waive impact fees on ADUs to meet public policy goals played a significant role in the subsequent increase in ADU development. Depending on municipal policy goals, there may well be a case for setting ADU fees below what would be charged for a standard single-family home or dropping them altogether.

Endnotes

1. Amanda Kolson Hurley, "Will US Cities Design Their Way Out of the Affordable Housing Crisis?" *NextCity*, January 18, 2016, https://nextcity.org/features/view/cities-affordable-housing-design-solution-missing-middle.

2. For a longer discussion of how an investor would consider an ADU, read the post on BuildinganADU.com about ADUs as an investment: http://www.buildinganadu.com/adu-blog/adus-from-an-investors-perspective.

3. Chris Botero, in conversation with the author, October 27, 2016.

4. The 2018 International Residential Code includes an appendix that allows for sleeping lofts and ladders to access the sleeping lofts. Oregon adopted this standard state-wide in 2018. Individual jurisdictions can choose to adopt this standard as well.

5. Martin J. Brown and Jordan Palmeri, *Accessory Dwelling Units in Portland, Oregon: Evaluation and Interpretation of a Survey of ADU Owners*, State of Oregon Department of Environmental Quality, last updated June 1, 2014, http://www.oregon.gov/deq/FilterDocs/ADU-surveyinterpret.pdf.

6. Karen Chapple, Jake Wegmann, Alison Nemirow, and Colin Dentel-Post, *Yes in My Backyard: Mobilizing the Market for Secondary Units*, Center for Community Innovation at the Institute for Urban and Regional Development at UC Berkeley, June 2012, http://communityinnovation.berkeley.edu/reports/secondary-units.pdf.

7. Patty Hastings, "Accessory Dwelling Good Fit for Man with Autism, Down Syndrome," *Columbian*, December 26, 2016, http://www.columbian.com/news/2016/dec/26/vancouver-man-accessory-dwelling-autism-down-syndrome/.

8. Bonnie Roseman, in discussion with the author, June 16, 2016.

9. Jake Wegmann, in discussion with the author, November 29, 2016.

10. Jordan Palmeri, email correspondence with the author, January 21, 2016.

11. Patrick H. Hare Planning and Design, *Accessory Units: The State of the Art* (Washington, DC: Patrick H. Hare Planning and Design, 1991).

12. Amy Dain, "The State Should Encourage Accessory Apartments," *CommonWealth*, October 28, 2015, https://commonwealthmagazine.org/opinion/the-state-should-encourage-accessory-apartments/.

13. City of Sierra Madre, *Planning Commission Staff Report*, September 3, 2015, http://www.cityofsierramadre.com/common/pages/DisplayFile.aspx?itemId=601744.

14. Patrick H. Hare, Susan Conner, and Dwight H. Merriam, *Accessory Apartments: Using Surplus Space in Single-family Houses* (Chicago: American Planning Association, Planning Advisory Service, 1981).

15. Patrick H. Hare Planning and Design, *Accessory Units*.

16. Missy Ryan, "Franklin's Apartment Rules to Take Time," *Boston Globe*, January 22, 2006.

17. Amy Dain, *Residential Land-Use Regulation in Eastern Massachusetts: A Study of 187 Communities*, Pioneer Institute for Public Policy Research and the Rappaport Institute for Greater Boston, Kennedy School of Government (Cambridge, MA: Harvard University, 2005).

18. Alan Durning, "ADUs and Don'ts," Sightline Institute, March 15, 2013, http://www.sightline.org/2013/03/15/adus-and-donts/.

19. Dain, *Residential Land-Use Regulation*.

20. Baltimore County, Maryland, Regulations, Article 4, Section 400 (2011).

21. Spencer Gardner, "The Challenges of Building Rental Housing," Strong Towns, March 9, 2016, https://www.strongtowns.org/journal/2016/3/9/the-challenges-of-building-rental-housing.

22. Samantha Kimmey, "Marin Hashing Out Revisions to Second Unit Rules," *Point Reyes Light*, December 28, 2016, https://www.ptreyeslight.com/article/marin-hashing-out-revisions-second-unit-rules.

23. Ryan Stanton, "See the Neighborhoods Where Accessory Apartments Could Be Built in Ann Arbor," *Ann Arbor News*, May 10, 2016, http://www.mlive.com/news/ann-arbor/index.ssf/2016/05/see_the_neighborhoods_where_ac.html.

24. Martin John Brown and Taylor Watkins, "Understanding and Appraising Properties with Accessory Dwelling Units," *The Appraisal Journal*, Fall 2012.

25. Phil Nameny, in conversation with the author, January 6, 2016.

26. Jake Fry, in conversation with the author, January 28, 2016.

27. Nicole Joslin, in conversation with the author, April 2, 2016.

28. David Foster, in conversation with the author, January 22, 2016.

29. Kevin Casey, in conversation with the author, April 11, 2016.

30. Seattle Department of Construction and Inspections, "Accessory Dwelling Unit (Mother-in-Law Apartment)," http://www.seattle.gov/dpd/permits/commonprojects/motherinlawunits/default.htm.

31. Adam Peterson, in conversation with the author, October 6, 2016.

32. Casey, interview.

33. Donald Shoup, *The High Cost of Free Parking* (Chicago and Washington, DC: APA Planners Press, 2011).

34. Dan Parolek, in conversation with the author, May 9, 2016.

35. Laura Lindgren, "ANOTHER VIEW: Keep Granny Flats Small," *Grunion*, October 6, 2017, http://www.gazettes.com/opinion/another_view/another-view-keep-granny-flats-small/article_2243fab6-a21c-11e7-850d-03e8a1654620.html.

36. Brown and Palmeri, *Accessory Dwelling Units in Portland.*

37. Shoup, *The High Cost of Free Parking.*

38. Elinor Hope Stege, "What Next for Accessory Dwellings?: Getting from Bylaws to Buildings" (master's thesis, Massachusetts Institute of Technology, 2009), https://dspace.mit.edu/handle/1721.1/50124.

39. City of Renton, "Customer Information Bulletin: Accessory Dwelling Units," Planning Division, 2015, https://rentonwa.gov/uploadedFiles/Business/PBPW/DEVSERV/FORMS_PLANNING/Accessory%20Dwelling%20Unit.pdf.

40. Renton city planner, in conversation with the author, September 14, 2017.

41. Casey, interview.

42. Dain, *Residential Land-Use Regulation.*

43. Jamal Kadri, public testimony to the Washington, DC, Zoning Commission, February 6, 2014.

44. Jason Furman, "Barriers to Shared Growth: The Case of Land Use Regulation and Economic Rents," remarks to the Urban Institute, November 20, 2015, https://obamawhitehouse.archives.gov/sites/default/files/page/files/20151120_barriers_shared_growth_land_use_regulation_and_economic_rents.pdf.

45. Casey, interview.

46. Staff reports, "Hillsborough Boards to Hold Jan. 19 Hearing on Collins Ridge," *News & Observer*, January 7, 2017, http://www.newsobserver.com/news/local/community/chapel-hill-news/article124794509.html.

47. Larry Wilson, "Granny Flats in Pasadena Are Good for the Whole Family," *Pasadena Star-News,* September 8, 2015, http://www.pasadenastarnews.com/opinion/20150908/granny-flats-in-pasadena-are-good-for-the-whole-family-larry-wilson.

48. Catherine Cruz, "Sewer Hookups Slow Accessory Dwelling Unit Approvals," KITV, March 6, 2017; updated March 27, 2017, http://www.kitv.com/story/34680754/sewer-hookups-slow-accessory-dwelling-unit-approvals.

49. Kol Peterson, "Building an ADU in LA: Part II," October 19, 2017, http://www.buildinganadu.com/adu-blog/building-an-adu-in-la-part-ii.

50. Brown and Palmeri, *Accessory Dwelling Units in Portland.*

51. Geoff Anderson, in conversation with the author, February 12, 2016.

52. Martin John Brown, "People in Portland Want and Build ADUs—With or Without Permits," *Architectural Therapy*, October 13, 2009, https://architecturaltherapy.files.wordpress.com/2009/10/portland-adus-permitted-and-not-2009-10-13.pdf.

53. Hare, Conner, and Merriam, *Accessory Apartments.*

54. Arthur C. Nelson, *Reshaping Metropolitan America: Development Trends and Opportunities to 2030* (Washington, DC: Island Press, 2013).

55. Nelson, *Reshaping Metropolitan America.*

56. Parolek, interview.

57. Ellen Marya, "Housing Cost Burdens Weigh Heavily on Low- and Moderate-Income Renters across the Country," *Housing Perspectives*, January 5, 2016, http://housingperspectives.blogspot.com/2016/01/housing-cost-burdens-weigh-heavily-on.html.

58. Marya, "Housing Cost Burdens."

59. "Housing Affordability Burden for US Cities," Governing the States and Localities, http://www.governing.com/gov-data/economy-finance/housing-affordability-by-city-income-rental-costs.html.

60. Wegmann, interview.

61. Brown and Palmeri, *Accessory Dwelling Units in Portland.*

62. Jake Wegmann and Karen Chapple, "Understanding the Market for Secondary Units in the East Bay" (working paper, Institute of Urban and Regional Development, UC Berkeley, October 2012), https://escholarship.org/uc/item/9932417c.

63. Ashley Salvador, "Much 'ADU' about a Lot: How Social Relations Influence the Affordability of Accessory Dwelling Units in Edmonton, Alberta, Canada" (bachelor's thesis, Dalhousie University, 2017), https://dalspace.library.dal.ca/bitstream/handle/10222/72852/April%2017%2C%202017%20Final%20Honours%20Submission.pdf?sequence=1&isAllowed=y.

64. Jane Jacobs, *The Death and Life of Great American Cities* (New York: Modern Library, 1961 and 2011).

65. Brown and Palmeri, *Accessory Dwelling Units in Portland.*

66. Wegmann and Chapple, "Understanding the Market."

67. Heather Burpee, in conversation with the author, January 29, 2016.

68. Nelson, *Reshaping Metropolitan America.*

69. Brown and Palmeri, *Accessory Dwelling Units in Portland.*

70. Lloyd T. Keefe, "History of Zoning in Portland 1918–1959," August 1975, https://www.portlandoregon.gov/bps/article/147441.

71. Keefe, "History of Zoning."

72. Hare, Conner, and Merriam, *Accessory Apartments.*

73. Bureau of Planning and Sustainability, *Growth Scenarios Report*, City of Portland, Oregon, July 2015.

74. Nick Christensen, "Portland Region Grows to 2.35 Million Residents, Census Estimates, with Newcomers Leading the Way," Oregon Metro, March 26, 2015, http://www.oregonmetro.gov/news/portland-region-grows-235-million-residents-census-estimates-newcomers-leading-way.

75. Nelson, *Reshaping Metropolitan America.*

76. Kerry Gold, "Laneway Homes Are Vancouver's Past, and Future," *Globe and Mail*, October 10, 2014, https://beta.theglobeandmail.com/real-estate/laneway-homes-are-vancouvers-past-and-future/article21055654/.

77. City of Vancouver, *The Role of Secondary Suites: Rental Housing Strategy—Study 4*, December 2009, http://vancouver.ca/docs/policy/housing-secondary-suites.pdf.

78. Aidan Devine, "Granny Flat Boom Engulfs Western Sydney as Homeowners Adjust to Soaring House Prices," *Daily Telegraph*, February 20, 2015, http://www.dailytelegraph.com.au/realestate/news/sydney-nsw/granny-flat-boom-engulfs-western-sydney-as-homeowners-adjust-to-soaring-house-prices/news-story/a4dad9be7e8ee114992d891b5fd12b19.

79. Burpee, interview.

80. Brent Jang, "Greater Vancouver House Prices Jump 20 Percent to Average $1.47 Million," *Globe and Mail*, September 2, 2015, https://beta.theglobeandmail.com/report-on-business/economy/housing/the-real-estate-beat/vancouver-house-prices-jump-20-per-cent-to-average-147-million/article26197722/.

81. 2011 Census Total Population Results, BC Stats, http://www.bcstats.gov.bc.ca/StatisticsBySubject/Census/2011Census/PopulationHousing/MunicipalitiesByRegionalDistrict.aspx.

82. Fry, interview.

83. Nelson, *Reshaping Metropolitan America.*

84. Housing: Density Bonuses, California Assembly Bill No. 1866 (passed Sept. 29, 2002).

85. "Population and Households Quick Statistics," Office of Planning and Community Development, Seattle.gov, http://www.seattle.gov/opcd/population-and-demographics/about-seattle.

86. City of Novato, General Plan 2035 Policy White Paper, April 2014.

87. Richard Scheinin, "Homeowner's Dilemma: Building an Accessory Unit without Breaking the Bank," *Mercury News*, July 26, 2016, updated August 12, 2016, http://www.mercurynews.com/2016/07/26/homeowners-dilemma-building-an-accessory-unit-without-breaking-the-bank/.

88. Johnny Sanphillippo, "Affordable Housing That Might Have Been," Strong Towns, June 16, 2016, https://www.strongtowns.org/journal/2016/6/15/affordable-housing-that-might-have-been.

89. 89. Casey, interview.

90. Wegmann, interview.

91. Wegmann and Chapple, "Understanding the Market."

92. Vinit Mukhija and Anastasia Loukaitou-Sideris, eds., *The Informal American City: From Taco Trucks to Day Labor* (Cambridge, MA: MIT Press, 2014).

93. Fannie Mae, *Selling Guide: Fannie Mae Single Family*, 2011, https://www.fanniemae.com/content/guide/sel122011.pdf.

94. Brown and Watkins, "Understanding and Appraising Properties."

95. Fannie Mae, *Selling Guide: Fannie Mae Single Family*, 2016, https://www.fanniemae.com/content/guide/sel022316.pdf.

96. Village of Euclid v. Ambler Realty Co., 272 U.S. 365 (1926), https://supreme.justia.com/cases/federal/us/272/365/case.html.

97. *Euclid v. Ambler*, 272 U.S.

98. *Euclid v. Ambler*, 272 U.S.

99. Martin Gellen, *Accessory Apartments in Single-Family Housing* (New York: Routledge, 2012).

100. Gellen, *Accessory Apartments*.

101. Dan Parolek, interview.

102. Gellen, *Accessory Apartments*.

103. Michael Lowrey, "Court Sides with Property Owner," *Carolina Journal*, March 10, 2008, https://www.carolinajournal.com/news-article/court-sides-with-property-owner/.

104. Mukhija and Loukaitou-Sideris, *The Informal American City*.

105. Maya Srikrishnan, "Encinitas Tries to Salvage Failed Granny-Flat Experiment," *Voice of San Diego*, February 10, 2016, http://www.voiceofsandiego.org/topics/land-use/encinitas-tries-to-salvage-failed-granny-flat-experiment/.

106. Stephanie Chavez and James Quinn, "Substandard Housing: Garages: Immigrants In, Cars Out," *Los Angeles Times*, May 24, 1987, http://articles.latimes.com/1987-05-24/news/mn-2558_1_one-car-garage.

107. Chavez and Quinn, "Substandard Housing."

108. Hare, Conner, and Merriam, *Accessory Apartments*.

109. Mendez, "Ambiguity at Home."

110. Mendez, "Ambiguity at Home."

111. Eli Spevak, in conversation with the author, January 13, 2016.

112. Dan Borchelt, *The Hidden Housing Supply: Accessory Apartments in the Boston Area* (Boston: Metropolitan Area Planning Council, 1988).

113. Tessa Melvin, "Legally or Not, 1-Family House Is Often Home to 2 Families," *New York Times*, February 5, 1995, http://www.nytimes.com/1995/02/05/realestate/legally-or-not-1-family-house-is-often-home-to-2-families.html.

114. Jamal Kadri, email correspondence with the author, August 18, 2017.

115. Brown and Watkins, "Understanding and Appraising Properties."

116. Jay Romano, "Your Home: When Owner Rents Out Part of House," *New York Times*, May 2, 2004, http://www.nytimes.com/2004/05/02/realestate/your-home-when-owner-rents-out-part-of-house.html.

117. James Borchert, "The Rise and Fall of Washington's Inhabited Alleys: 1852–1972," *Records of the Columbia Historical Society, Washington, DC*, 71/72 (1971/1972): 276–288.

118. Borchert, "Rise and Fall."

119. Borchert, "Rise and Fall."

120. The Octavia Hill Association, "Certain Aspects of the Housing Problem in Philadelphia," *Annals of the American Academy of Political and Social Science* 20 (July 1902): 111–20.

121. Sam Bass Warner, Jr., *The Private City: Philadelphia in Three Periods of Its Growth* (Philadelphia: University of Pennsylvania Press, 1987).

122. Borchert, "Rise and Fall."

123. Borchert, "Rise and Fall."

124. James Borchert, *Alley Life in Washington: Family, Community, Religion, and Folklife in the City, 1850–1970 (Blacks in the New World)* (Champaign, IL: University of Illinois Press, 1980).

125. Mary Corbin Sies and Christopher Silver, eds., *Planning the Twentieth-Century American City* (Baltimore: Johns Hopkins University Press, 1996).

126. Gellen, *Accessory Apartments.*

127. Maurizio Antoninetti, "The Difficult History of Ancillary Units: The Obstacles and Potential Opportunities to Increase the Heterogeneity of Neighborhoods and the Flexibility of Households in the United States," *Journals of Housing for the Elderly* 22, no. 4 (2008), http://www.tandfonline.com/doi/abs/10.1080/02763890802458320.

128. Stege, "What Next for Accessory Dwellings?"

129. Gellen, *Accessory Apartments.*

130. Gellen, *Accessory Apartments.*

131. Gellen, *Accessory Apartments.*

132. John Wildermuth, "SF In-Law Units May Emerge from Shadows via Proposed Law," *SF Gate*, March 13, 2014, http://www.sfgate.com/realestate/article/S-F-in-law-units-may-emerge-from-shadows-via-5312544.php.

133. Chapple et al., *Yes in My Backyard.*

134. Melvin, "Legally or Not."

135. Pratt Center for Community Development and Chhaya Community Development Corporation, *New York's Housing Underground: A Refuge and Resource*, March 2008, http://prattcenter.net/sites/default/files/housing_underground_0.pdf.

136. Chavez and Quinn, "Substandard Housing."

137. Borchelt, *Hidden Housing.*

138. Mendez, "Ambiguity at Home."

139. Gellen, *Accessory Apartments.*

140. Gellen, *Accessory Apartments.*

141. Richard F. Babcock, "The Egregious Invalidity of the Exclusive Single-Family Zone," *Land Use Law and Zoning Digest* 35, no. 7 (1983), http://www.tandfonline.com/doi/abs/10.1080/00947598.1983.10394895.

Index

Page numbers in *italics* denote images; those followed by a *t* indicate tables and those followed by a *f* indicate a figures.

About the Author

Kol Peterson catalogued his personal ADU development process on a blog (pdxadu.blogspot.com), open-sourcing the project. This blog turned into a valuable ADU resource locally in Portland, Oregon, as it allowed other prospective ADU homeowner developers to better understand the costs as well as the ins and outs of the development process. He later launched AccessoryDwellings.org with some fellow advocates and colleagues and remains an editor of the site.

After completing his ADU, Peterson began teaching classes about the ADU development process to provide homeowners with the chance to learn about the basic framework of becoming ADU developers themselves. The class provided an opportunity for homeowners to learn about the process from him firsthand, to meet others who were hoping to build an ADU, and to visit the sites of ADUs under construction that other homeowners were actively building. He has now taught this daylong class to more than a thousand Portland residents.

Peterson then started teaching a half-day class to real estate agents through Earth Advantage, a green building certification organization based in Portland. He also provides an ADU Specialist designation for real estate agents through the organization.

In 2013, Peterson and his wife, Deb, started Caravan- The Tiny House Hotel, the first of its kind. They used it as a venue to promote small housing and began a tiny house tour event series to spread awareness about small housing alternatives. He then started running Portland's ADU tour through Caravan- The Tiny House Hotel.

In 2015, Peterson started an ADU consulting company to offer on-site consultations for Portland homeowners. In 2017, he launched an online ADU course with a national focus: BuildinganADU.com. He continues to do ADU-related education, speaking, policy, advocacy, and consulting.

Image AA.1. Caravan- The Tiny House Hotel on the day of an ADU tour.

Image AA.2. A full bike rack of registrants parked outside one of the ten ADUs featured on the tour.

Image AA.3. Eli Spevak speaking with the homeowner and the architect of an ADU while leading a guided tour.

Made in the USA
San Bernardino, CA
03 September 2019